CULTURE SHOCK!

A Survival Guide to Customs and Etiquette

W9-BGJ-680

CANADA

Guek-Cheng Pang
Robert Barlas

Marshall Cavendish
Editions

This edition published in 2006 by:
Marshall Cavendish Corporation
99 White Plains Road
Tarrytown, NY 10591-9001
www.marshallcavendish.us

Other Marshall Cavendish Offices:
Marshall Cavendish International (Asia) Private Limited. 1 New Industrial
Road, Singapore 536196 ▪ Marshall Cavendish Ltd. 119 Wardour Street, London
W1F 0UW, UK ▪ Marshall Cavendish International (Thailand) Co Ltd. 253 Asoke,
12th Flr, Sukhumvit 21 Road, Klongtoey Nua, Wattana, Bangkok 10110, Thailand
▪ Marshall Cavendish (Malaysia) Sdn Bhd, Times Subang, Lot 46, Subang Hi-Tech
Industrial Park, Batu Tiga, 40000 Shah Alam, Selangor Darul Ehsan, Malaysia

Marshall Cavendish is a trademark of Times Publishing Limited

ISBN 10: 0-7614-2491-1
ISBN 13: 978-0-7614-2491-8

Please contact the publisher for the Library of Congress catalog number

Printed in Singapore by Times Graphics Pte Ltd

Photo Credits:
Photos by Bill Murtha, Bob Barlas and Guek-Cheng Pang. Dinner menu
on page 185 used with permission of Pierre Berton. ▪ Cover photo:
Photolibrary.com

All illustrations by TRIGG

ABOUT THE SERIES

Culture shock is a state of disorientation that can come over anyone who has been thrust into unknown surroundings, away from one's comfort zone. *CultureShock!* is a series of trusted and reputed guides which has, for decades, been helping expatriates and long-term visitors to cushion the impact of culture shock whenever they move to a new country.

Written by people who have lived in the country and experienced culture shock themselves, the authors share all the information necessary for anyone to cope with these feelings of disorientation more effectively. The guides are written in a style that is easy to read and covers a range of topics that will arm readers with enough advice, hints and tips to make their lives as normal as possible again.

Each book is structured in the same manner. It begins with the first impressions that visitors will have of that city or country. To understand a culture, one must first understand the people—where they came from, who they are, the values and traditions they live by, as well as their customs and etiquette. This is covered in the first half of the book.

Then on with the practical aspects—how to settle in with the greatest of ease. Authors walk readers through topics such as how to find accommodation, get the utilities and telecommunications up and running, enrol the children in school and keep in the pink of health. But that's not all. Once the essentials are out of the way, venture out and try the food, enjoy more of the culture and travel to other areas. Then be immersed in the language of the country before discovering more about the business side of things.

To round off, snippets of basic information are offered before readers are 'tested' on customs and etiquette of the country. Useful words and phrases, a comprehensive resource guide and list of books for further research are also included for easy reference.

CONTENTS

ACKNOWLEDGEMENTS

When we first met each other, we remarked upon the happy chance that we were indeed 'opposites'—Caucasian and male, long-term resident of eastern Canada complementing Asian and female, a newcomer to western Canada—and could bring different viewpoints to *CultureShock! Canada*. Since then, many hours of cross-Canada telephone time have gone into the creation of this book, and a friendship has been formed. What we lacked ourselves, we supplemented with information solicited from many sources and with suggestions from our own friends.

Writing this book has therefore placed us in debt to a large number of people. To all of you who made contributions in one way or another—thank you for your support. Special thanks must go, however, to those who so ably helped us research the facts which we needed to make this book accurate:

From Bob: to Robert Amesse, Elizabeth Mitchell and Norm Tompsett—first-class librarians all—to Denise Maxfield, Mike Filip, and Jim and Joanne Rich, whose contributions to various parts of the text were invaluable, and to Vern Shute and Charles Clarke, who proofread my text with great accuracy and precision. Finally, especial gratitude to my good friends Bill Murtha and John Mortimer, whose artistic suggestions and contributions helped immensely in visualising the text as it was being written.

From Guek-Cheng: thanks especially to Shirley Hew and Shova Loh who made me an author; to John Bartle, Mark Looi and Diane Quinn, for their invaluable help; to Bob and Clare Looi, who introduced me to this beautiful country; and to my Canadian friends who have welcomed me into their midst.

Last, but by no means least, our gratitude and love to our families whose constructive criticism and moral support have been invaluable during the weeks and months it took to put this book together.

From Guek-Cheng:
To Pius, Christopher and Kimmy, my fellow-adventurers in
exploring a new country.

From Robert:
With love to my wife, Nancy, my children, Richard and
Sharine, and my mother, Ann.

MAP OF CANADA

ARCTIC OCEAN

GREENLAND

BEAUFORT
SEA

ALASKA

DAVIS STRAIT

GULF OF
ALASKA

LABRADOR
SEA

NORTH
ATLANT
OCEAN

HUDSON
BAY

NORTH
PACIFC
OCEAN

C A N A D A

OTTAWA

UNITED STATES OF AMERICA

FIRST IMPRESSIONS

CHAPTER 1

'Canada is a broad land—broad in mind,
broad in spirit and broad in physical expanse.'
—President Truman,
address before the Canadian Parliament in Ottawa,
11 June 1947

It is always difficult to reflect on a country as diverse as Canada through the eyes of only one person—or even two—and first impressions of anything always depend greatly on the context and circumstances of the person doing the observing. When Guek-Cheng and I met to discuss how we would approach writing the following section, we agreed that, since first impressions are so unique, full justice to a topic as subjective as this could only really be done through the eyes of one of us. This would be better than us attempting to make some kind of visual compromise between us. So the text which follows was written by Guek-Cheng and primarily reflects her first impressions of arriving in western Canada as an Asian immigrant. However, what is strange but rather comforting is that my own first impressions of Canada as an Englishman who came to the eastern part of Canada some years before Guek-Cheng are not at all dissimilar. In fact, had I written the chapter which follows, much of what I would have said in it would be exactly the same. Where my account would differ is only in the smaller details of location and time, and hardly at all in the substance of what first impressed—and continues to impress—me about Canada as a whole.

ARRIVAL

I arrived in Canada without ever having set eyes upon any part of the country before. My port of entry was Vancouver, British Columbia. It was June 1989. Making one's first entry as an immigrant is a necessarily stressful experience. We were met and interviewed by a Canada Customs and Immigration official who went through our documents and asked us a few questions about our possessions, what we had brought in with us, what was to follow, and so on. The experience was somewhat of an ordeal, but not due to any unpleasantness experienced. It is probably a common experience that interacting with officialdom is generally difficult, no matter in which country, and when one is making one's first entry into the country, there is a feeling of being at a disadvantage and experiencing a lot of uncertainty during the encounter. So it was a feeling of great relief that overwhelmed me when we finally shook hands with the official who formally welcomed us to Canada at the end of the interview, which must have taken about an hour.

As we passed through the glass doors that took us into the waiting hall for arrivals, I got my first glimpse of Canada. The arrival hall seemed rather small when compared to a number of other international airports that I had encountered, especially that of the Singapore airport which is enormous, full of glass and gives a feeling of spaciousness, sometimes a feeling of being lost. But the smallness of the Vancouver airport was not unpleasant or constricting; it was warm and woodsy—there were two carved wooden totem-like figures in the middle of the area to welcome us—and this seemed most appropriate for Canada, especially British Columbia, where wood is such an important element. The space was filled with people full of expectation and anticipation for the arrival of friends and family. I was struck by the cosmopolitan atmosphere presented by these eager faces that were turned towards the doors. I had thought of Canadians as being mainly Caucasian in composition, but there were so many Asian faces in that crowd that it gave me a sense of comfort.

SIZE, CLIMATE, PEOPLE

Considering the fact that I am Asian, born and bred, and have spent my entire life living in a city, and that I come from the tropics, it is not surprising that these factors—the size of the country, its climate and people—should have made the greatest impact upon me during the first days of being in Canada.

We (I had arrived with my husband and two children, aged 14 and 10) had decided that we would not dally in the city but would catch the Greyhound bus the next day and head to the interior of the province, to the small town of Merritt, where my cousin was living. So my first impressions of the country, specifically that of British Columbia, were that of rural and not urban Canada.

That first journey into the interior of the province was the most impressive introduction to the vastness and magnificent beauty of the Canadian landscape. The three-hour coach trip begins on Highway 1, cutting through the farmlands and suburbia of the Lower Mainland onto Highway 5, also known as the Coquihalla Highway, which takes you inland and away from the coast. Remember when you read the next bit that I am a city person and from Singapore where it is hard to catch a view of the horizon that is not broken every few feet by a towering office building or condominium block. British Columbia's mountains are especially impressive if the highest hill one has been accustomed to is just a few metres high. The Coquihalla Highway follows the valley of the Coquihalla River as it cuts through the Cascade mountain range to the Nicola Valley in which Merritt is happily nestled. Travelling along the 'Coq', your ears become plugged with the pressure of the climb as the road rises to a summit of 1,240 m (4,068 ft). If it is your first trip on this highway, and even if it is not your first, take the time to have a break at the rest stop which offers a magnificent view of the most breathtaking scenery—that of the imposing Zopkios Ridge and the bare granite slopes of Yak Peak.

No matter the season, the Coquihalla drive never fails to impress with its mountainous slopes covered with forests of fir, pine and spruce, interspersed with stands of cottonwood, birch and aspen trees. When the slopes are snow-covered, they are soft and beautiful with animal tracks meandering up and down impossibly steep sides. For a short time in the spring, penstemons add bright purple circles to the otherwise bland brown and green slopes. But the most beautiful time of the year is arguably in autumn when the shivering leaves of the aspen, bushes and other trees turn golden yellow, rich brown and the willow branches go dark red. There is just a short window of time during which the leaves hang on the branches. Then the wind, which often blows through the valley, takes them off and leaves the branches bare and colourless. All is then bare and waiting for the snow.

It is not a cliché to say that there is always a surprise waiting around every bend. British Columbia was opened up by explorers and adventurers in the late 19th century. Often, when I drive through these mountain ranges, I wonder, how did these adventurers know which way to go, what valley to follow, which land to settle, where to place the railroad tracks that would link the country from sea to sea?

At the end of the three-hour drive, the vista changes dramatically as the mountains open up to the more gentle and undulating landscape of the beautiful, softly rolling hills of the Nicola Valley. Although I have seen this view of the valley many times, its beauty continues to charm and I am not alone in believing it to be one of the most beautiful valleys in British Columbia. Possibly, however, this is a biased viewpoint as we all live in the area. Nevertheless, it is one reason that I continue to live in Merritt more than 15 years after my arrival in Canada.

The expanse of the Canadian countryside is a hard thing to become accustomed to. Unless one is prepared to remain most of the time in the city and to commute by public transport, the automobile is a necessary possession, especially in smaller towns where there is no public transport.

The sudden disappearance and lack of trees is an astounding contrast to the heavily treed mountains from which one emerges. The Nicola Valley is part of a large ecosystem consisting of rich natural grasslands that have supported an extensive cattle ranching industry. It is home to the largest working cattle ranch in Canada, the Douglas Lake Ranch. This ranch, which covers several hundred thousand acres, owes its existence and wealth to the abundance of the indigenous Bluebunch Wheatgrass, known locally as bunch grass. The irony of this is that, when I had my first extended view of the grasslands while driving from Merritt to the town of Kamloops about an hour away, I thought in my ignorance: 'My goodness, what the environmentalists say about the clear-cutting and deforestation in Canada is right; there are hardly any trees left in this valley!' This is now a great joke at my expense and has become a 'when I first came to Canada' story at which friends laugh whenever I have occasion to relate it.

The immensity of the country is one of the very first things that impresses a first-time visitor. The land just extends itself endlessly, it seems; no matter where one is, it is easy to get in a car and be out in the wilderness in just a short time. Rough logging roads and wooded trails lead one on and on into the forest making it so easy to get lost here. A short upward climb and one is poised on some viewpoint with a 360 degree angle of the world all around. One could drive for miles on a major road without meeting any other traffic. The size of the country and the sparseness of human habitation are transformed from being just statistics on a page to becoming visually obvious.

In town, I was struck by how the sense of space was preserved so that even though residential estates were divided into city lot sizes, the visual divisions between neighbouring properties were generally blurred. Individual lot sizes were naturally much larger than what I had been used to, so that houses had quite a bit of room between them. The front lawns blended into one another, emphasising this visual expansiveness, and even when there was a fence built around a property, it tended to be low in height. All this was very different for me, who had been used to housing estates in which the demarkation of one property from another was very clear and where high fences, padlocked gates and fierce barking dogs to keep out the stranger were the usual occurrence. In Canada, one tries to keep the neighbourhood looking warm and friendly. There are now a growing number of fences being put up, especially in the heart of town and in larger urban centres, but 16 years ago there was less of that, and people are fond of saying that there used to be a time when they never had to lock their doors.

One with Nature

In a small town, too, many housing estates on the edge of the town often back onto crown land, that is, forested tracts of public land. Therefore, those houses that are on the periphery do not have fences to show where their backyards end. My cousin, with whom we stayed during the first few weeks in the country, had a house with a backyard that merged so naturally into wilderness that it was possible to go out the back door and continue walking from her lawn into a forest of ponderosa pines and firs without pause.

In Canada, it is spacious everywhere and everything seems big, both outdoors and in. The shops are huge, groceries can be bought in warehouse-size packages that fill shopping carts large enough to hold provisions for a week for a family of at least eight people, or so it seemed to me. Yet there are also contradictions in size, and while I have concentrated upon how the vastness of the country has made a big impression upon me, I should also point out that another 'first impression' regarding size belonged at the other end of the scale—that of the smallness of a Canadian small town.

Admittedly, there are many other Canadian small towns much smaller than Merritt, but as I am speaking of my first impressions, I shall have to relate it to this particular town. Merritt, when I arrived in 1989, had a population of just about 7,000 people. It had four banks when we first arrived (there are only three now), two traffic light junctions (there are four now), and a small cinema that soon closed its doors (there is still no cinema) because it could not compete with the three video shops (only one is left) then in existence. It seemed as if one could take a deep breath while at one end of the main street, and if the lights were in one's favour, it would be possible not to have to draw another breath until one got to the other side of town, just two blocks away. I say 'it would be possible' because I have not tried doing it and today it would be a lot harder, not because the centre of town has grown larger, but because there are marginally a few more cars on the road. I also enjoyed the ability to get the necessary things done without getting caught in gridlock, the fact that I could walk the children to school in less than five minutes, that there was no queue for the use of the tennis courts and other recreational facilities, and there was no parking fee to pay.

Merritt is typical of many other Canadian small towns in another respect—that in these 15 years it has not grown or changed much and some years it even seemed in danger of dying out. The smallness of such towns as Merritt delivers a charm of its own—people are friendlier, there is more time to get to know each other, and the pace of life is gentle. However, even as I write, it seems that this charm is being threatened. Recently, a number of big corporate retail companies have opened up shop here and that seems to indicate that they believe in the growth of the town. Local residents look upon this with mixed feelings, grateful for the jobs that these companies bring but hating the fact that they take away the uniqueness of the community.

The community of Merritt is unique. Its demographic make-up is roughly one third Caucasian, one third Indo-Canadian and one third First Nations. It is this interesting mix of people that makes it easier for a new immigrant like myself to be assimilated into the existing society. Naturally the ability to speak the language (English) and the fact that one is in many ways 'westernised' in thought, behaviour and appearance means that it is easier to blend in. I did not feel very different visually from other people when I walked about town.

A Learning Experience

Due to an ignorance of Canadian history when I first arrived, I harboured a stereotypical though vague idea of the country as a place that was overwhelmingly 'white' in population. Although I knew that the First Nations people had been on the continent long before the arrival of the first adventurers from England and Europe, I never gave this much thought outside of history and geography books. As for the number of Indo-Canadians in Canada, I was surprised to learn how much they, as a group, had contributed to the economic development of the country from its early days.

They had helped with opening up the western part of the country in various ways, but mainly by working on the railroad. While the number of Chinese families in Merritt were fewer than 10 when I arrived, I discovered that there had been Chinese people in the valley from its earliest days. Today, the old Chinese launderette shopfront with its fascia board peeling paint remains in evidence and there is still a Chinese general store beside it. The old shop owner no longer sells his wares, though his display windows are still filled with merchandise that date back several decades. Both the launderette and the general store belonged to a Chinese family, the survivors of railroad workers and market gardeners that had been in the valley since it was first opened up in the early 1900s.

People are friendlier in a small town. There is a greater inclination to catch a person's eye as one walks down the street and to nod and say 'good morning' or 'hello'. This is very different from walking about in a busy city street, where everyone seems to be in a hurry to go somewhere, engrossed in their own worlds and actively avoiding eye contact. Again, because I had come from a big city where most people remain anonymous and 'invisible', I was struck by this show of friendliness and general helpfulness that was exhibited by small town Canadians. A welcoming smile and a friendly 'how are you today?', 'can I help you?' and 'did you find everything you needed?' greeted me each day as I went about my daily chores, buying groceries at a supermarket, collecting letters from the post office or borrowing a book from the town library. Although the cynic might say that, in the shops, the sales personnel were just mouthing automatic 'friendly' responses to their customers, it is still better than being served by unhelpful, impassive workers. Fifteen years later, however, I have noticed that there is now less informality, helpfulness and spontaneous friendliness. I, too, can bemoan the loss of 'those good old days'. I tend to lock my car more often than leave it unlocked, especially if there are packages on the seat that might tempt the wandering eye.

In order to get a younger person's first impressions of the differences in living in Canada, I asked my daughter, who was 10 when we arrived, for her first impressions especially of her peer group. Generally speaking, friendliness and informality in relationships with people is a good thing, but for a child raised in a strict Asian society where the rules of behaviour between children and adults are quite formalised, the considerably more relaxed and informal interactions between these two levels of Canadian society were shocking. To address an adult by his or her first name and be on a first name basis was unthinkable behaviour and almost impossible to do, even though asked to do so by some adults. It was not uncommon for friends to visit each other at home and ignore the presence of any adults there, even if they were the parents of the friend. At best, they would say 'hi' or 'hello'.

She also found that young Canadians were quite forthright about expressing their thoughts and would venture an opinion about anything that they were asked. This was encouraged in school, where student responses to not just school subjects but to current events, were elicited by teachers who always wanted to know 'what do you think?'. It was different from her previous experience of school where students were often reticent in expressing their opinions and concentrated more on being 'receptacles' for the knowledge and wisdom of books and teachers.

School was out when we first landed, it being the summer holidays. That timing was calculated to give us an opportunity to register our children for the coming school year and become accustomed to the weather. This was a decision I certainly recommend to anyone planning to emigrate, work or study in Canada for the long term, especially if they come from any part of the world more temperate in climate. When we arrived in June, the daily temperature must have been above 20° C; this and the summer holidays allowed us to experience our adopted country at a more relaxed pace. By our second week in Canada, we had decided to go to the Canadian Tire shop, equip ourselves with a tent, stove and other camping equipment, and travel around a bit. It was a good way to see the country, driving around and camping at various provincial parks. While the weather was warm, it was not always dry and there were occasions when we had to erect our tent in the rain.

As the summer drew to a close and the temperature began to fall, I recall marking my calendar each time the thermometer registered another one or two degrees less than the week before. I find that the time goes by more quickly here and attribute part of the reason to the changing seasons that help one to mark the passing of time. 'Making hay while the sun shines' has much more meaning here than in the tropics. Shop flyers (advertising supplements that come free with newspapers and are also stuffed in the post box) begin to feature 'back to school' specials and clothes shops fill their shelves with winter stock. This gave us time to shop for the colder weather and being in the country helped as we were assured of buying clothing that would be appropriate to the climate. This was easier than trying to imagine what type of clothing would be warm enough for a Canadian winter and trying on long johns and winter jackets in hot and humid Singapore.

That first autumn, I was pleasantly surprised to notice that I was going down to play tennis at the nearby community tennis courts early in the morning in my shorts when it was only 10° C, something I would never have thought comfortable before; it was a little chilly perhaps, but I knew by then that it would quickly warm up once the sun rose from behind the mountain. I enjoyed thinking that I was walking about in temperatures that resembled the interior of a refrigerator. I was delighted that I felt quite comfortable despite the fact that where I had come from, 30° C was the norm, and I recall a Singapore newspaper once splashing '15° C' in huge point size across a Page One article in astonishment at some freakishly cold weather we had experienced.

The changing climate obviously made a huge impact upon me. I had to divest myself of stereotypical images of 'Eskimos' (whom I now know are called Inuit) and igloos and snow-covered ground and come to terms with the reality of the Canadian climate. It is hot here in summer, the temperature soars above 30° C and the ground is not permanently covered with snow. Initially, I found it difficult to look at the summer greens and browns of the earth, grass and trees and comprehend that all that expanse could be totally made white and blanketed with several inches of snow. Living in a rural environment brings a person into extremely close contact with nature. For the first time, I understood what it felt like to have the day drag out gloriously long during the summer and have it dramatically cut dark and short in the winter. The tilt of the earth's axis is clearly demonstrated each day; geography lessons from school days become palpable.

Wildlife Watching

But there was one aspect of nature I wished to experience but had to wait for the longest time before that wish was fulfilled. Like many newcomers to Canada, I wanted to see the wildlife close at hand, to watch a bear, deer, and with luck, a moose wandering by. Whenever we drove through the country or went into the forests, I would watch for any sign of movement on the hillsides, hoping for my first glimpse of some wild animal, but I never saw much except cattle and horses and other domestic animals. It was hard to believe that I was living in a country rich in bears.

I think it took at least two years before I finally got to see my first bear, and then it was at such close quarters that it shocked me. I was with the local ski club checking out the trails in the summer time, just driving along slowly, when a bear that had been spooked by the voices of other people further up the trail came dashing down the rough road towards my car. When he saw me, he did a quick right hand turn off the trail and into the bushes. I could not tell who was more shocked, the bear or me! Deer were easier to spot, and I soon learned to pick them out from amongst the trees. They were also less shy of humans and could be seen grazing even by the side of the road. But it took many more years before I encountered my first moose: that happened one winter when I was out cross-country skiing and a mother moose and its young one could be spied among the trees close by the ski trail. Other skiers also stopped to watch them, which shows how rare a sight this is. These early sightings have been special, but

Now that I live a little outside of town, with countryside all around, I often catch glimpses of deer and bear. I have even learned to pick out moose grazing in a swampy area as I drive by in the morning.

they, like the other first impressions and surprises, have never lost their impact. After more than 15 years here, I continue to enjoy the vast and open country around me, the ability, still, to go out into the wilderness and drive, walk and ski for miles with no one else about. The sight of a deer grazing around the house continues to amaze. I have not moved towns because the community I am now a part of is still one of the friendliest I know, and while I, too, sometimes bemoan 'the good old days', I know that I would not want to give up small-town living and move into the big city.

OVERVIEW
OF CANADA

CHAPTER 2

'If some countries have too much history,
we have too much geography!'
—William Lyon Mackenzie King,
former Canadian Prime Minister

GEOGRAPHY

'Humongous' is a Canadian word that aptly describes the country. Here are some facts to give you an idea of what it means:

- Canada's width from the Atlantic Ocean to the Pacific Ocean is more than 7,700 km (4,784 miles), more than four times the width of India. It would take a good two weeks to drive across the country from coast to coast.

- From its southernmost point, where Pelee Island rises out of Lake Erie, to Ellesmere Island in the Arctic Ocean, Canada is about 4,800 km (2,982 miles), or more than five times the length of Japan.

- All in all, Canada covers nearly 10 million sq km (approx. 6 million sq miles) in area. It is the second largest country in the world. It is larger than the United States and even China, and is exceeded only by the republic of Russia.

- Yet Canada is one of the least populated countries in the world. There are just over 32 million people in Canada. That works out to roughly three people per square kilometre. In fact, much of the countryside is under-populated and more than three-quarters of the population live in urban centres. Two-thirds are concentrated within 200 km (124 miles) of the border with the United States.

- There are more than a million rivers, streams and lakes, which make up a quarter of the world's fresh water supply. The Great Lakes, which Canada shares with the United States, are the world's largest body of fresh water.

- Canada is divided into six different time zones: Pacific, Mountain, Central, Eastern, Atlantic and Newfoundland. If you arrived at 8:30 am in Saint John's in Newfoundland and telephoned a friend in Vancouver, British Columbia, to relay the good news, he would probably be fast asleep as it would be only 4:00 am there and his welcome might be lukewarm!

From Sea to Sea

Visitors may have difficulty grasping the immensity of Canada. One way of making it more comprehensible is to divide it into smaller, 'bite-size' pieces that can be digested one at a time. Canada can be divided into six main geographical regions: the Atlantic Provinces, the Canadian Shield, the Great Lakes-Saint Lawrence Lowlands, the Interior Plains, the Cordillera and the North.

The Atlantic Provinces

The three maritime provinces of New Brunswick, Nova Scotia and Prince Edward Island, together with the island of Newfoundland on the eastern coast of Canada, form the Atlantic Provinces.

This region differs physically from the rest of Canada because of its forested hills and low mountains, and its rugged and indented coast. These physical characteristics have resulted in separating the people of this region into small communities and scattering their settlements. Therefore, there are few areas of high population density in the Atlantic Provinces.

The provinces are a cluster of peninsulas and islands which form the north-eastern extension of the Appalachian Highlands and are greatly affected by the Atlantic Ocean. They are home to only about 10 per cent of the country's population and have always been the poorest provinces of Canada. The main industries are resource-based, relying on fishing and forestry. Often the economy and survival of a whole town can depend on a single industry.

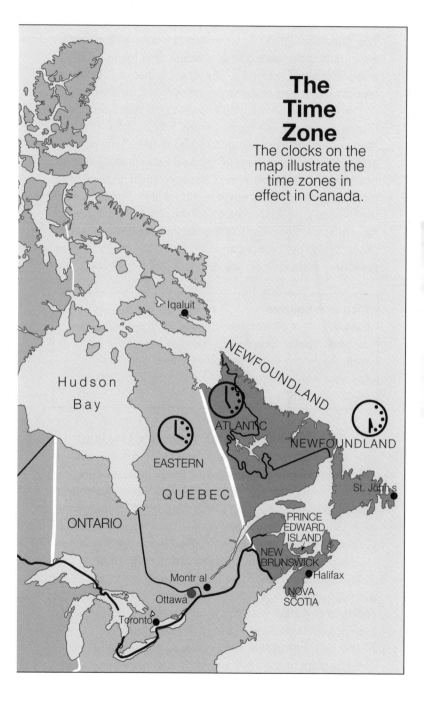

The Time Zone

The clocks on the map illustrate the time zones in effect in Canada.

The Canadian Shield

The Canadian Shield is an enormous area that occupies about half of the mainland of Canada. It is made up of the northern half of Manitoba, Ontario, Quebec and Labrador (the mainland part of the province of Newfoundland).

The Canadian Shield, also known as the Pre-Cambrian or Laurentian Shield, was formed more than 2 billion years ago. This ancient, glacially eroded region is full of rivers, lakes and forests, making it a hunter's and fisherman's paradise. Practically uninhabitable, the Canadian Shield is responsible for keeping Canadians closely hemmed in to the border with the United States, and accounts for the physical separation of eastern and western Canada. But the area is rich in resources, producing 40 per cent of Canada's minerals—cobalt, copper, gold, iron, nickel, silver, uranium and zinc—and wood.

Rich in Resources

Canada is one of the two major pulp and paper producers in the world. The Canadian Shield's other great resource is water, supplying the area further south, the lowlands of the Saint Lawrence, with 70 per cent of its electricity (hydroelectricity or 'hydro-power').

The Great Lakes and Saint Lawrence Lowlands

This very small area of Canada extends across the south of the two provinces of Ontario and Quebec. Despite its size, it is here that more than half of Canada's population lives. This densely-populated part of eastern Canada contains more large cities of over 100,000 people than any other part of Canada of similar size. The metropolitan centres of Montreal, Quebec City, Toronto and Ottawa are all situated here.

This area also includes the heartland of French Canada; yet there are also strongholds of British settlement. Some of the contrasts of the land are due to cultural differences between French and Anglo-Saxon patterns of settlement.

The rich agricultural land, once all cultivated, attracted many settlers in the 18th and 19th centuries, but much of it has now become a great urban and industrial area. This region produces about three-quarters of all the country's manufactured goods in an area known as the Quebec-Windsor corridor, which stretches between those two cities and along the shores of the Saint Lawrence River and Lake Ontario. Another factor which makes this the richest part of the country is the great waterway formed by the Saint Lawrence River and the Great Lakes. This waterway is ice-free for most of the year, thus giving the inland region around it access to the Atlantic Ocean and the rest of the world.

The Interior Plains or the Prairies

This region can be simply described with one word—flat. This part of Canada is roughly made up of the central provinces of Alberta, Saskatchewan and the southern part of Manitoba. It is bounded on the west by the Rockies and on the east by the Canadian Shield. The plains are flat and, as you travel by train through it, level as far as the eye can see. This region has always been, and still is, Canada's 'bread basket'. Half of its area is forested and most of the other half is devoted to the growing of grain, especially wheat, making Canada the second largest exporter of grain in the world behind the United States.

A quarter of the population in the prairies is made up of immigrants from Germany, Eastern Europe, the Ukraine and Russia, whose ancestors transformed the barren plain into today's fertile farmland. The domes of Russian and Greek Orthodox churches are especially visible in this region. The Métis, of mixed French and native ancestry, form a small but significant part of the population.

The Cordillera

This mountainous region starts from the Rockies in the east. It consists of plateaux and valleys in the middle and ends with another mountainous range along the edge of the Pacific Ocean in the west. It corresponds roughly to the political divisions of British Columbia, the Yukon and part of Alberta.

Great contrasts can be seen in this region—there are the English gardens of Victoria, the wilderness of the Rockies,

A spectacular waterfall in the Canadian Rockies.

the rolling hills and plateaux of the interior and the coastal forests. Most of the population is concentrated in the south and near the coast, where the main cities of Vancouver and Victoria are located. Forestry and the paper and pulp industry, cattle and other animal farming are vital to the population in the interior of British Columbia. This is easily one of the most scenic parts of Canada, rivalled only by the mountains of the North-west Territories. The spectacular scenery has made tourism an important industry in British Columbia.

The Great White North

Comprising the North-west Territories, Nunavut and the Yukon, this region covers about 40 per cent of Canada's land area. Much of it is cold, isolated and almost entirely uninhabited. About 17,000 of the world's Inuit population live here. (Inuit, meaning 'the people', is a name they prefer to Eskimos, which means 'meat-eaters'.) Another native people in the far North are the Dene (Dene also means 'the people'). A third of people are the Métis, who trace their ancestry to the unions between the French *coureurs de bois* and native women in the early days of the fur trade. The remainder of the inhabitants of this great white land are made up of a mainly transient community of adventurers, hunters, trappers, missionaries, people who work for the mining, oil and other natural resource industries and their support services.

Biologists divide the North into two regions: the boreal forest and the tundra. The boreal forest is a broad band of coniferous forest extending across Canada from Newfoundland to Alaska. The tundra, which reaches from the boreal forest northwards to the Arctic Ocean, comprises 20 per cent of Canada's landmass. It is treeless. The two regions meet along the tree line, a transitional zone several kilometres wide. This boundary also separates the traditional lands of the Dene and the Inuit.

The Inuit occupy the shores of the Arctic Ocean and of the Hudson Bay, the Dene the Yukon and the Mackenzie Valley.

The native communities are located around bays, river mouths and inlets, reflecting their basic lifestyle of hunting, fishing and gathering.

Looking at it another way, the region can be sub-divided into the sub-arctic Mackenzie River valley in the west and the arctic area of the northern islands and the north-central mainland.

In the middle of summer, it is never dark in the North. And in mid-winter, the only daylight is a combination of sunset and sunrise. Summers can be pleasantly warm with temperatures rising above 20°C but the season is short and often wet. Rainfall and snowfall are light because the Arctic is really semi-desert. Yet the ground is often wet and swampy because there is a layer of ground below the surface that is permanently frozen. When the snow thaws, the water remains on the surface and cannot drain through the frozen ground.

Mineral resources are the economic mainstay of this region, but the forbidding climate and extreme isolation of the area make exploitation of the land difficult. Nevertheless, it is non-renewable resources like gold,

Attractions

Tourism is a short-term, basically summer industry. Visitors come mainly from the United States and the southern parts of Canada to view nature's breathtaking and unspoiled beauty—the treeless landscape, alpine scenery, ice floes, icebergs and glaciers, and the mountains of Baffin, Devon and Ellesmere islands which are the highest in eastern North America.

silver, lead, zinc, copper, oil and natural gas that have spurred the economic development of the North. These industries do not produce widespread permanent settlement, but rather promote the rise of 'instant' towns with labour imported from the south. A large part of the white population in the North is transient in nature. Even government employees regard their time in the North as just a 'tour of duty' limited to several years.

Regional Quirks and Quarks

Politically, Canada is made up of ten provinces and three northern territories. The provinces, from east to west, are Newfoundland, Nova Scotia, Prince Edward Island, New Brunswick, Quebec, Ontario, Manitoba, Saskatchewan, Alberta and British Columbia. They have their own governments which are primarily responsible for public schooling, health and social services, main roads and local government. The three northern territories are the North-west Territories, Nunavut and the Yukon. The territories are governed by the federal government in Ottawa and by territorial governments which may legislate where the federal government has given it the necessary authority.

Newfoundland

In a Nutshell	
Total land area:	393,173 sq km (151,804 sq miles)
Total fresh water area:	34,030 sq km (13,139 sq miles)
Coastline:	19,720 km (12,253 miles)
Population (2001):	513,000
Capital:	Saint John's
International airport:	Gander

Newfoundland (pronounced 'newf-n-land') is the furthest east of the Canadian provinces. The main part of the province is the island of Newfoundland, which has a mountainous and lake-strewn interior and a rocky, rugged coastline. There are few big cities, and life is mainly centred around small fishing communities on the coast, known as 'outports'. These 'outports' are dispersed along the coast in sheltered bays, near headlands or on islands, and even today, there are some that are only accessible by boat. These are mainly along the south coast where no road linking them has yet been built. The isolation of these villages means that today's way of life and culture have not changed much since the arrival of the early settlers from Europe. Cars are a luxury, but who needs them here anyway? Access to the 'outports' is difficult. Some are on ferry lines, others are not. These little communities are some of the most remote settlements in North America.

Labrador, the mainland portion of the province, is mainly wild and sparsely populated. Many of the communities in this region are extremely isolated and travel is commonly accomplished on water. Newfoundlanders (or 'Newfies' as they are sometimes referred to by other Canadians) are mainly descended from British immigrants. They have a very distinct culture, most noticeable in their language, which is full of colourful and unique slang and idioms. Some words which cannot be heard in any other part of the country are 'ballycater' (a narrow band of ice which forms along the foreshore in winter), 'kinkhorn' (the throat or windpipe), 'sparbles' (shoemaker's nails) and 'yaffle' (to gather in a pile). Also unique is the fact that the island of Newfoundland has no snakes or skunks.

Fishing is the main occupation of Newfoundlanders. Other industries are mining, hydroelectricity and forestry. The weather is cool throughout the year, with the moderating influence of the sea reduced by the cold waters of the Labrador Current. Winters are mild and summers cool and short. It is relatively wet.

Saint John's is the capital of the province and its largest town. It combines the feel of a high-rise city and a coastal fishing village. It is also the oldest city in North America and England's first overseas colony, the very beginnings of the British Empire.

Access to Newfoundland from the mainland by ferry is from North Sydney, Nova Scotia. There is a year-round service to Port aux Basques and a seasonal service to Argentia on the Avalon Peninsula.

Nova Scotia

In a Nutshell	
Total land area:	55,491 sq km (21,425 sq miles)
Total fresh water area:	2,650 sq km (1,023 sq miles)
Coastline:	5,934 km (3,687 miles)
Population (2001):	908,000
Capital:	Halifax
International airport:	Halifax

Nova Scotia is very much like Newfoundland, and as it is a peninsular province, no part is too far from the sea. The climate is wet and cold, but the summers and winters here are more moderate than in areas of the same latitude in the interior of the country. Winters may be stormy, however, and there is a problem with fog all year round. The rugged coastline is cut by numerous bays and inlets, ideal sites for fishing villages. The catch includes cod, lobster and scallops. However, the main industry is manufacturing, along with shipbuilding, and the production of dairy goods and paper. Scenically, the mountainous landscapes of the Cape Breton Highlands, which jut out to the north, contrast with the relatively flat agricultural land which lies around the south of the peninsula. An area with a difference is the beautiful Annapolis Valley, along the Bay of Fundy, which is famous for its apples and is most beautiful in spring when pink and white apple blossoms cover the trees.

The population is mainly of English and Scottish ancestry, but there are French, German and Dutch communities scattered throughout the province. Nova Scotia means 'New Scotland', and the Scottish influence is strong everywhere, especially in Cape Breton in the north. Highland games are a highlight of the summer months. In some areas, you can still hear Gaelic being spoken.

Due to its favourable position on the Atlantic, Nova Scotia has always been strategically important. Halifax, with a population of about 359,000, is the capital of the province and the largest city in the maritime provinces. It is the headquarters of Canada's small navy and a major port owing to its year-round accessibility.

Prince Edward Island

In a Nutshell	
Total land area:	5,656 sq km (2,183 sq miles)
Total fresh water area:	None
Coastline:	1,107 km (687 miles)
Population (2001):	135,000
Capital:	Charlottetown

Prince Edward Island is the smallest province of Canada and the most densely populated. Its rich, red soil supports a mainly farming community that produces potatoes as the main crop. Fishing—for lobsters, oysters and herring—is

Strange formations abound in the sea-eroded flowerpot rocks at Hopewell Cape, jutting out into the Bay of Fundy.

also important. The warm ocean currents that wash the Gulf of Saint Lawrence where the island lies give Prince Edward Island a climate that is much warmer than most of Canada. But the island is also wet and there are occasional extreme low temperatures in winter.

Charlottetown, an old, quiet country town with a population of about 32,000, was named by its Loyalist settlers after Queen Charlotte, the consort of George III. It claims to be the 'Cradle of Confederation', site of the historic meeting which took place in 1864 and which eventually led to the unification of Canada in 1867.

Prince Edward Island is accessible by ferry from Caribou, Nova Scotia; it can also be reached by road from mainland Canada via Confederation Bridge, built in 1997, and one of the longest bridges in the world.

New Brunswick

In a Nutshell	
Total land areas:	73,437 sq km (28,354 sq miles)
Total fresh water area:	1,350 sq km (521 sq miles)
Coastline:	1,524 km (946 miles)
Population (2001):	729,000
Capital:	Fredericton

New Brunswick is rectangular in shape and has an extensive sea coast. The proximity of the sea has a moderating influence on a climate that has mostly cool summers and cold winters. The land is covered with forests; the wooded highlands are cut by many fast rivers and deep valleys. As can be expected, forestry, pulp and paper are the two main industries. Descendants of the Acadian French settlers make up a sizeable part of the population, as do descendants of the United Empire Loyalists who migrated north during the American War of Independence.

Fredericton, the province's capital, was named for the second son of George III. It is a quiet tree-lined city which retains the grace and dignity brought to it by its Loyalist founders. Many old buildings and elegant houses remain. Fredericton is the home of the province's lieutenant-governor and its legislature.

An interesting spectacle is the 'bore tide' on the Bay of Fundy, which New Brunswick shares with Nova Scotia. When the incoming tide reaches its peak, it creates a wall of water which roars all at once into the towns of Moncton, New Brunswick and Truro, Nova Scotia. This surge of water occurs twice a day and the exact times are predicted in advance. Special viewing platforms are provided for visitors to watch its arrival. A similar phenomenon occurs in Saint John, New Brunswick, when rushing water up the Saint John River creates 'reversing falls'. In reality, these are a series of rapids which appear to change direction under the pressure of the incoming tide. Another New Brunswick geographical oddity is the 'Magnetic Hill' near Moncton, on which cars appear to coast backwards without any power—uphill!

Quebec

In a Nutshell	
Total land area:	1,540,687 sq km (594,862 sq miles)
Total fresh water area:	183,890 sq km (71,000 sq miles)
Coastline:	10,839 km (6,735 miles)
Population (2001):	7,237,000
Capital:	Quebec City
International airports:	Mirabel, Dorval (Montreal), Mirabel (for charter flights)

Quebec got its name from *kebec*, an Algonkian Indian word meaning 'where the river narrows'. It is Canada's largest province and almost half of it is forested. North of Montreal and Quebec City are the Laurentian Mountains. The area south of Montreal is mainly farmland. In the Saint Lawrence Valley, there is a long frost-free season from early May to September, but the northern and western parts of the province experience more extreme winter temperatures and cooler summers.

'*La belle province*', as it is called, is the heart of French Canada. For many people, it is the existence of Quebec as a province that makes Canada unique. The mainly French population has a culture that makes it distinct from other parts of Canada, indeed the whole of North America. This is reflected in the language, architecture, music, food and religion of the region. For more than 85 per cent of the people of Quebec, French is the mother tongue. Many of these francophones or Quebecois, as they are known, speak only French. About 90 per cent of them are Roman Catholic. They tend to think of themselves more as Quebecois than as Canadians, and regard themselves as a different nation, though politically linked with the rest of Canada.

The countryside is rich in tradition and the remnants of the old 'seigneurial system' can be seen in much of the countryside. The Gaspe region is a unique part of the province; an area of wild beauty where land ends in sheer cliffs falling into the Gulf of Saint Lawrence.

A regular feature of Canada is the long winding river, as illustrated by this aerial picture of the Northern Ontario landscape.

Quebec's wealth lies in its abundant natural resources. Nevertheless, it is manufacturing that is the main industry. Other important industries are aluminium, minerals and timber.

Montreal is Canada's second largest city, with a population of 3 million people. About 12 per cent of all Canadians and 40 per cent of Quebecois live here. Two-thirds of the people are French-speaking, but the downtown core of the city is surprisingly English. Montreal is a major port and a centre for finance, business and transport. It is an arts centre as well, particularly for French Canada.

If Quebec is the heart of French Canada, then Quebec City is its heartbeat. The town is unique in many ways, but mostly in its European appearance and Old World atmosphere. The old section of town has been designated by UNESCO as a World Heritage Site. This is the seat of the provincial parliament and Laval University. Quebec City has been the centre of French nationalist thought for hundreds of years and talk of independence and separatism may vary in intensity but never ever dies. The overwhelming majority of the people here are francophones (as opposed to anglophones who are more influenced by Anglo-Saxon language, thought and culture).

The climate is very changeable. Summers are fairly hot and not as long as in southern Ontario. Winters can get really cold, especially in January and February.

Ontario

In a Nutshell	
Total land area:	1,068,587 sq km (412,583 sq miles)
Total fresh water area:	177,390 sq km (68,490 sq miles)
Coastline (on lakes):	1,210 km (751 miles)
Population (2001):	11,410,000
Capital:	Toronto
International airports:	Pearson (Toronto), Ottawa

The name Ontario is derived from an Iroquois Indian word meaning 'rocks standing high near the water', which is probably a reference to the Niagara Falls. It is by far the richest province, with about a third of all Canadians living here. Ethnically, it is also the most diverse. Here, French and English are mixed with other European and Asian languages. The majority of the people are city dwellers and congregate in the area between Kingston and Windsor along the shores of the Great Lakes. The northern part of the province is, however, very under-populated. Most commercial activity is linked to the abundant natural resources—forestry and mining. The southern part of Ontario around the lakes has long, hot summers and mild winters, but it gets colder the further north you go into the province.

Manufacturing is the major industry. The cluster of cities around the western end of Lake Ontario is known as Canada's 'golden horseshoe'. It includes Hamilton (centre of Canada's iron and steel manufacture), Oshawa (centre of the automotive industry), Windsor (Detroit's twin city) and Toronto (Canada's largest city).

Toronto is the undisputed economic heart of the country, the nation's financial, business, publishing and fashion capital, and home to more than 200 of Canada's leading corporations. It is the centre for hundreds of suburbs and satellite towns and Canada's most ethnically diverse city—one of every four immigrants to Canada finds his way to Toronto. But despite its high-rise, big-city image, one of the most impressive things that usually strikes the visitor to Toronto is its cleanliness and orderliness. Much of the city is either new or has been rebuilt in the past 15 years. It has a reputation for being safe at night—the streets are busy, the restaurants and entertainment centres open, the parks and metros used in the way they are meant. There is none of the litter, graffiti and crime, no areas of concentrated poverty that can often be found in big cities. CN Tower, one of the tallest free-standing structures in the world (533 m / 1,748 ft), is the city's symbol and landmark. At the top, you can find a restaurant, a disco and two observation decks. Toronto is also the busiest Canadian port on the Great Lakes.

Besides Toronto, the attractions of Ontario include Ottawa, the country's capital, and the Niagara Falls, the tourist attraction which Canada shares with the United States.

Manitoba

In a Nutshell	
Total land area:	650,090 sq km (251,001 sq miles)
Total fresh water area:	101,590 sq km (4,088 sq miles)
Coastline:	917 km (569 miles)
Population (2001):	1,120,000
Capital:	Winnipeg
International airport:	Winnipeg

The name Manitoba was derived from an Algonkian Indian word. In Lake Manitoba, there is a strait where the water makes an odd echoing sound which the Indians associated with Manito, the great spirit. So they named the place Manito Waba, meaning 'Manito Strait'. Northern Manitoba, which is part of the Canadian Shield, is hilly and forested, while the south is low and flat. The latter is ideal for farming, especially wheat, which is the province's most important crop. The main industry is manufacturing. Food processing and the clothing industry are also important. Winters are long and cold and summers can be hot.

Winnipeg, the capital, became the first stop of the great Canadian land rush of the late 19th century with the arrival of the Canadian Pacific Railroad. It is still home to the descendants of European immigrants who opened up the country—Ukrainians, Mennonites, Hungarians, Poles, Jews, Italians and Portuguese. Winnipeg grew into a railroad hub, the centre of the livestock and grain industry, and is today the centre for grain handling and transport. It has a population of 671,000 people.

Saskatchewan

In a Nutshell	
Total land area:	651,903 sq km (251,701 sq miles)
Total fresh water area:	81,632 sq km (31,518 sq miles)
Population (2001):	979,000
Capital:	Regina

Saskatchewan is Cree Indian for 'river that turns around when it runs'. This province produces two-thirds of Canada's wheat crop. Other grains grown are barley and rye. Oil and potash are Saskatchewan's most important resources. The province has the world's richest deposits of potash. Two-thirds of Saskatchewan is very flat, prairie lowland, where there is often not a tree in sight. The climate is continental, with cold and long winters and warm and short summers.

Regina was originally dubbed 'Pile O'Bones' in reference to the bones left by the buffalo-hunting natives who butchered their kill and left the remains here. It became the capital of the North-west Territories and was the headquarters of the North-west Mounted Police. Its name was changed to Regina (Latin for 'queen') in honour of Queen Victoria. In 1905, it became the capital of the newly-formed province of Saskatchewan. When oil and potash were discovered, Regina became the province's commercial, financial and industrial centre.

Saskatoon is the province's largest city (population 226,000). It was founded in 1882 by a group of Methodists from Ontario who were granted land to form a temperance colony. The coming of the railroad, combined with the resources of oil, potash and wheat, made Saskatoon one of Canada's fastest-growing cities.

Alberta

Alberta, the westernmost of the central provinces, is in the interior plains region. In winter, the south is subject to the cold, dry air masses of the continental polar air, but summer is warm and full of sunshine. Alberta came into its own in the 1970s with the discovery of oil and natural gas. Besides these, Alberta also has other minerals, such as coal. Agriculture is also an important source of income.

The province is known as 'dinosaur country' as more dinosaur bones have been found here than anywhere else in the world. You can see the remains of dinosaurs in the south-central badlands and at the Dinosaur Provincial Park in the south-eastern part of Alberta. The park was created in 1955 and has been declared a World Heritage Site.

Edmonton is the capital of Alberta and its second largest city. It is known as the 'Gateway to the North' because it is situated on an economic divide between the highly productive farmlands of central Alberta and a vast resource-rich northern hinterland.

Calgary, which has grown to become Alberta's largest city, is strategically situated on major air, rail and road corridors, and is therefore an important transport centre. It is also the financial centre of western Canada and the headquarters of Canada's oil and natural gas industries.

In a Nutshell	
Total land area:	661,188 sq km (255,286 sq miles)
Total fresh water area:	16,796 sq km (6,484 sq miles)
Population (2001):	2,975,000
Capital:	Edmonton
International airports:	Edmonton, Calgary

British Columbia

British Columbia is, for many, the most beautiful province in Canada. The visitor can head for the mountains, hills, forests or lakes—there is every kind of scenery you could wish for. This makes tourism a big money spinner for the province. The province is Canada's window to the Pacific and Asia.

The fishing industry emphasises the use of modern, long-range fishing vessels that trawl the deep seas rather than the coastal fishing that has resulted in the quaint villages of the Atlantic Provinces. There is little arable land here, and what there is is mostly given over to the growing of fodder for animals. There are rich mineral resources, however, and tremendous hydroelectric power and huge forests which fuel the forest industry. There is a major fruit growing area in the interior of the province, known as the Okanagan Valley, while in the south near Osoyoos, there is the only desert in Canada.

The climate is mild, due to the warm westerly winds and the Pacific Ocean. Along the coast, it is often cool and wet. Winters are never severe, but mild and wet, and summers are warm. The interior is much drier and hotter in summer and colder in winter.

The capital of British Columbia is Victoria, on Vancouver Island. It is British Columbia's second largest city and sits on the south end of Vancouver Island; a genteel town with a distinctly British air.

Vancouver, which sits on the mainland just opposite, is the province's largest city and Canada's third largest. Picturesquely situated between mountains and sea, it is blessed with a very mild, though often wet, climate. There is a large and vibrant Chinatown which covers eight square blocks, and Cantonese can often be heard in the shopping areas.

One feature unique to British Columbia is the Adams River Sockeye salmon run, when adult salmon struggle up the river to reach spawning grounds where they find a mate, spawn and die. This occurs every year around the month of October, and once every four years, a bumper run occurs when millions of salmon return in such abundant numbers that they turn the river a crimson colour. The last such run was in October 2006.

North-west Territories

In a Nutshell

Total land area:	1,479,698 sq km (571,314 sq miles)
Population (2001):	37,000
Capital:	Yellowknife

The North-west Territories occupy a vast area—more than one-third the area of the whole country. It is Canada's frontier land—the land of the fur trader, hunter/trapper, explorer/adventurer and missionary.

In 1789, Alexander Mackenzie, one of Canada's great explorers, travelled the length of the river that is now named after him. In his wake came traders, missionaries and prospectors. The area was monopolised by the Hudson's Bay Company, which had sole trading privileges in the territories for many years. When, in 1870, the Hudson's Bay Company sold its privileges, the area was opened to free traders. Gold discovered in Yellowknife Bay in the early 1930s caused prospectors to flock to the area.

The western part of the North-west Territories and the Mackenzie River valley are the best-known and most accessible parts. The capital is Yellowknife, which has a population of about 17,000. This represents almost a quarter of the total population of the region. Yellowknife is a modern city with high-rises, hotels, restaurants, a museum and two gold mines. The old part of the town is a picturesque collection of old gold rush buildings. Tourists use it as a base for trips to the more remote regions of the north. Access to Yellowknife by road is from Edmonton, 1,600 km (994 miles) along the Mackenzie Highway. Apart from this main road and its network of offshoot roads, the rest of the territories are accessible only by air.

Yukon

In a Nutshell	
Total land area:	482,517 sq km (186,300 sq miles)
Total fresh water area:	4481 sq km (1,730 sq miles)
Coastline:	343 km (213 miles)
Population (2001):	29,000
Capital:	Whitehorse

Yukon in the native language means 'greatest'—an apt name indeed for a land that is full of jagged mountains, boundless waterways, infinite wildlife and sharply contrasting seasons.

It has vast mineral wealth, and mining is the Yukon's major industry. However, most of its resources have yet to be unearthed because of the harsh climate and rugged terrain.

The Yukon is almost synonymous with gold, which was discovered in the area in the late 19th century. The discovery resulted in the world's last great gold rush. People flocked to the Klondike from all over the world. Dawson City became boom city, with a population of more than 30,000 people then. Today, only 2,000 keep it alive.

Whitehorse was the stopping point en route to the Klondike, and when the gold turned to dust, it was also the stopping point for those who made it back. Today, it is the administrative capital of the Yukon, and about 19,000 people live here.

Nunavut

In a Nutshell	
Total land area:	1,900,000 sq km (733,594 sq miles)
Population (2001):	27,000
Capital:	Iqaluit

On 1 April 1999, the map of Canada changed for the first time since 1949 (when Newfoundland joined Canada) and the new territory of Nunavut came into being. The creation of Nunavut is the result of lengthy negotiations between the Inuit, who have long aspired to control their own land and future, and the Canadian government.

The Nunavut government is made up of a legislative assembly that reflects the ethnic make up of the territory (85 per cent Inuit) and makes decisions by consensus. That means its decisions are made with the unanimous agreement of the majority of its members rather than along party lines. The members of the legislative assembly (MLAs) hold a secret ballot in order to elect a speaker, who oversees operation of the assembly. Also elected in a secret vote by the MLAs is the premier of Nunavut, as well as the executive (cabinet).

There are three distinct regions of Nunavut: Qikiqtaaluk, Kivalliq and Kitikmeot. Most of the people are Inuit. The capital, Iqaluit, has a population of over 5,000 and lies roughly 3 degrees south of the Arctic Circle. Nunavut is rich in mineral deposits such as copper, gold, silver, lead, zinc and diamonds.

HISTORY

The history of Canada is one of immigration and the filling up of empty spaces. Much larger than their continental neighbour to the south, the lands that are now part of the sovereign nation of Canada have been the scene of constant challenges between one group and another for supremacy. Today, Canada brings together 10 provinces and three territories, stretching from the Atlantic to the Pacific Ocean and from the 49th parallel to the frozen lands of the Arctic Circle. The people of the provinces and territories are united into one nation with a common identity and many similarities in its vision of itself. However, there are still differences and tensions within Canada. Both the similarities and the differences are the result of historical events which have shaped the country into what it has become today.

'The People'

The first two groups of people to come to North America in the earliest times were almost always referred to by later European arrivals as 'Indians' or 'Eskimos'. In neither case is this an accurate indicator of their origins nor even pleasing to themselves as a description of their people. In fact, native Canadians prefer to refer to themselves in their own languages simply as 'the People'—the undisputed first inhabitants of the land.

It seems likely that the first group of 'the People' to come to Canada crossed from somewhere in Asia by means of a now non-existent land bridge sometime during the last Ice Age.

Hunting to Survive

Grouped in small wandering tribes, they roamed the ice-covered land in search of food. As much of the surface of Canada was still covered by glaciers and vast sheets of ice, game was not always easy to find. The animals that they managed to hunt and kill provided them with food, shelter, warmth and clothing, and for many centuries, this way of life suited 'the People' perfectly.

However, as the ice began to recede and vegetation took its place, the nomadic hunting tribes began to gather some of the wild plants for food. When this happened, it was a short move from the gathering stage to the point at which agriculture itself started to develop. So some of the original tribal groups stopped wandering and began to cultivate the land deliberately. Maize—often called Indian corn—made its first appearance, and although the crops that the early cultivators farmed did not encourage anything like the stage of agricultural development that took place in Europe, gradually a stable and prosperous group of gathering communities began to emerge, scattered across the face of North America. There was very little, if any, communication between these groups due to the enormous distances involved. But the People had begun to stake their claims to the land—claims that would be hotly contested later. For the time being, however, the People's settlement process continued gradually and mostly peacefully over many centuries—until the beginning of exploration in North America by European navigators and the inevitable cultural conflicts that followed.

The Arrival of the Europeans

It is still not known exactly who the first Europeans to come to North America were, but legends—and some recently recovered artifacts—suggest that the Norsemen of Scandinavia landed on the east coast of North America (including Newfoundland) long before the arrival of Christopher Columbus in the New World. Probably other European fishermen also discovered the New World before Columbus—the Grand Banks off the coast of Newfoundland were known for centuries as one of the most prolific fishing grounds in the world, and there may have been permanent fishing communities in the parts of Canada adjacent to them, such as Newfoundland, as early as the 13th century. However, it was not until the early European colonisers came that the native people received the first significant challenge to their way of life. The French were the first to

A re-enactment of a famous battle in an Ontario park.

realise the enormous potential of this vast undeveloped land and particularly the abundance of natural resources which it possessed—in fact the same kinds of resources that the native communities had been relying on for centuries. French explorers (and later English ones too) were initially looking for furs, much in demand for the European fashion styles of the day, thus fetching a high price in the markets of Europe. As a result, men such as Samuel de Champlain and Pierre de la Verendrye became the first Europeans to penetrate the interior of Canada, and through their travels, spearheaded the first contacts between the original peoples and the European settlers who soon followed and began to take possession of the land for themselves.

The Hudson's Bay Company

The British weren't far behind the French in the race to exploit this new country. The Company of Gentlemen Adventurers into Hudson Bay (now known simply as the Hudson's Bay Company) was created in 1660 under the auspices of the British King Charles II, and the rivalry between the English and the French, which has coloured much of the development of this new land, began in earnest.

At first, the native peoples with whom these early adventurers came in contact were more than eager to sell to the newcomers all the fur they wanted for the new wonders they could get in exchange: knives, copper pots, clothing and guns. But relying on the native people to satisfy the supply could not last long.

Struggle for Supremacy

Settlement almost always follows trade and so the next 100 years had a profound impact on the way of life that had been carried on uninterrupted by the native peoples over the preceding centuries. In one way or another, the next period was one of almost continuous wars between the English and the French over rights to both trade and settlement. The Hudson's Bay Company staked its claim to all the land which fell into the watershed of Hudson's Bay, where it had first established trading posts, while the French, using their system of *coureurs de bois*, had penetrated with their large canoes further and further into the mainland surrounding and leading away from the Saint Lawrence River. Of course, no attention was paid to the rights of the native people and any interference from them usually resulted in either attempts to convert them to the European way of thinking (often accompanied by religious conversion) or outright extermination. As a result of this invasion, by the early 1700s, French settlement was well established, particularly along the shores of the Saint Lawrence River, while the British had extended northwards from their southern colonies and established strings of trading posts close to, or even on, the

It did not take long for these new British settlers to have an impact on the way Canada was governed, and to tip the balance even further away from the previous domination of the fledgling economy by the fur trading interests located in Quebec and Montreal.

territory claimed by the French. The rivalry between the British and French finally came to a head in 1759 when the French forces, under the command of General Montcalm, were besieged by the English troops of General James Wolfe in an attempt to capture the French stronghold of Quebec. The British success in this battle became one of the pivotal points in the course of Canadian history by entrenching British supremacy over those areas of Canada which were later to become Quebec and Ontario, and by laying the foundation for the resentment and distrust which persists into modern Canadian life.

Spread of British Culture

The British domination of settlement and trade in North America was not to go unchallenged, however. And not only by the French. In 1776, Britain's own American colonies rebelled against their colonial masters in the American War of Independence. As a result, some of the British immigrants began to move northwards to stake their claims to new land in Canada which was still firmly within the jurisdiction of Britain and so removed from the influence of the rebellious

American colonists. These Loyalists, as they became known, settled mainly along the shores of northern Lake Ontario and in the Maritime Provinces, establishing a formal British presence. They brought with them a culture which was very different from both that of the natives and the French culture which was still flourishing not many miles away up the Saint Lawrence.

The Creation of Canada

In 1791, the old Province of Quebec, created after the fall of New France to the British in 1763, was divided into two parts: Lower and Upper Canada. Lower Canada, with Quebec City as its centre, remained mainly French in character in spite of the fact that it was now under British rule, while Upper Canada was controlled by the British elements who had settled in the area after the American War of Independence. The capital city of York (now Toronto) was very much influenced by these staunchly British Loyalist settlers.

However, the antagonism between the remaining British colonies in North America and the newly independent country to the south, did not subside. Much of the conflict centred around the insistence of the British to retain control over shipping in the Saint Lawrence River and the Great Lakes. This meant, in the British opinion, that they had the right to stop and search American ships to see if they were carrying aid to France, with whom the British were once again at war. The Americans finally declared war on Britain and its colonies in 1812. There were several land skirmishes during the two years that this war lasted. Several naval battles were also fought on Lake Ontario, but in the end, neither side gained a strategic advantage over the other and the War of 1812, which was the only occasion when Canada and the United States have come into actual armed conflict, was eventually terminated by the Treaty of Ghent in 1814. The issues that had led to its outbreak were finally settled three years later in the Rush-Bagot Agreement between Britain and the United States.

Following the resolution of the War of 1812, there was considerable growth in population in both Canadas with the result that a sense of nationalism began to emerge for the first time. The governors of both provinces, appointed by the British king, began to feel and see challenges to their formerly undisputed authority, some of them resulting in outright political rebellion. Lord Durham, sent out by the British to investigate the cause of the political unrest, suggested in his report of 1839 that the two provinces be united once again (partly to facilitate the total assimilation of the French Canadians) and that this new single entity be given its own legislature with considerably increased political powers. The British government agreed and this union took place in 1841, creating the new Province of Canada.

During this period, the provinces close to the Atlantic had also been growing in population and were establishing their own identities. New Brunswick, Nova Scotia and Prince Edward Island, as well as Newfoundland, had attracted their share of settlers from both the French and British communities. Although all these areas had a certain degree of autonomy, they were still under the direct control of the British government in London, as was the Province of Canada. During the 1840s and 1850s, all the new provinces began to face problems brought about by a rapidly industrialising world. To cope with these problems and to help spread the load, talks began among the leaders of the various areas on the possibility of union. In 1867, the provinces of Canada, Prince Edward Island, Nova Scotia and New Brunswick joined together under the British North America Act into one country. This Confederation, as it was called, was only a limited beginning to the creation of what we now know as the country of Canada, but it did set the stage for Canada to become more than a reflection of the cultures and beliefs of France and England.

The Making of Modern Canada

Confederation brought together two peoples very different in culture and outlook who had reached a political agreement purely for economic reasons. It was an uneasy partnership as the history and culture of the British and French pulled them in such different directions. Canada had become, in effect, a bicultural country, but not yet a multicultural one.

An historic pioneer village. Here, young schoolgirls have their hands inspected before entering the classroom.

Up to and following Confederation, the native population had been steadily pushed westwards by the increasing British and French settlement in the east. The rock masses of the Canadian Shield had now become the great physical and psychological dividing line—to the east there was civilisation and sophistication, while to the west were the empty lands of Indians and buffaloes all the way to other British settlements along the Pacific shore in British Columbia. As a result, there was considerable concern among some Canadians that these empty lands would soon be swallowed up by the ever-expanding United States if steps were not taken to populate them with Canadians. The British-controlled Hudson's Bay Company still owned much of this empty land and so arrangements were made by the Canadian government to purchase it from them. This led quickly to the establishment in 1870 of the first Canadian political unit west of the Canadian Shield, called the Province of Manitoba. Following this, British Columbia agreed to join in the Confederation in 1871, following a promise that a railway line would be built, linking coast to coast. After some political tribulations, this line was indeed completed and the last spike hammered in at Craigellachie, high in the Rockies, in 1885.

Colonisation of Empty Lands

At last, the vast empty lands that stretched for miles between Manitoba and British Columbia had become accessible from the east and so could be populated. Thus a concentrated effort was made to attract new settlers from outside the country to fill this new but still very desolate land. Through a massive publicity campaign, promising free farm land to those who came to Canada and successfully established themselves there, new immigrants were attracted from all over Europe to Canada. They were taken westwards on special trains run along the newly completed Canadian Pacific transcontinental line. Some of these new settlers were experienced farmers who had never had the good fortune to own their own land and who were overjoyed to accept and develop the tracts of virgin land that were given to them by the Canadian government. Others were new both to the country and to the type of backbreaking labour they had volunteered for. Although some of the newcomers gave up and went home, the descendants of many of the original settlers still farm the same prairie land today, though on a scale and in a style that must have been unimaginable to their hard-working ancestors who had to develop the land with basic farming implements and their own bare hands.

Eventually, this vast influx of new settlers resulted in the formation of the new provinces of Saskatchewan and Alberta in 1905. With the exception of Newfoundland, which after many years of deliberation finally joined the Canadian Confederation in 1949, the physical structure of Canada as we now know it was essentially in place.

As Canada grew and prospered, individual communities both contributed to and benefited from this prosperity. The first three decades of the 1900s were a time of great growth for Canadians, and even though the simmering dispute

The maple leaf is today a symbol of Canada. Its adoption as the national flag gave Canadians a greater sense of unity.

between English and French flared up again briefly over the issue of conscription into the British army during World War I, on the surface Canada appeared to be becoming an extremely prosperous and successful multi-cultural experiment. However, this sense of pride and harmony began to crumble when the Great Depression of the 1930s hit Canada hard. New protest movements were formed, especially in Quebec and the farming communities of the west, leading to the development of new left-wing political parties, such as Social Credit. This popular unrest, although briefly halted by Canada's involvement in World War II, drew attention to the fact that some of the original underlying tensions between the peoples and regions of the country had never been completely dealt with or satisfactorily solved.

Conflict and Resolution

The externally imposed tension of World War II, which had temporarily diverted attention away from the internal problems of Canada, had receded. After this, a number of independence movements surfaced during the 1950s and 1960s, a definite sign of the growing feeling of disunity among the very different ethnic populations. The 'Quiet Revolution' in Quebec was an attempt by the Quebec and federal governments to work together to pay more attention to the specific problems of the French Canadians in Quebec, by methods such as the establishment of the Bi-lingualism and Bi-culturalism Commission in 1965. Prime ministers John Diefenbaker and Lester Pearson also tried to give Canada as a whole a greater sense of unity by the adoption of the Maple Leaf flag and the holding of Expo '67 in Montreal on the country's 100th birthday. However, these efforts did not go without opposition, as embodied by the FLQ (Front de Libération de Quebec), a home-grown terrorist organisation. Prime Minister Pierre Eliot Trudeau, a French Canadian himself and an extremely popular choice as national leader at the time of his election, may be best remembered for his tough stand against Quebec separatist terrorism during the early 1970s. But he is probably more well known for being the prime minister who finally won Canada's own written constitution, with the right to amend and change it without resorting to the British Parliament as had formerly been the case.

However, in spite of all the federal efforts to define the best possible relationship between Quebec and the rest of the country, political unrest in Quebec culminated in the election of the Parti Quebecois in 1976 on a separatist platform of sovereignty association with Canada (which would grant political but not economic independence from the rest of the country). In the event, a referendum in 1979 rejected any form of outright separation, but did little to reconcile French Canadians with their English neighbours.

Unrest also resurfaced in the western provinces of the country, which had long felt neglected by the concentration of political and economic power in eastern Canada. The need for change in the region began to be emphasised, even leading to talk of the formation of a western-based Reform Party if the problems of western Canadians were not soon addressed satisfactorily by the government in Ottawa.

During the 1970s and 1980s, native Canadians too began to demonstrate dissatisfaction with their lot and with the land sacrifices that their ancestors had been called upon to make. Some of the earliest treaty arrangements had been negotiated with individual bands and were little more than licences for outright exploitation of their lands and resources. Legislation during the 20th century had begun to redress this imbalance by providing special privileges, such as tax relief, for registered native Canadians, but most of the native population were still encouraged, by law, to live on their own reserves and not to mix with their non-native neighbours.

As a result, political agitation among the various native groups centred around these three issues:

- to have the aboriginal peoples of Canada recognised as a 'distinct society'—a phrase first used by the French Canadians to describe themselves—to include special provisions in any constitutional legislation;
- to define clearly their place in Canadian society; and
- to settle, once and for all, native claims for land and legal rights.

To counter all these feelings of alienation, the federal government continued its efforts in trying to bring a sense of unity to Canada, especially with the repatriation of the Canadian Constitution in 1982 and other specific regional legislative attempts to heal the rifts that seemed to be developing in all areas of the country.

Canada in the 21st Century

Although the tensions that exist beneath the surface are real and in need of solution, Canada is still more than just the sum of its parts. However, much economic, social and linguistic issues threaten to disunite the country, more profoundly now than they have ever done since Confederation. There is still a desire among most Canadians to make their country work and to resist its disintegration and subsequent inevitable absorption by the United States.

To achieve this, both the federal and the Quebec governments began initiatives in 1990 to find out what needs to be done to reunite the country in a meaningful way. In spite of growing regional anti-French and anti-English sentiments, these commissions represent a serious attempt to prevent further disunity. The issue of aboriginal rights and land claims is also being actively examined by the federal government, through a series of high level meetings and Royal Commissions, in an attempt to reach an agreement on the rightful status of the native Canadians in their homeland.

The need for action on these divisive issues is becoming clearer for Canada in the 21st century and its citizens are undergoing a fundamental change. What is needed, and what the current government commissions are seeking, is the promotion of a common vision of what unites all Canadians and makes them contribute equally to the success of the country. Finding this will not be easy, especially given the historical legacy of Canada, and it will require compromise and sacrifice. But if it can be achieved, Canada in the 21st century will be a strong and united country, having renewed its basic traits of tolerance and understanding, and having found peaceful solutions to its problems of division.

THE POLITICAL SPECTRUM

Canadian politics obviously play a very important part in defining what Canada is now and what it will become in the future. The Canadian democratic traditions are very open, and Canadians have strong opinions about their politicians and their multi-level system of government, federal (national), provincial and municipal.

Canada is a member of the Commonwealth of Nations and a constitutional monarchy. As such, it is headed by a Governor General, who acts as the representative of Queen Elizabeth II in Canada and exercises the monarch's functions on her behalf. The Governor General is appointed by the Queen on the recommendation of the prime minister of Canada, and usually stays in office for five years. He/she is granted the use of his/her own personal standard which flies over his/her two official residences: Rideau Hall in Ottawa and the Governor's Wing in the Quebec Citadel. Some of his/her functions are the summoning and dissolution of Parliament, the appointment of ambassadors and the commissioning of officers in the Armed Forces. He/she also gives royal assent to any new law passed by the House of Commons and is consulted in the same way that the Queen would be if she lived in Canada.

The headquarters of the federal government have moved location many times, but since Confederation, they have been in Ottawa, formerly Bytown, at the head of the Rideau Canal. The Canadian Parliament is divided into two houses, the House of Commons and the Senate. The former comprises elected representatives and the latter appointees for life by the prime minister. All new bills require the support of both houses and the assent of the Governor General before becoming laws. The federal parliament is responsible for matters that affect the country as a whole: national defence, citizenship, foreign policy, economic policy and currency.

The Governor General
The first Canadian to hold the post of Governor General was Vincent Massey who was appointed in 1952, and the first woman Governor General was Jeanne Sauve, who was appointed in 1983. The current Governor General is Michaëlle Jean who was born in Haiti and is the first African Canadian to hold this post.

Provincial parliaments are located in all the capital cities of the ten Canadian provinces, and are responsible under the constitution for the administration of all provincial matters, including main roads, social services, education, health care, industrial growth and the environment. The three territories have their own administrative councils for the same purposes, but, due to their much smaller populations, these do not have the same degree of autonomy as the provincial parliaments.

Local government is headquartered in small towns and cities all over the country, and looks after schools, libraries, public utilities, parks, recreation facilities and urban planning.

Political Parties

There are four political parties in Canada which are represented in the federal parliament in Ottawa, the Canadian capital. At the time of writing (2006), the party in power is the Conservative Party, led by Stephen Harper, which forms a minority government. The main opposition is the Liberal Party.

The Bloc Quebecois is the next largest party in terms of seats. It is composed mainly of members of parliament elected from ridings in Quebec. Its main reason for existence is to ensure that Quebec voters receive the special treatment from the government which they feel is their due and to assist these same voters in their movement towards the emergence of an independent Quebec, politically and economically separated in some manner from the rest of the country.

The remaining party, the New Democratic Party, led by Jack Layton, is the closest the Canadian government gets to socialism.

At the provincial level, there are also a number of significant political groups, once again mainly in Quebec and in the west. Two votes for separation have already been held, in 1976 and 1995. Both were unsuccessful. Although the 1995 referendum was a close call for the Federalists, the enthusiasm for separation from Canada seems to have waned somewhat in Quebec over the last few years. The Liberal Party is currently in power in Quebec, while the Bloc Quebecois, the Separatist Party, forms the official opposition. In the west, the Social Credit Party, although with nothing like the backing of the Parti Quebecois in Quebec (and not even as strong as it has been in the past), remains a strong political force in western Canadian politics.

The municipal governments, which control all local activities, are not as politically oriented as their federal or provincial counterparts. They are also more directly responsive to those they represent because of their proximity. But they are still subject to persuasion from the political parties on issues that involve funding from higher levels of government.

Regrettably, however, there is a strong cynicism among the Canadian population at the moment about all political processes and the politicians who control them. Politics in Canada is not regarded as a noble profession but more of a self-serving one. It will take strong commitment from aspiring politicians in the future to overcome this and restore trust among the electorate that the government and its policies really operate in the best interests of the citizens of the country as a whole.

The Canadian Charter of Rights and Freedoms

On 17 April 1982, Canada gained, for the first time, a written constitution, which among other things, gave certain legal guarantees to all Canadians. This Charter of Rights and Freedoms includes four fundamental freedoms—of conscience and religion, of thought, belief, opinion and expression, of peaceful assembly, and of association—and a number of other rights associated with these. These rights include the right to life, liberty and security of the person, the right to perform certain actions if suspected of a crime and to be presumed innocent until proven guilty, and rights guaranteeing equality under the law, regardless of race, national or ethnic origin, colour, religion, sex, age and mental or physical ability. Each of these areas is clearly defined in the Charter of Rights and in any provincial legislation dealing with these areas, and any violation can be challenged in court. Most provinces also retain an ombudsman who investigates alleged breaches of civil rights and rectifies any miscarriages of justice.

Canadians take the rights and freedoms granted to them very seriously—more seriously perhaps than any other legal aspect of their lives—and there is always great pressure from the community when it is felt that one of these rights is being infringed upon. Laws relating to contentious social issues, such as abortion, have frequently been the subject of challenges, and in spite of sometimes strongly-held conflicting prejudices, the rights of the individual are usually upheld and safeguarded. This gives rise to controversy and occasionally social unrest, but one thing most Canadians do accept is the fairness of the concept that an individual has the right to make his own decisions in situations which do not affect others.

These constitutional rights override and nullify any federal or provincial law which conflicts with them—subject to a successful court challenge—and cannot be repealed or amended by any parliament or legislature. The only possible exception to the operation of the Charter of Rights and Freedoms is its provision for the federal parliament or a province to declare that one of its own laws shall operate within its jurisdiction in spite of an obvious conflict with one of the stated rights and freedoms. This provision for 'opting out' is valid for five years but can be renewed for a further five-year period.

THE CANADIAN VISION

CHAPTER 3

'Americans have great and noble principles
and they go to hell trying to live up to them.
Canadians also have great and noble principles but
they go to heaven figuring out ways to get around them'
—Noam Chomsky, philosopher

IT IS PROBABLY BECAUSE CANADA'S HISTORY has been so full of cultural conflict and confusion, that there has been interminable discussion among Canadians in an attempt to define what a Canadian really is and what vision of the world he espouses. The debate continues to this day, so narrowing down the nature of Canada and its view of itself is nearly impossible. All that anyone can really do is to examine what has been said, written and implied about the nature of this country, but any final understanding must always be the responsibility of the individual to reach by drawing conclusions from both the concrete and abstract clues that Canada and its citizens provide from their daily lives.

John Porter, a Canadian social historian, in a well known book about Canada published in the 1960s, referred to Canada as a 'vertical mosaic' in which different ethnic groups and social classes lived in a clearly defined relationship to one another. It is this concept of the 'mosaic' rather than the more American concept of the 'melting pot' which has had the major influence on what Canada has become today. The difference between 'melting pot' and 'mosaic' lies in the way in which a country and its inhabitants integrate new arrivals into the social fabric of the country. In Canadian terms, what the mosaic concept has really meant is that newcomers to Canada—and nearly all Canadians are either newcomers themselves or have fairly recent ancestors who were new arrivals—have been encouraged both to retain their own cultural identity and to attempt to become part of some overall Canadian identity at the same time. This has never been an easy task as it has really meant trying to do two things at the same time, one of which was very ill-defined. This has led to considerable discussion and confusion within Canada itself as to whether the Canadian identity is different from or the same as the sum of all the various cultural parts which have been contributed to it.

Thus, anyone who lives in Canada for any length of time will be confronted by the two questions that Canadians are continually asking themselves: what does being Canadian mean and how should I view myself in terms of my own Canadian identity?

WHAT IS A CANADIAN?

Pierre Berton, one of Canada's best known authors and historians, writes in his book *Why We Act Like Canadians* that Canadians have come to terms with the tensions that obsess them, slowly and cautiously in the Canadian fashion, and that they are beginning to understand that these tensions will not go away. Instead, they must learn to live with them, adapt to them and survive them, just as they have survived their appalling geography.

In talking of the Canadian obsession with tension, Berton may have put his finger on something fundamental to understanding how most Canadians think of themselves. Dealing with tension does lead to caution and most Canadians will agree that they are a cautious people. Certainly Canadians lack the flamboyance of the Americans who insist on 'liberty at any price', and as Berton claims, seem to prefer the concept of a democracy which 'is dispensed from the heavens like gentle rain' rather than the American kind which 'sprouts upwards from the grass'.

Perhaps Canadian cautiousness comes mainly from the fact that the Canadian people have always been caught between the demands of two cultures. They are also caught between the paternalism of Britain and France on the one hand, and the aggressive egalitarianism of the United States on the other. Many people—both inside and outside the

Although once common in the countryside, traditional blacksmiths like this one can only be seen in a special historical village.

country—see Canada as a compromise between the two, without either the reserve of the British or the brashness of the Americans, and this seems to be borne out in the attitude that Canadians try to project of themselves to others. But in trying to incorporate the best of two worlds into one national identity, some of their original strengths may have become diluted. As a result, many Canadians still say that there is no truly Canadian vision per se—though most Canadian writers, poets and dramatists would tell you differently—and that what Canadians are in effect is simply a pale reflection of some vast cultural and sociological mix. However, this ignores the fact that the perceived identity of the country as a peculiarly successful blend of understanding and acceptance is a vision shared by many Canadians, and that this could only have been achieved through a unique set of circumstances which have shaped the special nature of the Canadian people as a whole.

Statistics tell some of the story that makes Canadians a special people. Out of a Canadian population of nearly 32 million, more than 15 million now live in big metropolitan areas like Toronto, Montreal and Vancouver, and have adopted the outlook of big city dwellers. On the other hand, two million people still live in a completely rural, and predominantly traditional, lifestyle on the farms that dot the countryside. However, this represents a significant population shift in such a comparatively young country, as up to World War II, 25 to 30 per cent of Canadians lived away from the cities and on farms. Today, these farms are fast disappearing, changing the face of the country, and its attitudes, in the process. The remainder of the population live in the smaller towns and cities spread across the country, reflecting both the traditional values of a rural society and the more progressive attitudes of the urbanite. This mix of traditional and progressive attitudes is peculiarly Canadian and accounts, in no small measure, for both some of the special ways in which Canada sees the world and also for its internal divisions.

Thus, although Canada today is predominantly an urban, mobile society with a progressive contemporary vision, it is still tempered by the fact that many city dwellers are newcomers to city life. They are either recently transplanted from smaller Canadian communities or from completely different communities in other countries who have come to Canada seeking a new life and a new vision for themselves. For this reason alone, any static definition of what a Canadian is is extremely hard to achieve, and will continue to be as long as the sociological mix of Canadians is constantly changing through internal population shifts and constant immigration from a variety of foreign cultures.

CANADIAN STEREOTYPES

Although an actual definition of a true Canadian might be hard to reach, there is no shortage of Canadian stereotypes, most of them unflattering. In the 1980s, the Canadian comedy team of Bob and Doug Mackenzie specialised in portraying the stereotypical Canadian as a boozing outdoorsman whose ignorance of the world around him was only exceeded by his own stupidity. Bob and Doug's stereotypes were limited in their vocabulary and their conversation—liberally sprinkled with the addition of 'eh', a supposed Canadianism—revolved round fishing and the price of beer. Most Canadians found the observations of Bob and Doug Mackenzie funny, but also a little disturbing as there was no doubt a grain of truth in the picture.

Observations from the Side

Here are some comments on Canadians made by a cross-section of current observers of Canada:

'Historically, a Canadian is an American who rejects the revolution.'
—Northrop Frye, literary philosopher

'I think our identity will have to be something which is partly British, partly French, partly American, partly derived from a variety of other influences which are too numerous even to catalogue.'
—Eugene Forsey, government senator

'Dull and introverted and all the rest of it though we may be, Canadians have, as a people, a national gift for tolerance and an acquired skill at compromise.'
—Richard Gwyn, newspaper columnist

'Years ago, the British critic Ron Bryden said to me, "Canadians are nice, very nice and they expect everybody else to be very nice"; and I have yet to come up with a better definition.'
—Mordecai Richler, novelist

'The problem is that Canada is not so much a nation, more an act of faith ... I asked dozens of people what made them specifically Canadian and every single one defined their country purely in terms of not being American.'
—Simon Hoggart, journalist

'A Canadian is somebody who knows how to make love in a canoe.'
—Pierre Berton, media personality

'Sociologically I am an American. Psychologically, a Canadian. Sentimentally, a Quebecois... Everywhere I see dualities.'
—Clark Blaise, author

'Well it's a good place to live. But that's all Canada is—just a good place to live. Canadians have lost their destiny.'
—Donald Creighton, historian

'Perhaps then, Canada is not so much a country as magnificent raw material for a country: and perhaps the question is not "Who are we?" but "What are we going to make of ourselves?"'
—Alden Nowlan, poet

In 1952, noted Canadian actor Don Harron created the character of Charlie Farquharson, a rustic who has since become one of Canada's most endearing, and enduring, comic stereotypes. Charlie is an uneducated man with an interesting vocabulary and strong opinions about his country, its history and the way it is run. As Charlie Farquharson, Don Harron has often appeared on television and radio to comment on Canadian society and to encourage it to look at itself in a humorous way. Charlie Farquharson's comments have also been collected into a series of books which have found their way onto most Canadian bookshelves, the most famous of which is *Charlie Farquharson's History of Canada*.

But if you ask many Canadians today to describe the way in which Canadians are stereotyped, both by themselves and by outsiders, especially by Americans, you will get comments about Canadians being seen as a fundamentally boring people, living in a land of perpetual ice and snow, and surrounded by polar bears and men in red coats. Most Canadian stereotypes are rarely positive and seem to emphasise either only the scenic beauty of the country or the backwardness and conservatism of the people. To be fair, however, in a more positive light, Canada and Canadians have also achieved an international reputation as constructive compromisers, especially negotiators and peacemakers, capable of seeing all sides of a position.

MULTICULTURALISM IN CANADA

Just as there are many views of what a Canadian is, there are also many myths about the nature of Canada's multiculturalism. The most enduring is that Canada is not really a multicultural country, but a creation of the British, to which all other cultures have become subservient. Up to the end of the 19th century there might have been some truth in this as there can be no doubt that the British government did try to create Canada in its own image, especially at the expense of the French. But ever since the arrival of the large waves of immigrants from Europe before World War I and after World War II, Canada's character has changed and its population base includes people whose origins are as diverse as the world itself. In the last two decades, more than 1 million immigrants came to Canada from more than 100 different countries, settling in cities and small towns, and changing their characters for ever. Surprisingly perhaps, this influx of ethnically diverse newcomers into what were predominantly enclaves of western culture does not seem to have led to any kind of overt racism, as it has done in some areas of the United States. Canada and Canadians have a remarkable record for tolerance and this characteristic seems to ease the absorption of newcomers. As a result, there is little evidence of racial conflict in the country, even in its major cities.

In fact, the ever-growing multicultural nature of the country is now reflected in the attention that is paid to it by both private and public agencies. The federal government's Department of Citizenship and Immigration as well as the corresponding provincial departments have a number of services and publications designed specifically to assist

The Mennonites were among the first Europeans to come to Canada.

newcomers to Canada. The right to an interpreter in a court of law is now enshrined in the Canadian Charter of Rights and Freedoms, while many educational authorities are introducing both extensive English as a Second Language and Heritage Language programmes in the schools. The concept of the vertical mosaic with the Anglo-Saxon cultures at the top is now thankfully a dying one and does not seem to be replaced by any other kind of national stereotype.

The mosaic is still growing and increasing in complexity, with the result that, as Canada settles into the 21st century, there are more Canadians with origins outside North America than there are from within. This fact alone will change the nature of the country and its needs forever. Acceptance, understanding and tolerance of many cultures has become part of the Canadian way of life and those who come to this country in the future will find that these Canadian traditions are alive and well. However, the Canadian stereotype may well undergo some change over the years while, probably, Canada's seemingly unending search for its true identity will still go on.

CANADA'S YOUNG AND YOUNG AT HEART

The typical Canadian family is small and usually includes father, mother and two children. There are few extended families. The average family size has dropped from 3.9 people in 1961 to 3.0 in 2000. This is due mainly to lower fertility rates, but also to an increasing number of single-parent families. The birth rate has declined rapidly. In 1971, the average woman gave birth to 3.2 children. By 1981, that figure was 2.8. Today it is only 1.7.

Family lives have changed dramatically. Social changes, a decline in religious beliefs and liberal divorce laws have resulted in an increasing proportion of marriages that end in divorce. By the mid-1980s, almost 50 per cent of all marriages ended in divorce. More Canadians are living alone than used to be the case. The number of single-parent families is increasing at a fast rate and in 1996 represented 14.5 per cent of all families with children. There has also been a big increase in families with no children at home, either because these are childless families or because the children have left home. However, two-parent families with children are still the norm. A new family unit that has recently emerged and is increasingly accepted is that formed by two people of the same sex.

The average age of marriage for men is 27 years and for women 25 years. When speaking of marriage, one can differentiate between marriages that take place in church, civil marriages performed outside church and by a justice of peace, and 'common-law marriages' in which two people live together without having been legally married. Increasing numbers of Canadians are living in common-law relationships. In 1996, the number of couples that reported living in such common-law unions represented a 28 per cent increase over 1991.

Canada's Young

As in many other industrialised countries, where both parents are in the workforce, day care for pre-schoolers and children of school age is a major problem. Figures from Statistics Canada show that 68 per cent of women in the full-time workforce have a child under the age of three.

Parents, therefore, have to resort to the costly solution of sending their children to an assortment of child-minding facilities, such as nursery schools, child minders who will babysit in their own homes or at the child's home, after-school centres, child-minding centres and all-day child care centres. Some of these facilities are funded by the federal or provincial government, but child care is, unfortunately, still very expensive. In order to help such families, the federal government offers tax credits and subsidies. The various provinces may also have different programmes, such as the day care subsidy programme in British Columbia for families with a low income to meet the cost of day care services for their children.

The Block Parent Programme

This is a Canada-wide programme that aims to get each neighbourhood to protect the children in its area. Quite

Cheering children show their enthusiasm on Canada Day.

simply, a Block Parent is a responsible adult who cares about the well-being and safety of children and volunteers his or her home as a refuge for children in distress. After being screened by the police, the Block Parent is given a recognisable red and white sign (that of an adult holding a child by the hand) that he displays in the window of his home where it is clearly visible from the street. A child in trouble—either ill, lost, being bullied, alarmed by strangers or vicious animals, or caught in bad weather conditions—will know he can go to such a house for help. Police are supportive of this programme because it acts as a deterrent to criminals and troublemakers.

The Paper Chase

Constitutionally, education is a provincial matter, which means that educational policies are determined by provincial governments and not by the federal government, and so there is a great diversity across the country regarding the primary and secondary school system. Each province has its own department of education and its own system for training teachers. The schools are supported with money derived from local taxes as well as government grants. These schools account for more than 90 per cent of the school population. All Canadians have access to public education up to graduation at Grade 12, and both public schools and secondary schools are free of charge and open to all.

In all provinces, there are some elementary and secondary schools which are private or independent, and provide an alternative to the public school. These schools are operated by private bodies for specific religious, language, social or educational purposes. They may or may not be denominational, and are all privately funded, although some do receive additional financial support from their provincial governments. There are also private kindergartens and nursery schools for children of pre-elementary age and in five provinces—Newfoundland, Quebec, Ontario, Saskatchewan and Alberta—there are separate schools. These schools are affiliated to certain religious bodies but remain within the public school system. Roman Catholic schools form the largest group. Other separate schools are run by Protestant churches (a combination of Anglican, United Church and Salvation Army) as well as Pentecostal churches and Seventh Day Adventists.

When the children have progressed from day care to school, they are usually about five or six years old and are

Young children can join a variety of activity groups, such as the Girl Guides.

ready to begin their primary or elementary education, which is general and basic. Elementary school may start with either the kindergarten years or Grade One. Students remain in an elementary school until they are about 13 years old, and by that time, they should be in Grade Seven or Eight, depending on the province.

Children who might have been accustomed to a more regimented school life, having to wear school uniforms and conforming to many rules and regulations concerning colour of shoes, hair accessories, hair length and so on, will be surprised to find that, by contrast, there appears to be a lot of personal freedom in Canadian schools. Except perhaps in some private schools, students are not required to dress uniformly. They attend school wearing their everyday clothes and 'runners' or sport shoes.

Unconventional Schooling

Many students who live in rural areas travel in to their schools in special yellow school buses, while those in even more isolated areas can often take their lessons by correspondence or via the Internet.

It is not uncommon for schools to gain and lose students at any time of the year, due to the high mobility of the Canadian lifestyle. Many Canadian families relocate from one town to another or change provinces, often as a result of moving to where the jobs are. There are generally few problems enrolling a child in a school. A student is normally accepted into the school nearest the area in which he lives and placed in the grade that is appropriate to his age. Parents should have the child's leaving certificate from his previous school and his latest school report, in order to facilitate enrolment. They can either go directly to the school nearest their new home or to the school board in charge of the area. The child may be required to sit for an assessment paper that will determine which grade he will enter.

The Canadian school year begins in the first week of September and ends in June. There are two weeks of holiday during the Christmas-New Year period, and about 10 days of 'spring break' in March. Canadian students look forward to the months of July and August, during which they enjoy their longest holiday, the 'summer break'. A typical school day begins at 9:00 am and ends at 3:30 pm. There is a one-hour lunch break at noon, during which students either have their lunch in school, or at home, if home is near enough.

From Grade Eight or Nine to Grade 12, students attend secondary or high school. If one were to compare the Canadian grade system to that of schools following the British educational system, Grade 10 would be equivalent to the General Certificate of Education 'O' level, and Grade 12 to the GCE 'A' level.

Throughout these years, progress from one grade to another is usually determined by standards set by each individual school board. In the junior grades of high school, there is some opportunity for students to select their courses of study according to their interests. This choice is increased at the higher secondary level, when students are offered more subjects. Within the provincial educational requirements, they build their own programme from a number of subject areas. In the past, secondary schools were mainly concerned with preparing students for university, and vocational schools were separate, catering to those not going on to a post-secondary education. Today, however, while there are still technical and commercial high schools, most secondary schools provide a mixture for all types of students. Thus, depending upon resources available, a school may, besides providing the normal and basic academic subjects in the sciences and arts, allow students to study technical subjects such as woodwork, metal-work and auto mechanics; attend commerce courses in business management, data processing and typing; and explore many other possibilities such as home economics, choir and band, peer counselling and tutoring.

However, the number and variety of courses is dependent also on enrolment (the number of students who want to take a course) and the availability of a teacher.

After graduation from Grade 12, students are either absorbed into the job market, or continue their formal education through community colleges, technical institutes or universities. Those over 15 may leave school and enter the workforce. In Ontario, school is mandatory until the age of 16.

Admission to university usually requires graduation from high school with specific courses and levels of achievement in them. Depending on the university, a general bachelor's degree course in arts or science takes about three to four years to complete, with an extra year for an honours degree. Some faculties leading to the professions, such as law, medicine and engineering, may require the student to have part of or a complete first degree before he can be admitted. The University of Toronto, University of British Columbia and McGill University are three institutions with a well-established international reputation, but there are many other universities in Canada for the graduating secondary school student to choose from. There is even a virtual university, Athabasca University, which offers courses solely online through the Internet. Tuition fees vary according to the institution and the course of study, but a resident of Canada can expect to spend at least C$ 10,000 to C$ 12,000 a year for tuition, books and other materials and living expenses, and a foreign student at least twice that amount.

Community colleges, institutes of technology, applied arts and sciences, and colleges for training in specific areas such as agricultural technology, fisheries and marine technologies, etc. provide an alternative to a university education. Admission usually requires secondary school graduation. Most college courses, when successfully completed, furnish the graduate with a diploma or certificate. Some community colleges also offer what are called transfer courses, that is, students taking these courses may, after one or two years, apply for a transfer into a university where they will complete their course of study. Other colleges may be accredited to one or more universities, so that they may confer on their students taking a degree from that university.

Education for adults is a rapidly growing area of Canadian education—departments of education, school boards, community colleges and universities may accept mature students who have left secondary school for a number of years and have the necessary academic requirements, and now wish to resume full-time formal education. There are also many part-time programmes and correspondence courses for adults who wish to gain credits at various educational levels, or to further their personal interests.

Adolescent Attitudes

Youths from culturally traditional backgrounds who come to Canada for further studies are frequently amazed and even shocked at the manner with which their Canadian friends treat their parents and elders. When visiting friends at home, they may find that the Canadian adolescent does not hesitate to, in the words of one horrified observer, 'scold his parents'.

Perhaps this is because the young Canadian is trained from an early age to voice his thoughts and opinions. Participation is important in school. When questions are asked, you are expected to respond without having to be called. Children are encouraged to speak up and voice opinions even on 'adult' affairs. For example, young fifth graders may spend some school time listening to the news on the radio and then discuss what they have heard. It is therefore not surprising that if you ask an 11-year-old about an issue that is currently being discussed, you would receive a fairly informed opinion. Students are encouraged to think about and discuss current and controversial matters, and even to write letters to the government giving their opinion on some current constitutional matter.

Contrast this with the emphasis in a more traditional society on respect for elders and a 'speak only when you are spoken to' standard, and where every elder, whether family or friend, is dutifully greeted with a 'Hello, uncle' or 'Hello, aunt'. A child from such an environment is expected to keep out of adult affairs and concentrate on school work so as to obtain a good grade, get a good job, earn a lot of money and be a success in the world. It

The youth of Canada are used to having their views taken into consideration as views held by future voters, leaders and decision makers. They often find themselves on an almost equal footing with adults around them, parents and teachers included.

is unlikely that an 11-year-old Chinese youth from Singapore, for instance, would be asked for an opinion on political events in the country or world affairs. Coming from a background with such expectations, it is therefore not surprising for a young foreigner or recent immigrant in Canada to suffer from culture shock and to wonder whether a friend who calls everyone, including those much older, by their first names, is not lacking in respect.

Making Friends

Socialising skills are learnt early in life. Schools are often co-educational, with a mix of boys and girls who have every opportunity to learn how to behave with the opposite sex. On Valentine's Day, for instance, an elementary school may host a dance for its students during break time or after school hours, with boys and girls encouraged to mix under the watchful gaze of their teachers. The adolescent begins, at an early age, to be concerned with such problems as how to be attractive and popular, go to parties, date and 'go steady'. These worries compete with studies for attention. Sex education is a part of school curriculum. At this time of increased social activity and the pressures of school, the adolescent is particularly susceptible to problems caused by drugs and alcohol. The only solution is for parents to be vigilant and keep a close eye on the kind of company their children are keeping, without meddling in their life of course.

Working Life

Working life is introduced also at an early age. Many children, even when quite young, undertake to do odd jobs to supplement their allowances. They may clean yards, wash cars and windows, or take care of plants and pets when their owners are away. As they grow older, they 'graduate' to delivering newspapers, babysitting, even tutoring or working part-time at the corner shop as a cashier or a delivery person, and earn quite a decent amount of money. This habit of earning money on a part-time basis continues through high school, college and university. For many students, the money earned through a part-time job or a job during the summer often means the difference between being able to pay for the fees for next year's college or university education and having to give it up altogether.

Leaving the Nest

Entering adulthood is a serious business in any community, and this is as true in Canada as anywhere else. Because of the nature of the Canadian educational system and also of the society as a whole, this passage into manhood or womanhood tends to take place when a young person leaves home for the first time. Very often, this is when he or she enters college or university at the age of 18 or 19 years old.

There is no ceremony or special event to mark this transition, but instead, the controlling hand of parents is removed all of a sudden and the young adults find themselves totally dependent on their own devices, and having to learn the two major survival skills in Western society; time and money management.

This means going without transition from the comparative ease of having someone to tell them what time to get up, being nagged (hopefully constructively!) about what to do during the day and how to plan for future events, to suddenly having to organise all this for themselves. This is by no means an easy step! Perhaps even more traumatic is the responsibility for budgeting money. Paying tuition and rent, buying groceries, planning for entertainment, organising travel to and from home—all these adult decisions are suddenly heaped on young people who also have to cope with the pressures of being in a totally new social group, removed from the influences of their family and traditional support group.

In many ways, this is just as much a rite of passage as any special ordeal, and it is a very difficult one for many young Canadians to handle. The best preparation for leaving home is for parents to gradually relinquish their control over a year or so before their child is to move away. Let them learn by their own mistakes in a supportive atmosphere before they have to learn the hard way without the benefit of someone close by to pick up the pieces. This isn't easy, however, as many parents live in fear of letting off the brakes too early.

But the transition from home to the university or college setting is a fact of life for many children in Canada, and those who are best prepared for it will succeed the best when the inevitable time comes.

A Profile of Canada's Youth

How do we know what Canadian youths are like—their values, concerns, image of themselves, sources of enjoyment and goals? It is to have them speak for themselves, as one study commissioned by the Canadian Youth Foundation has done. In this 1987 study, called 'Canada's Youth Ready for Today', more than 2100 interviews were conducted with youths aged 15 to 24 across the country. Here are some of the results:

- When speaking of their goals, Canadian youth ranked friendship and being loved as tops. Other choices in order of importance were success in what you do, freedom, a rewarding career, a comfortable life and a good education. Popularity was last in the list of 15 goals.

- Friendship and music were cited as the main sources of enjoyment. Relationships with parents and members of the opposite sex were next in importance. Then came television, sports, pets, reading and being by oneself. 'In practice, young people prefer an evening with their friends to being alone. They would rather spend their time listening to music than going to a structured group [activity] led by adults,' observed the study.

- The problems that really bothered the youths, like everyone else, were money and never seeming to have enough time. Life after high school and its unknowns were also important concerns.

- As for smoking, alcohol and drugs, the study revealed that just over a third of Canadian youth smoked cigarettes and drank alcoholic beverages at least once a week. Young men drank alcohol on a more regular basis than women, but they smoked at equal levels. Eighty per cent said they never smoked marijuana and 90 per cent said they never used illicit drugs. However, the young people agreed that drugs were readily accessible to those who wanted to try them.

SENIOR CITIZENS

Canada is still a country of young people, but its population is ageing rapidly. In 2000, the proportion of under-15s was approximately 19 per cent. This is expected to fall below 16 per cent by the year 2011. The senior citizen population, on the other hand, is growing more rapidly than any other age group. Those aged 65 and over currently make up 12.7 per cent of the population and this figure is expected to go up to 15 per cent or more by 2011.

Most of the elderly (91 per cent) live in private households, while 9 per cent are in nursing homes and other institutions. About a quarter live alone.

How long does a Canadian live? According to Statistics Canada, the current life expectancy of Canadian men is 76 years, while that for Canadian women is 82 years. In most provinces, the mandatory retirement age is 65 years. But in the provinces of Manitoba, New Brunswick and Quebec, there is no age limit.

Thinking Positive

The elderly generally have a very positive image of themselves and don't subscribe to the idea that when you are old, you are over the hill. The word 'old' to describe an elderly person seems almost rude. 'Senior' is the preferred form of reference. In the words of one advertising agency, it's '55 or better' not '55 or older'.

Senior Citizens

It often pays to be a senior. Shops offer special discounts on 'Seniors' Day', travel agencies provide cheaper travel, and hunting and fishing licences, camping fees and bus passes cost very much less. Even the income tax department or Revenue Canada recognises the special status of a senior who is 65 'or better' and allows a special deduction from one's taxable income.

Life is not over; rather, it often takes a new turn. Seniors join choirs, form musical and theatrical groups, go hiking, learn new hobbies, take college and university courses. (Have you ever heard the word 'opsimath'? It means 'someone who learns late in life'!) Bulletin boards in centres catering to the needs of senior citizens, local shops and supermarkets, and the community newspaper are good places to search for news of such activities.

A marriage between two seniors is not uncommon. Many widows and widowers seek a new life with another partner, and such weddings are often well attended and blessed by the presence of children and grandchildren.

Many activities and services are organised for people in this age group. The National Advisory Council on Aging delves into matters related to ageing and the quality of life for seniors. Canada Post runs a Letter Carriers Alert Programme which ensures that a watchful eye is kept on the homes of seniors and the handicapped. There are homemaker services that help seniors to live independently, offering help with house cleaning, shopping, preparation of meals and personal care.

Retirement Communities

In some parts of Canada, developers have built housing subdivisions especially for seniors, known as retirement communities. These communities are usually close to a small town, maybe near recreational centres, and contain social and recreational facilities like tennis courts, a golf course and a social centre.

Climate is often a major factor when choosing a place to retire to, especially in a country as cold as Canada. Older people who suffer from arthritis, rheumatism, respiratory and other problems feel healthier in warmer climates. In British Columbia, for instance, the beautiful seaside town of Victoria on the island of Vancouver, with its moderate climate, and the sunny Okanagan area in the interior of the province are popular choices for retirement. However, many are lured by the sun down to the United States, into Florida and California.

Is There Life After Retirement?

Recreation when one is a senior must necessarily be something not too physically demanding. Golf, lawn bowling,

A senior citizen enjoys the company of his dogs at a waterfront park.

curling, fishing, gardening and watching television are some that fit the bill. Knitting, quilting, painting and various crafts and hobbies are other interests. In British Columbia, for instance, there is an Annual BC Seniors Games in which active seniors compete in events such as badminton, bagpiping, chess, bridge, cycling, darts, bowling, curling, golf, swimming and track and field.

In summer, the main roads are well travelled by those who love the outdoors, and this can be done in a relaxed and not too rigorous way. Many seniors own recreational vehicles (RVs) which are remarkably well equipped, much like a house on wheels complete with bunks, stove, fridge and shower. They spend the summer travelling from campsite to campsite all over the country.

If one could, by a large stretch of the imagination, call volunteering a recreational activity, it is without a doubt that senior citizens take on the volunteer's role with gusto. Volunteers are an essential ingredient of Canadian society without whom life would be much poorer. This spirit is nurtured in the young (children go door to door on 'bottle drives', collecting empty bottles and cans to return to the shops for a refund on the deposits, or selling cookies, calendars, etc. to raise funds for various school activities). It is also kept alive in adulthood through volunteer work with many service organisations, and certainly carries on into retired life.

Many retired seniors also take on part-time jobs, and retirement can often bring new careers, such as managing apartments or selling real estate; hobbies can become small businesses.

One service of interest with regard to seniors is the Canadian Executive Service Overseas (CESO), headquartered in Toronto, which provides an opportunity for elderly volunteers to use their training, educational background, experience and skills in projects to help in under-developed countries and native communities. The Canadian International Development Agency gives an annual grant to CESO to fund its foreign projects. Retired persons who volunteer are paid travel costs, maintenance and out-of-pocket expenses. These volunteers are usually in the 60- to 70-year age group. They provide technical or management guidance and advice, such as feasibility studies, to manage or guide an established operation and to assist with training.

A senior citizen volunteers for an elementary school music class. Many old people remain active after retirement and volunteering is a most worthwhile activity.

Moving About

Getting around town can be a task as one gets older, but Canada's seniors are fortunate to be able to take to cycles at that age. Not bicycles, but adult tricycles or trikes. These are what they appear to be—adult versions of the three-wheeled cycle, often with a basket in front for carrying things.

Unfortunately, though, not all seniors are able to get out and about, especially during winter time, when the weather is a major factor in keeping them home. These elderly are commonly referred to as 'shut-ins'. Many towns and cities have volunteer-run organisations that provide essential services to shut-ins, such as 'meals-on-wheels'. The elderly person can, for a nominal fee, have his meals cooked and delivered by volunteers several times a week.

Money Matters

Housing, food, clothing and taxes are the biggest items of expenditure for a retired person. Money matters in particular need to be well planned.

The federal government helps out with Old Age Security pensions and Guaranteed Income Supplements, both of which are tied to the cost of living as measured by the Consumer Price Index.

The Old Age Security pension is paid to a Canadian citizen who is 65 years or older. To get the full pension, you must have lived in Canada for 40 years after the age of 18. A partial pension is available if you have lived here for at least 10 years after age 18. It is not necessary to have paid into this plan or to have worked in Canada.

The Canada Pension Plan is another federal programme that operates in all the provinces but Quebec, where its equivalent is the Quebec Pension Plan. But the senior must first have made contributions to it while he was working before being entitled to draw from it after retirement. The payment is related to how much one has earned and contributed to the plan.

The Guaranteed Income Supplement, based on your income and marital status, and Spouse's Allowance, are geared to the needs of those with a low income. In addition, some provinces have other plans to supplement the income of the elderly who are in financial need, for example, Ontario's Guaranteed Annual Income System.

The Registered Retirement Savings Plan (RRSP) is a private retirement savings plan that supplements federal and company pension programmes. It is a savings plan that is registered with the government so that contributions made to it can be deductible from one's income tax. The amount that is invested and the interest earned from it are not taxed as long as they remain and are not withdrawn from the plan. This is to give Canadians the incentive to save a portion of their income during their earning years to provide income when they are retired.

Any Canadian taxpayer, from any age until the end of the year he or she turns 69 years old, who has earned income, from salaries, bonuses, commissions, business, rental from property, can contribute to an RRSP. This scheme is available through banks, trust companies and investment brokers.

Senior Centres

These have been developed in every province and in the Yukon. They function as drop-in centres, activity centres or multi-purpose centres for older people. Increasingly, multi-purpose senior centres are becoming focal points for community social services to the aged. They offer a wide range of recreation, cultural and educational activities for older people to take part in and they provide services of various kinds. These services may include legal aid, help with forms, financial accounting procedures, health counselling and a housing registry. There may be programmes in which volunteers visit and meals-on-wheels are delivered. Children from schools are also encouraged to visit and share their experiences.

THE CANADIAN MOSAIC

Like many people in developed countries, Canadians as a whole have the luxury of being able to go beyond the bread and butter problems of everyday living and to devote much of their attention to matters such as the cleaning and greening of the environment, freedom of speech and minority rights. All these are issues that are often hotly debated and defended whenever they arise.

An Environment Conscious Society

It may seem fitting that a country like Canada, with such a huge pulp and paper industry, should have a voracious appetite for the products it manufactures. Government agencies and organisations, industries and business companies of every kind produce masses of booklets, pamphlets and advertisements to inform, explain and exhort the public to see their various points of view.

Visit the office of a government agent and you will find pamphlets containing all manner of information for every person conceivable—information for employers from the Workers' Compensation Board, a call to youth to join the Environment Youth Corps, budget explanations for the taxpayer from the Ministry of Finance, quick facts about the province from the Public Affairs Bureau, road maps, camping maps and forestry maps, a guide for parents through the changing educational system, information on programmes and benefits for seniors, regulations regarding rental housing, a how-to guide for someone contemplating a bed and breakfast business and, just in case, advice on how to *Help Yourself Survive A Tsunami!*

When you look into your letter box and open the morning's newspaper, you are often inundated by junk mail and flyers, which advertise every conceivable product. For example, you are informed about the latest bargains at the supermarket and department store, appealed to for help from the many charities, cajoled to try some miracle hair growth product, enticed to get your petrol from competing service stations by money-saving coupons. Even the local Member of Parliament adds to the paper pile with an 'I have your interests at heart' letter accompanied by a complimentary calendar at the end of the year while the funeral parlour tries to have the last word on how to avoid 'disadvantages when arrangements are made at time of need'!

Most of this eventually ends up in the bin. One newspaper reader wrote to say that he decided to find out how much junk mail he received. After keeping his flyers, newspaper inserts and junk mail for one month, he found the stack measured 21 centimetres!

Paper, be it newspapers, packaging, telephone books, glossy magazines, mail-order catalogues, etc., makes up about 40 per cent by weight, and about 50 per cent by volume, of rubbish. Plastics are estimated to be eight per cent by weight and 30 per cent by volume, of rubbish. The reason for the small percentage by weight of plastics is not because there is less plastic being used but because technology has produced lighter and more crushable plastics that are used in packaging today. The Canadian lifestyle is one that includes all kinds of plastic packaged products—fast foods in take-away throw-away boxes, bubble packs of cosmetics, soft drink or soda pop bottles, polystyrene trays of meat and vegetables, etc. Much of what is manufactured from Canada's ample resources ends in massive landfill sites where this waste material, some of it harmful or toxic, is simply buried beneath the earth and allowed to decompose. Yard waste makes up 18 per cent, metals 10 per cent, food waste eight per cent and rubber and leather two per cent by weight of the solid wastes that find their way to the landfill. However, decomposition is a slow process and some materials either decompose so slowly or do not decompose at all that they create a serious environmental threat to the country's ecology.

There is no doubt, however, that Canadians are becoming more environmentally conscious. The media do their part in this effort. Open the newspaper or switch on the television, and you often find a feature on cleaning up the environment, tips on how to be environmentally friendly, the preservation of forests, the effects of acid rain, the greenhouse effect, the disappearing ozone layer and more. Manufacturers must also jump on the bandwagon to retain the goodwill of the swelling ranks of the environmentalists. More household products, especially, are being sold in packaging which manufacturers claim are recyclable or biodegradable. Thus when out shopping, you might receive your purchases in a plastic bag that proudly advertises that it is 100 per cent biodegradable. However, '100 per cent biodegradable' does not mean that the plastic will ever be broken down completely, but that it will be broken into pieces small enough for them not to be noticeable. Eggs come in cartons that say 'made with no CFCs'. CFCs are chlorofluorocarbons that are responsible for the depletion of the ozone layer in our atmosphere.

'Reduce, re-use and recycle'. These are three words which have become much used by Canadians over the last decade in an effort to remedy the situation. It is also in recognition of the fact that it has become both an environmental and economic necessity to impose more stringent standards on the disposal of materials and to encourage the re-use and recycling of products where this is practical.

Practically speaking, this means that an environmentally-conscious family living in Canada must be prepared to

Canadians are becoming more and more environment conscious and they are doing their best to preserve what was given to them by Nature.

take the time and trouble to live up to its conviction that a cleaner world is the responsibility of every individual. The first step is taken when you, as a consumer, go shopping. As practically everything you buy comes in packaging that will end up in the bin, environmentalists suggest that you buy carefully, for example, choosing something that comes in a recyclable container rather than an equivalent product in a plastic blister pack. In addition to what you bring home, there is, as mentioned earlier, a tremendous flood of unsolicited material that arrives on your doorstep or is put into your post box. Everything needs to be disposed of, but hopefully not in a landfill site. In most Canadian towns and cities, household rubbish is picked up only once a week. The householder must therefore find the space and take the time to sort and store all recyclable items in his home until he is able to dispose of them in an environmentally safe way.

The Blue Box

Many Canadian communities have adopted the blue box programme in which each municipality is responsible for establishing a plant in which various kinds of waste products, particularly paper, glass and tin, can be processed for re-use in other forms. Each household is issued with a blue box into which items that can be recycled are placed for collection. The blue boxes are emptied at the same time when regular household rubbish is picked up, but instead of ending up in massive landfill sites, those items that can be re-used are treated appropriately.

Even in communities where there is no blue box programme, recycling is fast becoming a part of the lifestyle. Environmental organisations do what they can to encourage people to collect recyclable items and bring them to a collection depot. The types of recyclables accepted depend on the services available in the community, but generally, you are asked to rinse out containers, remove contaminants, and sort the different types of recyclable items first. Paper products are separated into different types such as newspapers, flyers, office paper, high quality paper like computer paper and cardboard. Sometimes some items like plasticised and waxed paper, styrofoam and certain types of glass may not be acceptable. The demands of each recycling depot vary, and it takes some patience and commitment to the cause to become a dedicated recycler.

The kitchen is one place in the home which generates lots of rubbish. Some households have a 'garburettor' installed to deal with this problem. The 'garburettor' is fitted to the bottom of the kitchen sink, where, at the flick of a switch, it will grind up most kitchen waste, even chicken bones, so that it can be flushed into the sewer system. It is even better to collect such kitchen wastes as fruit and vegetable peelings, egg shells and other organic material (but not fats or cooked foods) for composting in the garden together with grass clippings, leaves, wood shavings and ash from the fireplace.

Supermarkets have bins to take back all the plastic shopping bags that their customers have used, for recycling. In many cities, there are leaf collection and composting programmes in the autumn, during which householders are encouraged to collect their leaves in bags for picking up and recycling. Soft drink and beer bottles and cans can be returned to their place of purchase or to a bottle depot for a refund, 'white goods' or old refrigerators, stoves, washers and dryers are sent to a depot or second-hand dealer, used motor oil collected and sent to a service station which accepts it, and clean clothing in a usable condition can be donated to charitable organisations and second-hand shops.

THE GENDER ISSUE

During the last decade, gender equality has become a most important issue in Canada. Women, who were comparatively recently thought of as 'second class citizens', have begun to occupy a more just place in Canadian society, in both a moral and a practical sense. Nowhere more so has this been true than in the workplace, which has seen ever increasing numbers of women begin to move towards and occupy some of the most powerful and prestigious positions in public life.

Women at Work

Like many other countries, Canada's attitude towards women in the workplace was for many years patronising, to say the least. It was felt that there were certain jobs that were, by some kind of unexplained right, properly male. These were usually jobs that either demanded physical strength or which involved management skills, and there were similarly other jobs to which women were more properly suited (nursing, teaching etc.). For decades, this way of thinking was never really challenged.

By the 1990s, however, there was a significant and most timely change both in male attitudes and in the number of women occupying key positions in all sectors of the economy. More women were leaving their homes to work. In 1945, only one in four Canadian women worked outside their homes. Today, more than half of all Canadian women are employed in the workforce. Much of this has been brought about by a change in society's vision of the role of women and by women's perceptions of themselves, aided by significant legislation which has made this change both possible and permanent. Canada now has a Charter of Rights which forbids sexual discrimination in hiring and promotion. Pay equity legislation which mandates equal pay for equal work

Canadian Mounties in training. Women are a part of the Royal Canadian Mounted Police as well.

regardless of gender is now on the books in most Canadian provinces. However, in spite of such legislation, women tend to be employed in the more traditional occupations such as clerical, management and administration, nursing, teaching and sales jobs. For many women, work is largely part-time, with less likelihood of promotion and a lack of benefits such as medical, dental and pension plans.

There is still a dearth of women in some traditionally male professions such as engineering and medicine. Serious efforts are being directed at attracting women into those jobs into which they have not traditionally gone, and similarly to encourage men to take on roles which they have hitherto shunned. However, the process is slow and it will take at least a generation before the impact of this process is really felt. To encourage women to enter and remain in the workforce in greater numbers, such provisions as maternity benefits and pensions have been overhauled, and there is now even provision in many places of employment for paternity leave to enable the man to shoulder his share of child rearing. A husband and wife sharing one job, providing they hold equivalent qualifications, is not unknown, nor is the concept of the househusband where the man stays at home while the woman goes out to work.

Sexual Harassment

The issue of sexual harassment in the work place has also been addressed. In the past, women workers were often forced to endure sexual innuendos and sometimes even physical abuse by their male colleagues, but strict legislation has brought this situation under control in most places, so that this kind of practice has been substantially reduced.

The Changing Role of Women

Outside the workplace, the role of women is also changing, particularly as so many of them are now employed on a full time basis, either through choice or economic necessity. The Canadian male is now expected to shoulder his share of the domestic chores (although statistically it is still the woman who does the lion's share) and to be actively involved in the child rearing process. Domestic violence is still an issue in some homes, however, but once again, there is now a greater awareness of the problem in society at large, and more provisions both legal and societal to deal with it. In most homes, both boys and girls are brought up to believe that, apart from physical differences, there are few differences in capability between men and women and that most tasks in life can be performed equally by people of either sex. It will take another generation or two for this attitude to permeate Canadian society thoroughly but the process is well under way. The achievement of as total a sexual equality as possible is a goal that is actively sought by the majority of Canadians and is supported by the policies of the governments which represent them.

Famous Canadian Women

Canadian feminists have many models to emulate in their fight for justice and equality, not least of which were the 'Famous Five' of Emily Murphy, Henrietta Muir Edwards, Louise McKinney, Irene Parlby and Nellie McClung who challenged the law of the land.

Emily Murphy, born in 1868, was the wife of an Anglican pastor in Manitoba. She was one of the first advocates of feminism in Canada, campaigning for the property rights of married women, as well as for a women's court in which women involved in legal cases could testify without suffering embarrassment. When the first such court was established in the province of Alberta in 1916, Emily Murphy became the first woman magistrate in the British Empire and presided over it.

Later that year, another woman, Alice Jamieson, was made magistrate in Calgary, but both positions were challenged by Alberta lawyers who argued that women were not legally 'people' and could therefore not hold public office. Although the appointments were upheld by the Supreme Court of Alberta, this was not necessarily so in the rest of Canada. Emily Murphy and four other women, therefore, decided to challenge this and formally asked the Supreme Court of Canada for judgment on whether a woman could have a seat in Senate. The other four women were Henrietta Muir Edwards, a founding member of the National Council of Women, Louise McKinney, a former Alberta Member of Legislative Assembly, Irene Parlby, an Alberta cabinet minister, and Nellie McClung, another Alberta MLA. Together, they became known as the 'Famous Five'. When the Supreme Court decided that women could not be senators, the five appealed to the Privy Council in England, which ruled in 1929 that women were 'persons'. The following year, Cairine Wilson became the first woman to be appointed senator.

Freedom of Speech

Freedom of speech is another issue close to the heart of Canadians. Like their American neighbours, Canadians strongly believe in their right to speak out freely and without fear on issues which interest, annoy or frustrate them. Criticism of government policies and practices is commonly voiced both in public and private, and those who voice them do so without fear of retribution.

There are, of course, laws in Canada against both attacking someone with unjustified personal accusations either in print (libel) or by making unfounded and damaging verbal accusations (slander). Those who do this can be arrested and prosecuted. Politicians speaking in the House of Commons are exempted from this law, but otherwise it applies everywhere in the country and to everybody.

The press in Canada jealously guards its right to be free to say what it thinks and so newspapers, radio and television regularly discuss any topics which are timely and relevant. Their opinions do not always reflect or agree with those voiced by the government, nor even by the majority of Canadians, but the ideas and opinions voiced in the media are considered as an important part of determining the national position on matters both domestic and international. Naturally, there are some restrictions on offending public taste in public media to protect those who find some material offensive, though the issue of censorship is never very far below the surface in this regard and is one over which not everyone is in agreement!

Freedom of speech is seen by most Canadians as an important part of their democratic way of life, and both long-term residents and newcomers value their right to voice their opinion whenever it's appropriate to do so without fear of retribution, though always being prepared for an argument with those who do not agree with them!

The Volunteer Spirit

'Be a local hero' is the slogan of a public awareness programme across Canada that seeks to encourage a spirit of philanthropy among Canadians young and old. Certainly, the volunteer spirit is strong in Canadian society, probably because it is nurtured in Canadians from an early age. Schools play an important role. For instance, during Forestry Week, teachers take their charges out into the forests to plant seedlings, and on Earth Day or Environment Week, there are excursions into the countryside to pick up rubbish. Schools often hold fund-raising projects, and children and parents are expected to rally round and volunteer help during their free time to hold bake sales, garage sales, organise concerts and other activities. Many organisations and community services depend on volunteers to function. For example, Boy Scouts and Girl Guides leaders are often parents who volunteer their time after work so that their children are able to participate in these activities; similarly, the swim club, gymnastics club, baseball and hockey teams, too, depend on volunteers who are interested in providing these activities in their area. Services for the sick, elderly and handicapped and fund-raising for various charitable organisations are other areas where volunteers are needed—to deliver meals to the elderly who are house-bound (called 'meals-on-wheels'), to take the tea wagon around hospital wards and to visit the sick, to go door to door around the neighbourhood canvassing for numerous charities.

The 'Bee'

The 'bee' is a prime example of Canadian community spirit. 'Bees' began during pioneer days in Upper Canada when whole communities would get together to perform a

Originally, there were all kinds of occasions which called for a 'bee'—from erecting farm buildings and harvesting (the most common) to logging, stumping (the removal of tree stumps) and the butchering of livestock.

service for one of their members or to make some contribution to the progress of the entire community. If there is a large project which needs extra manpower to complete or if someone suffers a disaster and needs the help of the community. This kind of community spirit still survives in rural areas today.

Farmers' wives often held quilting, preserving or knitting 'bees' at the same time as their menfolk were outside at work on another project. And when the work was done, a huge meal would be served and the evening hours spent socialising.

In his book *Pioneer Days in Upper Canada*, Edwin Guillet quotes a contemporary observer as commenting that 'after the specific duties of the "bee" were ended, the young men indulged in trials of strength, while their elders discussed the crops, prices, local politics and the prospects of the ensuing year. The elderly women extended the circulation of the local gossip of the neighbourhood, while the younger ones were ready for the dance, the round of country games and the repartee of flirtation.'

LIVING IN THE CANADIAN MOSAIC

'...when I have been in Canada, I have never heard a
Canadian refer to an American as a 'foreigner'. He is just
an 'American'. And, in the same way, in the United States,
Canadians are not 'foreigners', they are 'Canadians'.
That simple little distinction illustrates to me better than
anything else the relationship between our two countries.'
—President Franklin Delano Roosevelt,
visit to Quebec, 31 July 1936

HAVING DISCUSSED MANY OF THE THINGS that make up Canada, such as the physical characteristics of the land, its history, the composition of Canadians, native as well as immigrant, and what they like to do, eat and how they socialise, there are still many other elements that characterise the Canadian lifestyle. These pieces, when added to the picture, help complete the colourful mosaic of Canada and its people.

A QUESTION OF SIZE

Huge, huge, HUGE—'humongous' describes the country and many things about it. Some humongous things are …

- **Buying in bulk**. In a large supermarket, you can usually find a section that sells almost anything in huge containers—soft drinks (or 'pop' as it is called here), pickles, condiments, flour, bird seed, etc. The customer takes just as much or as little as is needed. The advantage of this is you can buy any amount you like, without being limited by the manufacturer's packaging. Many other items, such as meat, are sold in family size quantities at prices that allow you to take advantage of the economy of size.

- **'Big wheels'**. Especially in the small towns and in the country, a common mode of transport is a truck or a 4x4 (four-wheel drive) vehicle. These are usually vehicles used for work or on the farms. Given the difficult winter driving conditions, a 4x4 is also a common vehicle for many people living in the country.

- **'Big money'**. This is what you have to pay for almost any kind of service. When you need some electrical or plumbing work done in your home, for example, you learn what expensive labour is all about. This is culture shock that hits the wallet. We had the electrician come and put in some wiring and heaters, a job which took less than a day's work, under five hours. When the bill came, it was more than a whopping C$ 300.

THE HONOUR SYSTEM

Much in Canada works on the honour system, that is, a system that does not depend so much upon authority, policing or penalties, as upon trust. It is a system that has evolved from the fact that many areas are vastly under-populated and often there isn't the manpower to keep a lot of activities and services functioning. So the honour system has had to be relied upon. People are expected to 'do the right thing' even when there is nobody looking.

Many of the examples of how the honour system works will obviously be found in the country rather than urban areas, such as at private as well as public campsites in the wilderness where campers are expected to deposit the camping fee into a money box because park rangers are not always on site. Numerous recreational facilities are provided for the enjoyment of many by a dedicated few who volunteer their time for the love of it, such as a ski group that maintains the trails outside a nearby town in the winter. These people are not able to collect fees from those who enjoy the fruits of their labour, but trust in the goodwill of skiers to give what they can towards the maintenance of such facilities into an 'honour box' at the start of the trail.

A woman whose interest in apiculture (the raising of honey bees) has evolved from a hobby into a small business, sells honey from her home. As this is a part-time business, and she and her husband have other work, this is done simply by putting jars of honey in a wooden shed by the gate, together with a money box and a sign displaying the prices. Customers

In many isolated areas of Canada, the honour system is part of the way of life.

are expected to serve themselves and put the correct amount of money into the box. This honour system has worked very well, she says, as most people are honest.

While there are always people who try to take advantage and beat the system, Canadians who have generally grown up with the honour system accept that if there is any cheating, it is to no one's benefit. Thus, even at the customs checkpoint at the US border, the honour system is used (though this is supplemented by the eagle eye of an experienced customs officer).

Border crossings have always been facilitated with the minimum of red tape, but the 9/11 terrorist attacks have severely curtailed the freedom of movement across the line. Border guards do their best to ease the traffic flow, relying much upon the honesty of travellers when they answer questions on how long they were out of the country and whether they have dutiable goods to declare, etc. The Canadian government prefers to re-establish the express lane programmes that allow frequent cross-border travellers to get through the checkpoints quickly. These travellers are screened in advance to determine that they are low-risk, do not have a criminal record and have not violated immigration or customs laws. They are then issued with special cards on which they declare their dutiable purchases. The cards are dropped into a box and the duties are then taken off their credit cards.

RIGHTS OF THE CONSUMER

Canadians are very conscious of their rights. Canadian laws ensure that the consumer's interests are protected by fair advertising and packaging and that market standards are kept. There are federal as well as provincial departments that one could go to with a complaint if one's consumer rights have been violated. In addition, there is a Consumers' Association of Canada that helps people who have problems resulting from buying goods and services. However, these are avenues of last resort and, hopefully, should not be necessary. In fact, many shops (especially those that are part of a big chain) and their sales personnel seldom object when you have bought something from the shop and wish to return it, if you have a good reason for doing so. Thus, a shirt or dress can be returned not only if there is an obvious flaw in it but even if you later decide you do not like the colour after all. Those who come from countries where the rights of a customer are vigorously defended may think nothing of this, but there are others who find such consideration enough of a novelty to be worthy of mention. Naturally, one's idea of a reasonable basis for wishing to return a purchase might not agree with another's, but the Canadian consumer has a fair amount of liberty, and the patience of the shop management and their wish to keep their customers happy are earnest.

Respect for the Customer

A driver who bought a new set of rims for his car brought them back, somewhat rusted, to the tyre dealer after one winter. The dealer accepted the man's argument that the rims should have lasted at least one season without showing signs of rust and offered him another set in exchange.

Shops seldom argue with the customer, but it is best if you have a receipt that proves you bought the item from that particular shop, and they will almost always exchange the faulty item or give you a refund. Some shops, however, have a 'no cash refunds, exchanges only' policy and others do stipulate a time limit within which any goods that you are not satisfied with should be returned. It is important to make a note of such policies when buying from these shops.

THE LUCK OF THE DRAW

"B 6, I 23, N 35, G 50, O 71..." the voice calls. In the hall, long tables take up almost every space, with just enough room for chairs back to back. As many as 100 to 200 people gather for bingo, at a different place each night of the week. It could be the Canadian Legion hall, church hall, civic centre or seniors' residential home. The games are complex and not really for the uninitiated because you have to be fast with the eye and quick with the hand.

Bingo is a popular form of entertainment and the games are often a means for many organisations to raise funds for their activities. If you pass by a community hall in the evening, for instance, and find a long line of cars parked outside, chances are there's probably a bingo game going on inside.

GARAGE SALES

You really learn what spring cleaning is when you live in a country with four seasons. After a long and cold winter during which one can feel very cooped up indoors, the gradual warming up of spring provides an opportunity to open up windows and let the fresh air in. The sunshine and warmer weather often encourage one to get some serious cleaning done. Attics, basements and garages are emptied and unwanted junk and white elephants put up for sale during weekends. Telephone poles in the centre of town sprout cardboard signs advertising garage sales. Notice boards in the local shops publicise the same. The avid bargain hunter scours these places and the classifieds in the town newspaper each Friday, so that he can be out early on Saturday morning to grab the best bargains. You learn to spot the house with the sale by the number of cars and trucks parked outside. While good purchases can certainly be made if you are a careful buyer who scrutinises each potential buy and does not succumb to every 'bargain', it is easy to come away with a handful of cheap items, only to find later that you have no use for all that junk you paid for. And if you have been weak and given in to the bargains all spring, then it's your turn to hold a garage sale of your own, so long as the weather stays sunny and warm.

DOOR-TO-DOOR

Be prepared to be bothered by a lot of door-to-door canvassing, which, however, is not a phenomenon exclusive to life in Canada but is certainly a part of it. Canvassers often have good reasons or worthy causes that bring them to your door—they may be volunteers trying to raise funds for charities or community projects, children trying to sell calendars, chocolates etc. to raise money for a school outing—but there is another category of door-knockers who can get on one's nerves. These are salespeople who can become nuisances when they refuse to take 'no' for an answer.

A variation of the door-to-door salesperson is the 'telemarketer' who resorts to telephoning people and bombarding them with all sorts of advertising gimmicks.

No Means No
An example of a persistent person is the salesman who periodically canvasses around the neighbourhood, trying to convince people that a freezer full of expensive frozen convenience-gourmet food is an essential household item to have in their basement.

ADDRESSING A POSTAL PROBLEM
Have you corresponded with anyone in Canada? Some people, mainly those who live in more urban areas, have 'regular' addresses, such as A Jones, who can be reached at 123, Main Street, Townsville. But as there is a large proportion of Canadians who live in small country towns, Canada Post has had to devise a different postal system to cope with the great distances the postal worker would have to cover to get from one address to the next, and the lack of people with which to do it. The post office in town, therefore, usually has a separate section consisting entirely of postal boxes. Each post box would be assigned to a household in town. If your friend, therefore, has a PO Box number for his mailing address, it is not because he wishes to keep his true address a secret from you. Even stranger is the address that looks something like a code, for example, RR#1 S23 C45! Addresses consisting of such an incomprehensible cluster of letters and numbers usually belong to those who live out in the country, and can be decoded like this: RR is short for 'rural route' (of which there are many in Canada and therefore they have to be numbered); S is a specific 'site' (in this case, site number 23 along rural road 1) at which there is a 'cabinet' or cluster of post boxes and it is usually at a road junction closest to the houses it serves; C stands for the 'compartment' or box, each of which is numbered and assigned, one to each household. With such a system, the person who delivers the post saves an enormous amount of time and energy and can deliver letters to 30 or 40 houses at a single stop.

A MANNER OF GREETING
"How are you today?" A girl from Hong Kong remarked that Canadians greet you by asking how you are doing. It upset her

to discover that they weren't really interested in her answer. "They expect you to say 'good', 'all right' or something like that and then to move on. If they don't really care how I'm doing, why ask?" she wanted to know.

Well, such disappointment can be avoided if one realises that the greeting has to be taken in the spirit of just a polite enquiry. You usually answer 'good' to this standard Canadian query, regardless of how you might really feel. That's not to say that the query is always a matter of just being polite and nothing else. Often, it might be genuine. A 'How are you today?' can often be a genuine question and a means of getting to know people.

PERCEPTIONS

Canadians are generally regarded by most people outside the country as being part of a tolerant and accepting society as a whole and this is mostly true of all regions of Canada. In fact, since most of Canada is itself made up of people whose ancestors were once immigrants themselves, there tends to be tacit understanding of the immigrant experience.

There is also a realisation that a country which was built by immigrants still needs to encourage people from other countries to settle here and continue the building process started by their forebears.

BECOMING PART OF THE MOSAIC

The United States is often described as a 'melting pot' of many cultures, while Canada is often described as a 'mosaic'. It is an image that was given wide currency by John Porter, who called his sociological study of social class and power in Canada 'The Vertical Mosaic'.

For those of us who come from the big cosmopolitan cities of other countries and speak English (or French, if you are settling into the French-speaking areas of Quebec), becoming a part of the mosaic and fitting into Canadian lifestyle comes more easily.

Fitting Right In

A migrant who moved from Asia to Canada said that during those first few months she had braced herself for the expected cultural impact her move would cause. But "the most interesting thing is that I have experienced no 'culture shock', but I seem to have blended right in," she said. She attributed this to the fact that she had travelled a fair bit and lived in a big, cosmopolitan city and had consequently been exposed to much cultural diversity. "The Canadians I have come to know (although not too many) seem to be able to talk on the same wavelength. Any difference in values and behaviour and expectations are very subtle and I haven't been able to put my finger on them yet."

But sometimes, our cultural traits do betray us. As a Chinese radio personality once said, he would have been saved a lot of pain if someone had told him that Canadians don't like people to talk loudly (a distinctly Chinese trait, he thought). This remark brings to mind an incident that happened in a supermarket, when a particularly loud conversation between two women could be clearly heard over the normal hum of noise in the supermarket. It came from several aisles away, and the speakers could not be seen, but most certainly were heard by all in the vicinity, speaking loudly in a foreign dialect. They were most definitely the focus of curious stares from shoppers all around!

It is comforting to seek the company of people who come from the same cultural and traditional background, hence there are often clusters of ethnic groups to be found in many cosmopolitan cities, not only in Canada but in cities all over the world. But, ultimately, interaction with the wider world, and learning to adjust to living in a new country, even though it may take a generation or two to do it, cannot be avoided.

> In Canada, there are often private social and government agencies, such as Employment and Immigration Canada, that will help people newly arrived in the country to adjust to their new surroundings, counsel them and help them especially to undergo job training and find employment.

Those who do not speak English, which is the language of interaction in most of Canada, are encouraged to learn it. Some schools and colleges conduct part-time and evening classes in English as a second language.

Naturally, not all newcomers to Canada will have problems adjusting to their new surroundings for various reasons. Perhaps they may merely have exchanged one western tradition for a similar one in Canada, or even if they had come from an Asian country, they may not have been so steeped in their cultural traditions as to make assimilation a problem. Even so, they may want to blend into their new Canadian surroundings as quickly as possible. Besides establishing relationships at one's place of work, it is a good idea to form other circles of friends. One way to do this would be to seek out people with similar interests. A look through the local newspaper will often provide a calendar of events, covering a wide selection of recreational, social and other community organisations. It only remains for the newcomer to the area to introduce himself and participate in his chosen activities, be it that of the town's darts club, tennis club, baby clinics, motorcycle association, arts and crafts group, weight watchers or overeaters anonymous, and he will soon find himself becoming a part of his community.

SOCIAL CUSTOMS AND ETIQUETTE

On the whole, Canadian society is very informal. Canadians are happy to entertain people in their homes and often belong to a number of local groups which provide either services or entertainment to their local community. However, the two most formal occasions in Canadian society tend to be weddings and funerals.

Weddings

Weddings can be big or small, highly formal or very informal, and can be held in a church, a community hall or even in a private home or garden. The cost of the wedding is usually borne by the family of the bride so the number of guests and the lavishness of the wedding will often depend on the financial situation of the family. Prior to the wedding, the bride-to-be is often given a 'shower', which is an informal gathering of her female friends and family at which small presents for use in her future home are given to the bride. Sometimes the bridegroom will also be treated to a 'stag night' by his male friends, but this tends to be a more raucous celebration of the end of his bachelorhood.

On the wedding day, the bride traditionally wears a white dress and veil, and the groom will wear formal clothing, which can range from a suit to a tuxedo. The actual ceremony is usually conducted either by some kind of religious leader or official or by a secular person licensed to solemnise marriages. The ceremony itself is usually relatively brief, but is followed by a reception to which all the wedding guests are invited, and at which a meal is usually served. Following the reception, the bride and groom

Drinks as well as entertainment are often also part of the reception, as are some short speeches made by members of the wedding party.

will usually leave for a honeymoon somewhere away from the community and the rest of the guests will disperse and go home. It is also important to note that, in many provinces of Canada, marriages between members of the same sex are now legal, and these often follow basically the same format.

Funerals

When a person dies in Canada, the closest relatives of the deceased will usually arrange for some form of ceremony to celebrate the life of the deceased. This ceremony can be arranged in many ways, but it is most often arranged by a funeral director working from one of several funeral homes in the local area. The funeral director will arrange things according to the wishes of the family and will take care of all the necessary arrangements, including the collection, preparation and burial or cremation of the body. Prior to the ceremony itself, an obituary notice will usually be placed in the local paper informing friends of the death and of the time and place of the funeral and also of the specific times for visitation at which family and friends can come to the funeral home to express their condolences to the close members of the family. On these occasions, the top half of the coffin may be open, in which case the deceased person may be viewed from the waist up, or closed completely as the family wishes.

Funerals can sometimes be quite costly, and it is increasingly the case in Canada that people will pre-pay for their own funerals before their death in order to prevent a sudden large financial burden falling on their family.

At the funeral service itself, the coffin is finally completely closed, and then a religious official or a member of the family may lead those present in remembrance of the deceased, after which the coffin will be transported either to the graveyard for burial or to the crematorium. Only close family and friends will usually attend this part of the ceremony. Following the burial or cremation, a reception will often be held in the home of one of the family members, or in a community hall, after which the formal funeral proceedings come to an end. On occasion, funerals can be private family affairs only, but a public service of remembrance is sometimes held instead a few days after the burial or cremation has taken place.

Ceremonies

Other social events common in Canadian society are the celebration of major family turning points such as baptisms, coming of age ceremonies such as *bar-mitzvahs* etc., special

Gatherings at home or in a local facility to celebrate sporting events, national celebrations, (such as Canada Day), are common. They can either be celebrated by a small group of individuals or by the whole community.

wedding anniversaries (40th, 50th, 60th, etc.) and birthdays (60th, 75th, 80th and above), promotions at work, retirements and any other event which marks a specific milestone in a particular person's life.

It is also important to realise that Canada is an extremely diverse country, both geographically and ethnically, and that many types of celebration can be found only in certain regions of Canada. These are often specific to certain ethnic groups in that area who may have their own social customs, traditions and etiquette on these occasions which is in addition to (or sometimes instead of) those commonly observed by most Canadians.

'I felt that no boy should have to depend either for his leg or his life upon the ability of his parents to raise enough money to bring a first-class surgeon to his bedside. And I think it was out of this experience ... (that) I came to believe that health services ought not to have a price-tag on them, and that people should be able to get whatever health services they required irrespective of their individual capacity to pay.'
—Tommy Douglas, Canada's 'Father of Medicare'

DOCUMENTATION AND FORMALITIES

Canadians are not required to carry any form of documentation with them while they are in the country, but there are two pieces of information for which any person born in Canada should have applied and which should be kept at home so that they are available for presentation if requested. The first of these is a birth certificate which is issued at birth by the province in which the person is born and which will be used subsequently to apply for other documents such as a passport or a driver's licence. The other piece of documentation is a social insurance number (most commonly referred to as a SIN number), which must be applied for from the federal government of Canada and will be used for identification in the work place and in subsequent dealings with any Canadian government office such as Canada Pensions or Canada Revenue. A SIN number is usually requested at the time someone enters the work force, but it can be obtained at any time after birth or legal entry into the country. Both these documents are protected by the Canadian Privacy Act and cannot be accessed by other people without the express permission of the holder.

In the case of a Canadian who is not born in Canada, a Citizenship Card will replace the birth certificate and a SIN number will be issued on application once the holder is eligible to work within Canada.

A Canadian passport is not automatically issued, but can be applied for once you have either a birth certificate or a citizenship card and a SIN number. Canadian passports are valid for up to five years, and can be renewed when they expire. It is possible to apply for a Canadian passport while still a citizen of another country, as dual citizenship within Canada can be held by agreement with some other countries, but the rules on this vary from country to country and will need to be checked before applying for a Canadian passport.

Federal Government Controls

Among other things, the federal government controls the licensing of such things that fall under national legislative control, such as customs and export regulations, firearms registration and national park permits.

The provincial, rather than the federal government, issues two other important personal documents; the health card and the driving licence. In order to obtain coverage under the terms of a particular provincial health plan, a health card will be required to be shown whenever you visit a doctor, the hospital or any medical facility, as it proves your entitlement to basic treatment. However, not all medical services are covered by all provincial health plans, and it can be sometimes necessary to pay directly for certain procedures and tests, even with a health card. At the present time, there is no system of private health care in Canada and all major medical and surgical procedures will be initiated through a local doctor's referral to the appropriate part of the provincial medical system.

A driver's licence can be applied for at different ages, depending upon provincial regulations. Most provinces will issue a conditional licence somewhere between the ages of 16 and 19 years old, but, before granting a permanent licence, all provinces will require a driving test first, often both written and practical. Driving licences have to be renewed every so often (usually every five years) and some provinces have a system of graduated licensing under which a novice driver is at first restricted as to which time of day he or she may drive a car and how many passengers may be carried.

Other licences issued by the province include things such as hunting and fishing licences, and entry permits to provincial parks.

Within your home, you will also need to make arrangements with various government or private organisations (depending upon the province) for the supply of such things as electricity service, natural gas or propane service for heating and cooking, cable or satellite TV reception and telephones. Suppliers of these services vary from province to province, and even from town to town, so it is necessary to find out what options are available in the area where you locate, and what the prices for these services are. Usually there is competition to provide these services, and this helps to keep prices from rising too high.

WHAT TO BRING

When one has to leave one country for another, one major concern is the consideration of what one should bring to the new country. It is comforting to know that there is very little that cannot be found in Canada as it is a very developed country. It is also a very multicultural society, made up of immigrants from all over the world. In Canadian cities, there are cultural enclaves such as Chinatowns, Little Indias, Little Italys, European quarters and Arab sections, where it is possible to find almost everything specific to one's culture, such as a special food or type of dress.

So in truth, one simple answer to the question of what to bring into Canada is 'nothing', that is, it is possible to obtain everything that you could possibly need so that you could come here without any of your possessions and easily replace every single one of them. Therefore, you might want to consider holding a large garage sale and getting rid of as much as possible before moving. Perhaps the consideration here would be to weigh the cost of getting movers to pack everything up and ship things over against the cost of buying what you need over here.

But no matter how 'ruthless' you are in dispossessing yourself of your goods, it is unlikely that you will be able to divest yourself of everything as many belongings have sentimental as well as financial value.

You will have packed up most of your possessions and stored them away until you can have them shipped to you. You may have brought with you a few of your personal effects, which you will bring in with you when you make your first entry into the country. In order to facilitate the customs and immigration process, make sure you have a list of everything that you have packed up together with an estimate of their value. The more comprehensive the list, the easier it will be when you go through customs.

Generally, you are allowed to bring in your personal and household possessions tax free, and this includes a large variety of items from your personal belongings like clothing, and books, and household furnishings and appliances, as well as collections of antiques that you may have, family heirlooms, and transportation items like cars, boats, trailers, even a private aircraft if you possess one.

The changing seasons in Canada require that you have with you clothing to suit the time of year when you arrive. Obviously it is easier to dress for the warmer months and for this reason, you should try to schedule your arrival in the summer. If you have to make your entry in the winter, bring some basic winter gear, including a winter jacket, scarf, thermal underwear, some mittens or gloves, headgear like a hat or toque and boots. If it is difficult to obtain these before you arrive, you should be prepared to buy them as soon as possible after your arrival. There are many shops where you can buy these new or second-hand.

With regard to antiques, bear in mind that the climate in Canada may have an adverse effect on wooden articles, especially if they have been used to a more humid climate. The drier air may cause the wood to shrink and crack, which would be very upsetting for you if the article is valuable or has sentimental value. I left a number of antique furniture pieces behind, preferring to do without them than to see them ruined. I did bring with me an old wooden table, which had sentimental value, and it developed some severe cracks. But as it was not an antique and it is still quite usable, it was not too disastrous for me.

As for appliances and any other electrical equipment, in order for them to be used in Canada, they have to be compatible with the voltage here, which is 110 volts, 60 Hz. Most audio equipment can be easily changed from 220 volts to 110 volts with the flick of a switch, but other types of appliances do not have this capability.

Obviously, bringing over old and used items will not cause a problem. But if you have anything that you have recently bought but not used, it might be subject to tax. It is best to have sales receipts and registration documents to prove that they are part of your allowed personal effects.

You may bring in any vehicles that you use as a personal effect, but these must have been genuinely in your possession and use before your arrival in the country. Moreover, Transport Canada has special restrictions with regard to some vehicles or transportation items. For instance, there may be a question of the age of the vehicle and of meeting the safety standards that have been set for Canada. (*For more information, see the* Resource Guide *at the end of the book.*)

The Registrar of Imported Vehicles is an agency that has been contracted by Transport Canada to administer a national programme that ensures that all imported vehicles comply with Canadian safety standards. The Registrar can be contacted at:

- (1)-888-959-2221 (toll-free in Canada and the US)
- (1)-416-626-6812 (from all other countries)

The informational pamphlet on Importing a Vehicle into Canada (RC4140) can be downloaded from http://www.cbsa-asfc.gc.ca/menu/CGCG-e.html. It can also be ordered by telephoning the Registrar of Imported Vehicles.

There are some items that cannot be brought into Canada at all, and if you have visited the country, you will have some knowledge of what these are because visitors are apprised of their restriction:

- Firearms, explosives, fireworks and ammunition, for obvious reasons. With firearms, there are some special cases when they can be brought in, such as for sporting and hunting purposes. However, any firearms brought into the country must be declared and a Firearms Act requires the owner to possess a valid licence or certificate.
- Drugs other than prescription ones.
- Meat, dairy products, fresh fruits and vegetables, because Canada is an agricultural country and there is always a concern that these might introduce some disease or pest into the country.

- Endangered species or products made from animal parts like skin, feathers, fur, bones and ivory.
- Cultural property belonging to another country, such as antique and cultural objects that have historical significance in their country of origin.

You have to be either 18 or 19 years old, depending on the province, in order to bring in alcohol and tobacco. There are also limits as to the amount of tobacco and alcohol that you can bring in without having to pay any duty, even if you meet these age requirements.

Pets

Pets are another concern for many people coming to Canada for an extended time. There are three general considerations:

- The age of the animal
- Whether it performs a necessary function for you
- The country of origin.

These considerations apply only to dogs and cats. It is natural that you will want to bring your family cat or dog with you, and if your pet is younger than three months old and is from the United States, no special documentation is needed. If your pet has a special function, such as a guide dog, the authorities also do not require special papers even if the dog is older than three months and comes from some other country other than the US, as long as it is with you when you make your entry into Canada. There is more red tape to encounter if your pet is an older animal. But if it is coming from the United States, the correct documentation will make things easier.

Rabies Certificate

A certificate from a veterinarian is required to show that your dog or cat has had its rabies shot in the last three years; this certificate must also identify your pet clearly with regard to its breed, age, sex, etc.

There are different requirements for animals other than a dog or cat and for all animals coming from countries other than the US.

The agency in charge of importing pets is the Canadian Food Inspection Agency. The CFIA has three import service centres that you can contact as follows:

- Eastern Import Service Centre (Montreal)
  (1)-877-493-0468 (toll free in Canada and the US)
  (1)-514-493-0468 (from other countries)
- Central Import Service Centre (Toronto)
  (1)-800-835-4486 (toll free in Canada and the US)
  (1)-416-661-3039 (from other countries)
- Western Import Service Centre (Vancouver)
  (1)-888-732-6222 (toll free in Canada and the US)
  (1)-604-666-9240 (from other countries)
  The CFIA's website is:
  http://www.inspection.gc.ca/

Bringing in Money

Useful Pamphlets

Information on the legalities of bringing large sums of money into Canada can be obtained from the Canada Border Service Agency at http://www.cbsa-asfc.gc.ca/menu/CGCG-e.html. Look for the pamphlet on 'Crossing the Border with $10,000 or more?' (RC4321). From the same site, you can find guides on 'Settling in Canada: Information on importing goods for people intending to settle in Canada' (RC4151) and 'Entering Canada to Study or Work' (RC4220).

Besides tangible goods, there is also the question of bringing in money. Canada does not have any restrictions on the amount of money one can bring in or even take out of the country, except that you are required to report to Customs if you are crossing the border with C$ 10,000 (or its equivalent in foreign exchange) or more. This is to reduce the incidences of money laundering offences and to fulfill Canada's commitment to the international fight against crime. Some countries, however, have restrictions on the amount of money that one is allowed to take out. In lieu of this, Canada will permit an immigrant extra time, up to three years, to purchase household items from the country that they are emigrating from and ship them to Canada free of duties and taxes.

WHERE TO LIVE

According to Statistics Canada, the majority of Canadians live in cities. Over 75 per cent of the population live in an urban rather than a rural setting.

This is a relatively recent phenomenon as Canada has strong rural roots. City dwellers, in fact, seem to belong to one of three groups: those whose ancestors moved to the developing cities as a lifestyle choice; those whose careers or occupations force them to live in urban areas; and newcomers to the country, used to cities in their native lands, who choose to band together with their ethnic counterparts in specific sections of Canada's largest metropolitan areas.

This has led to the population of Canadian cities becoming very cosmopolitan. The diversity of food shops, restaurants and entertainment available in the three largest cities of Montreal, Toronto and Vancouver as well as some of the smaller ones—namely Winnipeg, Edmonton and Halifax—bears witness to this social mix.

City Living

Physically, Canada's cities resemble those of many countries of the world. Relatively small central core areas, often dominated by high-rise office towers and expensive hotels, are surrounded by successive layers of residential communities. Each has its own infrastructure and character, often extending several kilometres from the city centre but all linked by an intricate and efficient public transport system.

The city dweller is freed from one of the obligations that Canada's vast size imposes on those who live in the country— that of owning a car. Those who live in the cities have access to efficient urban transport in the shape of an extensive bus network that is often supplemented by a mass rapid transit

As most Canadian cities are modern and upbeat, the sight of two work horses passing by the Parliament buildings in Ottawa inevitably attracts much attention.

Sense of Identity

For those who live in these suburban areas, there is often less sense of identity with the city as a whole than with their specific part of it. This gives rise to a sort of geographic identity but is, in a way, quite different from the social identity usually experienced in the close society of a small town or rural community.

system, such as the Montreal Metro, Vancouver Skytrain and Toronto TTC. In fact, many city dwellers choose not to own a car at all but to rent one on the relatively rare occasions when visits to friends, relatives or other family commitments take them out of the city.

Similarly, home ownership, often the ultimate dream for many Canadians, is not as common in a city where many live in rented apartments in high-rise blocks, deterred from owning their own home by the high cost of real estate, taxes and maintenance.

Interaction with one's neighbours also varies. Those in high-rise apartments tend to know little about and have little to do with their neighbours, except for those who live right next to them. In suburban housing estates, it is possible to have a nodding acquaintance with families who live on the same street.

All of Canada's major cities have professional sports teams too. There is usually ice hockey, Canadian football and basketball to watch in the winter months and baseball in the summer. The frequency of their games makes avid fans out of many of the city's residents.

Other pastimes include shopping which, for many Canadians, is more part of the culture than a simple necessity. Many also visit museums, art galleries and regular special events. All these are not available to the country or small-town dweller unless he is willing to make the long pilgrimage into the city and back for a specific event.

The development of a Canadian city lifestyle, relatively free of social obligations and with plenty of diversions, and tremendous employment opportunities, has resulted in the shift to Canada's cities over the last 20 or 30 years.

But there are drawbacks to living in a city. Rural and small-town values combined with a less hurried and relatively relaxed lifestyle and a strong sense of community are not easy to maintain in a city where the pace of life is faster. Another drawback is that the community's sense of being responsible for the welfare of all its members is not as strong in a city environment.

Culture and the arts, often sadly lacking in the countryside and small towns, are a positive feature of the bigger cities. Symphony orchestras, theatrical experiences, dance and art provide city dwellers with an abundance of cultural opportunities. This is often cited as the main reason for choosing to live in a city.

For those lucky enough to have a choice, living in the city has the appeal of convenience, but it also means adapting to a lifestyle quite different from that of the smaller communities.

Toronto (Ontario)

Toronto, Canada's largest city, used to be nicknamed 'Toronto the Good' because it was a rather staid and uninteresting—if comfortable—place in which to live. But few cities in North America have changed as much as Toronto in the last few decades.

The growth of the population over the last 50 years, with many people coming from different cultures and countries, has changed the city completely. It is no longer the rather Anglo-Saxon oriented, complacent and dull place it was at the end of the last World War but rather a dynamic, multicultural metropolis of more than four million people.

Remarkably, however, this rapid change has not brought with it many of the social ills which bedevil other major cities. Toronto remains one of the world's safest cities. Its transport system is efficient and fast, and its police force highly visible. Both these factors act as a strong deterrent to the various forms of personal attack becoming commonplace in other cities. The transport authority has even recently put in place a special programme in which suburban bus drivers have been authorised to let single women passengers alight directly outside their place of residence at night instead of having to walk there from the nearest bus stop.

The centre of Toronto is Bay Street, the financial heart of the country and the location of the country's largest stock exchange, the seventh largest in the world. Dominating the skyscrapers of Bay Street is the CN Tower, once the world's tallest free-standing building, at the top of which a public viewing platform allows visitors to get a panoramic view of the city.

Other attractions include the historic Fort York and Casa Loma, and The Art Gallery of Ontario; its ethnic shopping and dining areas such as Chinatown and Kensington Market; its wide variety of permanent entertainment facilities, ranging from symphony concerts at Roy Thompson Hall to rock concerts at Ontario Place. Theatres, cinemas and sports events abound. The Rogers Centre is home to the city's popular baseball team, the Blue Jays, and there is plenty of green space within and close to the city for those who enjoy outdoor pastimes in winter and summer.

Toronto is a Huron Indian word meaning 'place of meeting' and, through all that it has to offer, Toronto certainly lives up to its name!

Montreal (Quebec)

Montreal is an intriguing combination of modern North American dynamism and old-world European elegance. Home to more than three million people, just slightly smaller than its Ontario rival, Montreal shares with Toronto its reputation for efficiency and safety, but adds a cultural ambience which is all its own.

In fact, Montreal's reputation internationally is that of a very cosmopolitan city and it is its atmosphere which attracts visitors as much as its facilities. This is because it is very much a bilingual city and the home of a self-sufficient and thriving French culture. The way in which French and English cultures blend here is unique, and the recent addition of other ethnic influences from all around the world has made a visit to Montreal a truly special experience. In addition, Montreal has always had a reputation for good living, and the abundance of fine restaurants and cafés in its special 'quarters' help to keep this reputation alive.

Like Toronto, Montreal also has its share of historic places, museums, fine shopping areas, cultural activities and green spaces. Old Montreal, the Basilica of Notre Dame and McGill

University are all worth a visit, as are the Montreal Museum of Fine Arts, the Place Ville Marie, the city's vast underground shopping centre and Mont Royal Park in the centre of the city itself. The latter offers a fine panoramic view of Montreal and the Saint Lawrence River.

Despite having lost to Toronto the title of 'Canada's largest city', Montreal remains a major commercial and cultural centre, and the opportunity to experience its vitality and elegance is one no visitor to Canada should miss.

Vancouver (British Columbia)

Vancouver is the third largest city in Canada. In the beginning it was mainly populated by people of British ancestry, but with immigration over the years, Vancouverites are now of almost every race and colour. There is a huge Asian community, made up mostly of Chinese and including an increasingly visible number of Koreans and Vietnamese. Vancouver's Chinatown is the second largest in North America, next in size only to San Francisco's, and its restaurants serve a cuisine that, some would say, rivals even that of Hong Kong. There are also many Indians, mainly Sikhs, who have established a Punjabi market along a section of Main Street where Indian groceries, spices, saris and restaurants can be found. For many new Asian immigrants, being able to buy their 'local foodstuff' is a great comfort in strange surroundings.

Originally a small sawmill town, Vancouver grew in importance and size when it became the westernmost terminus of the Canadian Pacific Railway, outstripping both the 'royal city' of New Westminster and the present provincial capital of Victoria.

The city spreads over the rich delta lands of the Fraser River, with a seascape and mountain backdrop that has given it a spectacular setting. Many parks and gardens abound in this beautiful city so that much of nature's beauty, peace and quiet is within easy reach of its residents. Perhaps the most spectacular of these green oases is Stanley Park, a heavily wooded area of more than 400 hectares (more than 1000 acres) right in the heart of the city. In summer, Vancouver's beaches are covered with sun lovers, although braver souls test their mettle by jumping into English Bay during the

Polar Bear Swim, on the notoriously cold 1 January every year.

The original nucleus of the city is Gastown, now a renovated tourist-oriented area of shops, restaurants and nightclubs, complete with charming cobblestone streets and old gas lamps. The heart of the city and its financial and business district is now further south, centred around Robson Square. Stately homes in Edwardian suburbs like Kerrisdale, Shaughnessy and Mount Pleasant contrast with high-income, high-rise apartment living in the West End.

There is an international airport, two universities (the University of British Columbia and Simon Fraser University) and a prestigious art school (the Emily Carr College of Art and Design). The city is home to the Vancouver Symphony Orchestra and its sporting heroes are the Vancouver Canucks (ice hockey) and BC Lions (Canadian football).

Vancouver is linked to the interior of British Columbia by the Trans-Canada Highway. Within the city, the excellent grid-

A close-up view of the Lions usually seen from the Lions Gate Bridge in Vancouver.

like road network is supplemented by a public bus system and the mass rapid transit Skytrain.

Surrounding the core of the city are the municipalities that make up the metropolitan area known as the Lower Mainland. These are strung out along the delta of the Fraser River. North of the river, the mountains gradually close in and, as you travel east, the population centres of Pitt Meadows, Maple Ridge and Mission become less dense. The more open area to the south is made up of farms, interspersed with small communities such as those in the municipalities of Surrey, Langley, Abbotsford and Chilliwack.

Small-town Snapshots

Despite the fact that 75 per cent of Canadians are city dwellers, much of Canada is still country and small-town in nature.

Many small towns are built around a single industry, such as fishing, logging or mining. Others might owe their existence to their strategic location at the crossroads of rail or road communication. They are often separated from the next town by miles of open country, farm or ranch land.

The Canadian small town is easily recognisable. As you approach by road, you will often see a 'Welcome to Townsville, population 4,000' sign. Often, there is an accompanying signboard listing the churches that are active in town, be they Anglican, Roman Catholic, Baptist, Full Gospel, Evangelical and so on. A third sign might display the badges of service clubs, for example, Lions, Rotary, Kiwanis. Sometimes, a board will say 'This is a Block Parent community', meaning 'we look after our children here' (see *Canada's Young and Young at Heart*, Chapter 3, *The Canadian Vision*). All this gives the visitor the feeling that the small-town community is a close-knit and caring one.

The centre of town often consists of one main street that might be no more than two blocks in length. Here, you will find the general shop, hardware shop, pharmacy (drugstore), a couple of banks and perhaps some café-restaurants that often offer Chinese and Canadian 'smorgasbord' meals. The shopping centre is not quite as ubiquitous as you might

Small-town Canada with a relic of an earlier time.

expect but can usually be found in the larger towns. (One might even use it as a measure of whether a town has 'made it' in terms of size).

The Charm of Being Small

The resident of a small town is often friendly and open, even to strangers. Unlike in the city, where the rush is always evident and people seldom pass the time of day with a stranger, in a small town there is time to stand and stare and comment upon the weather.

One of the pleasing features about living in a small community is the ease with which you get to know your neighbours. The cashier in the supermarket, the bank teller, post office clerk and the sales attendant become more than familiar faces. You discover that the mother you meet at a school function attends the same church as you. You see her again when your children join the gymnastics club. When shopping one day, she turns out to be the cashier at the supermarket check-out counter. Thus a web of relationships builds between you that form the basis for a friendship. Walk around town, and chances are you will meet someone you know well enough to exchange a few civilities with.

The atmosphere in the town is usually casual, especially in summer, when the hot weather encourages the shedding of the many layers of clothing that were worn during winter. I once saw some guests at a wedding reception arrive in their bermudas.

On the outskirts of town, near the main road, there is usually a cluster of service stations that serve passing motorists, while the road into town is lined with motels and hotels for the overnight traveller.

Few people are in a hurry. There are no traffic snarls to fray the nerves, no horns being honked by impatient drivers. Pedestrians have right of way, and not only do they take it, they are also given it! You can stand at the street corner, waiting to cross, and a driver will stop and ask you to go. A car can pause in the middle of the road to let a passenger off, or two cars may halt the traffic while their drivers say hello. And those behind (granted, there is seldom more than one) will usually wait patiently until they are ready to move on again.

For the many people who choose to live here rather than in the city, these are the charms that more than make up for the lack of hustle and bustle, excitement and entertainment of city life. Nevertheless, even a small-town resident sometimes looks for entertainment, so where does he find it? (*See Chapter 7, Canada At Play, to find out*).

Small Towns, East and West
Merritt

'Welcome to Merritt, a lake a day as long as you stay'—that's what the signboard tells visitors to this little British Columbia town of just about 8,000 people.

Merritt is situated in the Nicola Valley, a high glacial valley about 600 m (1,968 ft) above sea level. It is a three-and-a-half hour drive from Vancouver, at an important junction in the Coquihalla Highway which connects the west coast to the interior of the province. As you enter the town, lumber yards feature prominently and they fill the air with the fragrant scent of pine, fir and spruce.

The town grew as a result of coal and copper mining, but the forest industry is the big employer now and there are several sawmills in town. The valley itself is rich cattle country and many ranches surround the town. In fact, the first settlers were cattle ranchers, attracted by the vast grasslands of the valley. Many of Merritt's streets bear the names of the early pioneers, whose descendants continue to live in town.

Remembrance Day Parade in front of the Court House in Merritt.

But before the settlers came, the valley was home to many native tribes. The valley was named after Chief N'Kwala, whose name was anglicised to Nicola. Today, there are five native reserves in the area. In 1983, the natives formed the Nicola Valley Institute of Technology, based in Merritt. It is an independent institution for natives and non-natives and provides degree-level courses in agreement with other universities.

Tourism is carefully cultivated. Merritt's boast of 'a lake a day as long as you stay' is not an idle one as there are about 150 lakes and streams within the area, kept well stocked with salmon, trout and other fish. There are numerous trails along which to go hiking, horse riding, skiing and snowmobiling. Thousands of country music fans descend upon the city every July for the Merritt Mountain Music Festival. Each Labour Day weekend in September, the Merritt Rodeo and Fall Fair provides local residents and tourists with the excitement of a rodeo, old time fiddling contests, pancake breakfasts and a community dance.

Campbellford

Set on the picturesque Trent Canal, Campbellford in Ontario has about 5000 inhabitants, many of whose families have lived in the town for several generations.

The one main street, naturally called Front Street because it parallels the water, is intersected by the only other street of any significance, called, also for obvious reasons, Bridge Street. Together, these two form the downtown area: a collection of small, locally-run shops with the post office, three banks and an off-licence (liquor store) thrown in for good measure.

Surrounding the downtown area, the majority of Campbellford's residents live in detached houses on other smaller streets, which also contain the town's facilities. For instance, Campbellford's ice hockey arena is tucked away at the back of the town behind the high school, on whose fields teams from other towns practise whatever sport is currently in season. Adjacent to the arena and high school, the community hospital is staffed by local physicians who see their patients there and take turns to be on call for the relatively few emergencies which crop up. The town's many service clubs meet on different days—Rotary on Mondays, Kinsmen on Tuesdays and so on—and many of the town's prominent citizens and business people belong to several of them.

A typical autumn scene in the small town of Campbellford, Ontario.

There are two small factories in Campbellford, but mainly the economy of the town and its survival depend on the success of the local area's small business and service ventures.

Most of the people here know each other—some of the town's doctors have brought several generations of the same family into the world and some of the teachers have taught them all too! So there aren't many secrets; indiscretions have an embarrassing way of surfacing no matter how hard one has tried to disguise them. But similarly, if there is someone in trouble, the community will always rally round to offer what support it can, be it financial, moral or social.

Campbellford has its local heroes—the scout leaders, the little league coaches, the leaders of the business community—and there is a strong community spirit in the town as a whole. Such a community spirit epitomises small towns everywhere—a sense of local identity, lacking in the biggest cities of the country, and which keeps people living in Campbellford and towns like it all over the country. It is this sense of local community and spirit which is still, to many, the essence of Canada's strength and of its most important values; tolerance, understanding and moral uprightness.

FROM LOG CABIN TO TRAILER HOME

The very earliest Canadian homes, if you discount the tents and tepees of the native peoples, were made from logs that the first settlers had hewn from the giant forests around them. Log buildings served as churches, mission posts, trading shops, family homes and shelters of every kind. Today, in spite of the many alternative materials that are available to the builder, log houses are still prevalent on farms and ranches and as holiday retreats in the country. This is because they are recognised as strong, durable and beautiful structures that are in harmony with their natural surroundings. The log house building, far from being a dying tradition, seems to be holding its own in a world where steel, plastic and glass are the universal building materials and wood, where it is found, has first to be chipped, stripped and otherwise treated before it is used. Canadian log homes have even found a niche in the export market. Several, often small, companies, have found it viable to first construct these homes log by log, then dismantle them for shipping and reassembling in Japan especially, where log homes are a popular trend.

Canadian suburban houses, however, are more standard looking, with the wood-frame house being more common than that of brick.

Constructing a wood-frame house

- Construction of the frame house usually begins with digging a foundation in which concrete can be poured to form a basement.
- A skeletal framework made of wooden planks forming the walls of the house is then erected on the concrete base.
- The frame is covered with sheets of plywood on the outside and gypsum board on the inside to complete the walls.
- These walls sandwich a fibreglass material that serves as insulation against the cold.

When building a wood-frame house, it takes just a short while to nail a wall together and erect it.

- The external plywood wall is commonly covered with vinyl or wooden siding, and sometimes a brick veneer, purely for cosmetic purposes.

Unlike a brick house, the wood-frame house can be completed in as a short a time as three months. Often a real estate developer will just clear the land and divide it into building lots.

The buyer, after purchasing his empty land, has many options as to how he wishes to get his dream house built:

- He can employ a draughtsman or an architect to custom-design his house.
- He can choose a ready-made building plan, available from magazines, books and building companies.
- If he is a true do-it-yourself handyman, he can take on the job of building from start to finish himself, without help from a professional builder.
- Alternatively, he may hire a builder to take the house up to a specific stage, such as seeing that the excavation, foundation and framing of the structure are done, after which he can take over and finish the job.
- He can also hire a builder to take the job from start to finish, but supervise the work himself.
- His most expensive option would be to hire an architect to take charge of the entire project, from the designing to completion of the house.

The house may have just a single level, or two or three levels, in which case the bottom-most storey is called the basement and can be below or at ground level. If the house stands by itself, it is a single-detached house. Although it can vary from neighbourhood to neighbourhood, most suburban properties tend to blend into one another, that is, front lawns often merge and there are no fences or gates to separate one property lot from another. Where there are fences or hedges defining the property line, they tend to be low and decorative. Back fences are generally higher and more protective of privacy.

Houses attached to another are sometimes called 'townhouses' and may be further distinguished by other names: duplex (two houses attached to each other on one side, or semi-detached houses), four-plex (four houses attached together), or six-plex (six houses attached to each other) and so on. The term condominium housing or 'condos' refers to high-rise apartment buildings or rows of low-rise buildings.

Given the regional disparities in economic and population demands, there is no single average price of housing for Canada. Prices fluctuate according to many factors, such as the health of the local economy, the rise and fall of mortgage rates, the movement of the population and consumer supply and demand. Nevertheless, average housing prices in the cities of Toronto, Vancouver and Victoria have risen above C$ 300,000 in the past 10 years. In Calgary, where there has been tremendous growth, the average price of a house in that period has risen above C$ 150,000. In Montreal, Ottawa and Edmonton, an average house costs over C$ 150,000.

While many Canadians continue to live in the suburban sprawls that spread outwards from the big cities in comfortable single- or double-storey homes with gardens to plant and lawns to trim, there is an increasingly new demand for housing in neighbourhoods closer to the downtown core. These homes are often apartments with a view in high-rise condominiums. An increasing number of old, often historic, buildings in inner-city cores are also being renovated internally. These are sold to those who eschew the traditional house on a large lot of land and commute along the main roads for the convenient lifestyle of city living, close to work and entertainment.

Renting or Buying a House?

Federal housing policy in Canada is mainly the responsibility of the Canada Mortgage and Housing Corporation (CMHC), established in 1946 to administer the National Housing Act. The CMHC works with the provinces to ensure that all Canadians have access to adequate housing at an affordable cost. The assistance may take the form of loans made, often at reduced interest rates, for the construction of affordable rental accommodation for low- and middle-income families and the elderly.

It is possible to discover which houses are for sale by just driving around housing estates. Those houses which are on the market often have 'For Sale' signs displayed on their

Typical rents may include heating costs, hot and cold water supply, and sometimes electricity and gas, and household appliances like kitchen stove, refrigerator, washer and dryer.

lawns. Some of these signs may say the house is 'For Sale By Owner' or the signs may belong to one of many real estate companies operating in the area. Another good way of finding a house to buy or rent is to go to a real estate agent who will have a listing of most of the properties that are available in his district. Although there are many different real estate companies, they all have access to the same pool of available properties that are listed for sale or rent.

Keeping Standards High

There are also special loans available to homeowners and landlords to help renovate and bring deteriorating housing up to minimum standards.

Some of the standard features that are included in houses for sale are cupboards, clothes closets, plumbing and electrical wiring. Sometimes, refrigerators and other appliances like kitchen stoves and dishwashers may also be included. Electricity for lights, radio and television and other small household appliances, is supplied at 110 volts.

In your search for a home, you might come across condominiums with a sign that says the housing is 'adult oriented' or one that might say 'seniors preferred'. This is accommodation reserved only for older people, who prefer to keep a quiet pace of life and not have it disrupted by crying babies or children playing in the yard. Families with young children are not welcome to live in these apartments. Similarly, some apartment building owners do not allow pets.

Trailer homes are a form of low-cost housing. Having said this though, it must be noted that costs can vary considerably depending on the amenities that are included in the home. A trailer park is one where you can rent a trailer home (which looks like a large container) already on site. Some people have their own trailers and rent a pad in the park on which to put their 'house'. Many of the families who live in these trailer parks are in the lower-income bracket and tend to be transient in nature, moving to towns where they can find work. Retired elderly people who do not wish to be encumbered with a large house and garden at this time of their lives also form a large part of trailer park residents. They spend a fair amount of their time in an RV (recreational vehicle) travelling around the country or travelling south to escape the cold.

How to Find a Home in Canada

The first choice that a newcomer to Canada has to make is whereabouts in the country he/she (or the whole family) wishes to live. Traditionally, many people immigrating to Canada have found themselves attracted to the major urban centres of Toronto, Montreal or Vancouver, but there is an increasing trend recently for newcomers to locate themselves in the smaller cities and towns, scattered right across the country where living costs may be lower.

The Canadian government has a number of agencies which will help newcomers decide on the best location for them in terms of finding employment, being able to afford reasonable housing and also to integrate themselves into a local community which already contains people of similar backgrounds. Once a city or town has been targeted as a desirable location, a decision has to be made as to what type of housing there would be most suitable.

There are several kinds of housing to choose from in most places, some of which can be quite small (sometimes as small as two units, known as a duplex) or quite large (sometimes apartment blocks as high as thirty or more storeys). Detached or semi-detached houses are also easy to find in most places, but are usually more expensive.

The next choice is whether to rent or to buy a place to live, and this generally depends on the amount of money that is available. If you choose to rent, there are several different types of rental accommodation commonly found throughout Canada. These can include:

- co-op housing, in which the rent is geared to income and all the tenants take part in managing and running the building
- rent-controlled public housing which is built by the provincial government and managed through a local housing authority
- or privately owned rental housing where you pay rent to an individual or a company and where market forces determine the appropriate rent.

Finding a Property

There are many ways to find an apartment or a house to rent. The agency which greeted you when you arrived in Canada may have workers who can help you find a place to live, or the community in which you have chosen to live may have an organisation which will help. However, to find the actual apartment or house which is most suitable for you, you will have to do your own search. This can be done by asking friends or family already living in the community, by searching the classified ads in local newspapers, or, most commonly, through a real estate company which handles rentals.

Tenant's Rights

You should determine exactly what your tenant rights are by contacting the tenant office or your local tenants' association, if your apartment building has one.

Once you have found a suitable place to rent, what your rental payment will include differs from province to province, and you should check carefully exactly what you will be responsible for paying for over and above your actual rent payment. (For example, electricity may or may not be included in the rent.) Once you have decided on the apartment you wish to rent, you will usually be asked to sign a lease, which is a legal agreement between you and the landlord and will specify what the rent is, what it includes and what the exact responsibilities of both tenant and landlord are. The provincial government often has rent-control policies in force which determine how far and how often your rent can be increased and, as a tenant, you will also have certain other legal rights.

If you want to buy a house, the process is slightly different as you are more likely to consider it a more permanent residence than you would a rental apartment. In any case, before you decide where to buy, check out the neighbourhood thoroughly and, if you can, find out something about its reputation. Ask where the schools are, the nearest shopping centres, the nearest places of worship and so on to make sure that this is an area in which you would feel comfortable living.

When you have determined that this is indeed the place for you, the best course of action is to contact a real estate agency in the area and ask them to show you what is available in your price range. House prices have a very wide variation, depending on the type and size of house and especially, where it is located. Take your time to look at as many available houses as possible before you decide on which one interests you the most and, once you have done this, you can make an offer to purchase the house. The offer you make will customarily be lower than the price which is being asked and it is then up to the sellers to decide if they wish to accept your offer.

Even after an offer has been accepted initially, all final agreements to buy a house should be subject to a building inspection, which you or your real estate agent will have to arrange for. The fee for this service is usually about C$ 300 and the home inspector you choose will submit to you a written report telling you how well built the house is and whether or not it needs repairs. If it does, the report will tell you which repairs need to be made first and at what estimated cost.

If the home inspection is satisfactory, you will then need to engage the services of a lawyer to complete the transaction and if you do not have sufficient cash, you will also need to visit a bank or other lending organisation to arrange for a mortgage. The Canada Mortgage and Housing Corporation is a very good source of information on how to do this and on advising you what you should expect to pay in mortgage payments, including interest. You will also need to arrange insurance on your house before you actually move into it.

Selling Your Property

If you decide that you wish to sell your house at a later date, you can do so privately through doing your own advertising or a real estate agent will also be able to arrange this for you. Payment for the services of a real estate agent is usually charged to the seller and can range from two to five per cent of the agreed sales price, depending on the agency and the location.

SHOPPING

So you have packed up all your possessions, set aside what you will bring with you on your flight over, which is mainly clothing and other personal effects, and left the rest for the movers to send along at a later date. Then you have worries about having forgotten to buy some items you consider essential, or you have packed away something you think you might require right now. Banish those fears! There is hardly anything that you cannot obtain in Canada, especially if you are in a fairly large urban centre, whether it be food, clothing or something for the house.

Shopping Centres For All

As in many other countries, the shopping mall or centre, which is a large building with many shops under its one roof, is a ubiquitous feature of Canadian cities. There is a predictability about the shopping centre that makes shopping easy for a newcomer to the country. In smaller towns, there may not be an 'all under one roof' shopping

Shopping centres are usually open seven days a week and those in the larger cities will have longer opening hours. During special times of the year, like the festive Christmas and New Year season, the shops remain open for longer than usual.

Many supermarkets issue their customers with membership cards that can be used to earn points or to be eligible for special offers. In addition, there are special deals every week on selected items, and other savings can be made by buying what you need in larger quantities or in bulk.

centre but a cluster of shops can still be found either around a big parking lot or in the form of a 'strip mall' of shops strung out side by side along a road.

Shopping centres generally have all kinds of shops in one place but there will be one or two big shops like a food supermarket and a department store to attract shoppers. In between these large shops, there are many smaller shops, selling clothing, shoes, sporting goods, lingerie and so on. The majority of these shops are branches of large chain stores.

In some cities, certain days of the week are informally designated as 'late shopping days', during which shopping centres may elect to stay open slightly later in the evening. This is handy for workers who can then do their shopping after office hours. The convenience of such one-stop shopping is most appreciated in the winter when it is uncomfortably cold outside or when it rains.

Bigger is Better

The supermarket or big grocery shop is the place to go shopping for food. In these big shops you will find not only food, but often also a variety of other household necessities, such as clothing, videos and music cds, books and magazines, medicines, pharmaceutical products and photo processing services. Large supermarkets also open seven days a week and for longer than the smaller shops. In bigger centres, some supermarkets are open 24 hours.

It seems that Canadians have thoroughly embraced the idea that 'bigger is better' if one is to judge by the increasing appearance of 'big box stores' in the cities. A 'big box store' eschews aesthetics for the practicality of size and quantity. The shop is seldom little more than an enormous rectangular, single-storey building filled from floor to ceiling with merchandise. This style of shopping first appeared in the 1970s in the United States and has found a firm foothold in Canada, too. It is not the place to go if you are looking for things that are unique or interesting but, if looking for mundane necessities, one can certainly find bargains. Many 'big box stores' can be found in one locality surrounding equally cavernous parking lots and, together, they are a signature landscape phenomenon of North America that would probably be visible on a photograph of the continent taken from outer space.

Small and Special

At the other end of the scale, there are, and hopefully will always be, small clusters of unique, individual shops that offer a more varied and local shopping experience. In these small shops, going shopping becomes a more interesting and inter-personal activity. There is the opportunity for customer and shopkeeper to form a relationship that is more complex than just an exchange of money for goods. Service is also more friendly and meaningful, and you can find more unique things to purchase. Often these shops form the heart of cultural enclaves, especially in the cities, and are places to go if you are looking for speciality items. For example, in Vancouver, Commercial Drive is the place for the shopper looking for Italian food like cheeses, pastas and olive oil. Chinatown and Richmond shops have everything Chinese like barbecue pork and electric rice cookers, and Punjabi Market has the widest selections of saris within the area of a downtown city block. Whatever your ethnic background might be, Canadian cities stock almost everything you need in the way of culturally specific food and other goods. This is especially true in Toronto and Vancouver, two very cosmopolitan cities. If you have moved into a small town, this may be more difficult, and you might have to schedule periodic shopping trips into the city that is nearest to you in order to get your cultural food fix of *sushi* or *borscht*.

Convenience Shops

Also in the category of small are the numerous corner convenience shops or newsagents (called *dépanneur* in Quebec) where one can buy a smattering of essential items like canned soup, fruit, milk, cereal, bread, snacks, newspapers, magazines and cigarettes. These may be small 'mom-and-pop' shops or part of a large chain of shops like 7-Eleven. The small retail businesses tend to have shorter opening hours and close on Sundays. Some close for the entire weekend, thus contrasting with the chain stores that remain open 24 hours, seven days a week.

Do Your Homework

When moving into a new neighbourhood, it is a good idea to talk to the neighbours and to go on a discovery walk or drive within the vicinity in order to source out the types of shops there are in the area.

Public Markets

When you have more time, it is worthwhile exploring the 'public market' for a more interesting shopping trip. The public market concept is about shopping under one roof, but in Canada you will find the public market to be a large warehouse-like space where the emphasis is on items that are small, local, fresh, unique and organic, so different from the plastic, pre-packaged offerings of supermarkets. The many individual vendors who have stalls in the market excel at displaying their wares. Piles of fresh fruit and vegetables invite you to reach across and pick them, glistening hunks of meat beckon from behind glass counters, cheeses and pickles swim in vinaigrette and olive oil baths and the sight and smell of fresh baking guarantees you will part with your money more easily. There is a greater intimacy between customer and produce, and customer and seller. The public market is such a colourful and pleasurable place to shop that it is often also an attraction for tourists.

Restricted Goods

In Canada, there are restrictions regarding the sale of alcohol and cigarettes. Each province has a liquor board that is

Know the Law

Be aware that there are legal age restrictions in Canada regarding drinking and smoking. Minors under the age of 19 may not buy alcohol or cigarettes. Shop personnel may ask you for your identification if you look younger than the age limit.

controlled by the provincial government. These boards are independent monopolies that operate the largest and the greatest number of shops in all urban centres. Except in Quebec, alcohol can only be bought in licensed outlets and not from grocery stores or newsagents, as in Europe and Asia. In addition to liquor board outlets, there may also be other smaller off-licences (liquor shops) operated by other businesses such as hotels, restaurants and bars. These are sometimes called 'cold wine and beer stores' because they keep some stock in refrigerators for customers making last-minute purchases for a party. These places tend to have longer shop opening hours than liquor board outlets, remaining open at weekends and later at night. They often charge a little extra for these conveniences.

Taxes to Pay

Environmental Health

Additional costs are charges that are added to certain types of goods to encourage consumers to recycle. These include a small bottle deposit of five or ten cents that is returned to you when you bring the empties back, and levies on items such as tyres, batteries, paint and motor oil. This is so that consumers bear some of the financial responsibility of disposing of such environmentally bad products.

When you are looking at the cost of goods, remember that there are taxes to add to the price you see on the tag. The federal government imposes a seven per cent Goods and Services Tax (GST) on top of the price. In addition, there is a sales tax that varies from province to province and that adds yet another seven to eight per cent to your bill. The provinces of Newfoundland and Labrador, Nova Scotia and

New Brunswick have chosen to combine the GST with the Provincial Sales Tax into something called the Harmonized Sales Tax, currently standing at 15 per cent. This is the biggest extra cost with goods sold in Canada and makes a difference when you bring your purchases up to the cashier to be 'rung' through.

Where and How to Pay

Large shops have cashiers set up in different parts of the shop for the convenience of the shopper. Some department stores which sell a variety of products have a row of cashiers at the front of the shop, just as in the supermarkets. There may be some 'express' check-out counters dedicated to serve shoppers who have just a few items to pay for and are in a hurry. Of course, cash is the universal means of payment. This is especially so in the smaller independent retail shops which may not have alternative credit or debit payment facilities. But you will often be given other means of paying for your purchases—you may set up an account with the shop if you are a regular customer, or you may pay by credit card or by directly debiting your bank account using a bank card. Some big shops also issue their own credit card that is usually linked with one of the major credit card companies, such as Visa, MasterCard and American Express. Payment by personal cheques is another option but one that is not always available. Most businesses prefer that you do not use cheques, and if you do, they will ask you to prove your identity by showing some identification bearing a photograph, such as a driver's licence.

You will be given a paper receipt for whatever you buy which is your proof of payment. It is important to keep this receipt in case you need to return the item you bought. Most shops will honour an unstated agreement to take back the item if you give them a reasonable explanation for bringing it back but it is best to check with the shops about their return policy. For the most part, shops will give you 30 days to bring back something if you are unhappy with it and if you have not used the item. Most of the time, they will give you your cash back, but some now insist on an exchange of goods only.

If you are buying a large item that is expensive, a 'big-ticket item' such as a household appliance or a vehicle, there will be a warranty on the product. Make sure you read the fine print, and if you are paying by installments, you should find out exactly what your payment terms are, and how long it will take you to pay fully for the item. Sometimes, shops offer 'deals' that look very attractive. They might be willing not only to accept payment in installments, but also to defer an initial payment or deposit for some time as well. Check on what the penalties might be if you are unable to pay up. Do the maths and work out what your purchase will cost you in the end. These financing deals are negotiated not with the shop that has sold you the product but with a finance company that will make it worth their while to advance you the money. You might decide that it is too much to pay.

As a consumer, you have rights and responsibilities. You can learn more about this from Canada's Business and Consumer Site at http://www.strategis.ic.gc.ca or call 1-800-328-6189 (toll-free in Canada).

Searching for Bargains

Be on the lookout for sales. For clothing, shoes and other personal items, there are often sales timed to coincide with the seasons. Each spring, summer, autumn and winter, the shops bring in new fashions and the unsold stock from the previous season is put on sale. After Christmas, shops hold Boxing Day sales to clear away whatever they did not sell during the rush to buy gifts. There are always bargains you can get if you know what it is you would like to buy and keep a look out for it. A good place to check on what's for sale is in the 'flyers' or advertising inserts that the shops put into your postbox and also come with the newspapers. Looking out for sales is quite acceptable, and Canadians will often pride themselves upon getting a 'bargain'. However, the process of bargaining itself, which is one way of obtaining a good price in some countries, is not acceptable here. Shoppers are expected to pay the price shown. The exception to this rule is when you are engaged in a private sale, outside a formal shop environment, such as when buying a used vehicle or transacting a purchase found in an 'items for sale' advertisement. Bargaining is to be expected when you buy something from a garage sale.

COPING WITH THE SEASONS
Winter's Chill

Humourist Stephen Leacock once said that life in Canada consists of preparing for winter, enduring winter and recovering from winter. And, being Canadian, he ought to know.

Indeed, the seasons play an important part in the life of the people. As winter approaches, the householder must look critically at his home to winterise it. Storm windows and doors are checked, the central heating is turned on. Cars too must be prepared for winter. Summer and all-season tyres are taken off and snow tyres put on. The engine oil is changed to one of thinner viscosity.

In winter, ranchers also bring their cattle down from the hills. The geese fly south and so do the 'snowbirds'. The 'snowbirds' *(see Canadianisms in* Chapter 8*, Canadian Language)* are Canadians who fly south every year to Florida, Hawaii, Mexico and other sun-bathed lands to escape the grip of winter.

But winter does not mean the shutting down of everything, or the suffering of 'cabin fever' when one is kept indoors by the inclement weather for weeks at a time. Life still goes on and some things come alive only during this time of the year. A really beautiful winter's day, when the air is crisp and clear, the sky a cloudless blue and the snow sparkling in the sunshine, has to be experienced to be believed. One good way to deal with the winter's cold is to get outside and be active. Some Canadians love to spend time and money at ski resorts, while others will just take their

Black Ice—Beware

'Black ice' is a particularly dangerous phenomenon on the roads. It occurs when there has been a sudden thawing or rain followed by freezing temperatures. The water on the road freezes into a thin layer of ice that cannot be seen, and a fast moving car loses all grip on the road. There is little control, so the vehicle spins out of control and may slide off the road into a ditch or onto the opposite side of the road into the path of oncoming traffic.

Snow lends an air of serenity to this small village in Quebec.

winter entertainment wherever they can find it, whether it be cross-country skiing, sledding, skidooing, ice skating and ice fishing—anywhere there is snow and ice. Frozen lakes are converted into ice-rinks by ice-skaters and become pockmarked with little holes that have been drilled by the ice-fishermen.

In Canada, snow is everywhere during winter. The softly falling snow is a beautiful sight and can even be mesmerising. A snow-covered lawn is often an invitation to children and the young at heart to play, making snowmen and throwing snowballs at each other. Shovelling the driveway can be an enjoyable task (though some might not agree) and making a snowman requires more skill and experience than you might think. (Snow conditions have to be just right before a snowman can be built. The light powdery stuff may be what skiers look for, but a snowman needs snow that will stick together.)

Driving is particularly hazardous at this time of the year. When there is blowing snow, visibility on the roads can be cut down to a kilometre or less, ultimately producing a condition known as 'whiteout'. In such conditions, driving is extremely dangerous and roads may have to be closed. With snow and ice everywhere, roads must be sanded to provide more traction for the tyres. The driver must learn different skills, such as how to handle a slipping and sliding car especially when the snow has been packed down into a layer of ice. In fact, a driver new to such conditions might be wise to find some open area like an empty car park to practise throwing his car into a slide and regaining control of it so that he can drive more confidently.

Cracked or shattered windshields and headlamps are common when the sand and gravel that have been spread on the road to give your tyres traction become missiles flung at you by an overtaking car or truck.

Dressing in winter is an art that really can only be learnt when you are in the country. It is difficult to predict how cold a winter can be as this depends on which part of the country you are in. However, it is safe to say that a visitor to Canada in winter must be prepared for temperatures below freezing.

Dressing in layers is often recommended, especially when you intend to exercise outdoors. You should wear top and bottom thermal underwear which is the first essential layer of clothing to put on. Its closeness to your skin helps you to keep warm. Unless you are going to the north, it need not be made of wool, which might be too warm and is often uncomfortably prickly to wear. Thermal clothing should be made of synthetic fabrics like polypropylene which will draw perspiration away from the body. (It may seem surprising, but it is possible to perspire profusely even though one is exercising in temperatures below freezing.) It is also essential to wear one or more knitted jumpers made of wool or acrylic. Then top it off with a winter jacket, of which the warmest and lightest is made of down. It should be water- and wind-resistant. It is also important to keep your head covered with a hat or toque made of wool or synthetic fabric, as 60 per cent of your body warmth is lost through the head. For the hands, gloves or mittens are important. Mittens are warmer as fingers are kept together and there is less surface exposed to the cold. Put your feet in wool or thermal socks and winter boots to keep them warm.

Winter Warmers

A word about winter boots:

- It is better if they are slightly too large rather than too small, so an extra pair of socks can be slipped over for more warmth.
- Tight boots can also restrict circulation and cause your feet to freeze.
- It is a bonus if the boots are also waterproof, as you will often be walking in snow or slush.
- Like winter tyres, the tread of your boots should provide good traction on icy pavements.

The air in winter is also drier, and lips may crack and peel, and skin become dry and flaky. Lip balms and moisturising creams for the skin are necessary. The hot, dry air that is circulated throughout the house with central heating compounds the problem. So too does the hot water that you use to wash your hands. But aside from the cold, dryness and wind, one culprit that is seldom recognised is the winter sun, whose ultraviolet rays can damage the skin. If you enjoy outdoor winter sports, you should use a sun block cream for protection.

Do not, however, get the impression that in Canada, one must always be heavily laden with clothes in winter. The above is only for times when you venture outdoors, and even then it depends on how cold it actually is. Indoors, you can wear as little as you wish, because of the 'miracle' of central heating.

Central heating makes even the harshest Canadian winter bearable. With it, you can stand at the window looking out on the knee-deep snow in your yard, yet be dressed in your summer shorts because the temperature in your house can be kept as high as you wish. (Of course, it would cause a corresponding high in your heating bill.) Over the years, Canadians have experimented with various ways to heat their houses, from simple fireplaces in each room to the most ingenious methods of creating and spreading heat from one source throughout the house, without having to sit in front of the radiator, burning your front and freezing your back.

By far the most common system nowadays involves a furnace, usually located in the basement, and connected by an extensive network of internal hot air ducts to all areas that need warmth in winter. These furnaces are powered by various sources of energy. Some use electrical power (usually expensive), some oil (expensive too and sometimes subject to fluctuations in supply) and some natural gas (usually the cheapest, but not always available). Wood furnaces, sometimes in combination with one of the other sources, are also quite common, especially in the countryside, where fuel supply is obviously greater. Wood stoves, refined and developed from the primitive models used by Canadian pioneers, are also popular for providing supplementary heat to individual rooms in a house, as are localised electric forced air and electric baseboard heaters. A more recent source, which is gaining more popularity with Canadians, is the heat pump which draws heat directly from outside the house (interestingly enough even in winter, there is always some heat residual either in the air or in the ground) and re-circulates it through the internal ducts.

Whatever the source, however, central heating has become a must and it would be extremely rare to find a house or apartment in Canada that is not equipped to deal centrally with the cold blasts of winter.

Signs of Spring

During late January and early February, most people will have had their fill of winter and will be looking for signs of spring.

'Spring is in the air'—but what does that mean? It could mean that, when you are out walking, you suddenly notice that the bare branches are starting to bud again. Others look for birds, and the first sight of a robin in the yard is often occasion for joy. Ranchers can tell that the cold weather's gone when their cows start calving.

And it is not just nature that tells you spring is just around the corner. Shop window displays also change with the seasons. Snow shovels give way to bicycles and racks of seed packets. Clothing shops put away their winter jackets and offer summer blouses and T-shirts. Every now and again, you see someone on a bicycle. Shorts and skirts are in vogue again. The first advertisement for a garage sale is also a definite sign that warmer times are here. The impatient gardener will take every opportunity when the sun shines to clear the dead leaves and winter debris, and ready his yard for the next season's plantings.

For a more authoritative opinion as to whether you've seen the last of the snow, wait for Groundhog Day on 2 February. On that day, everybody watches with bated breath for a special little groundhog called Wiarton Willie, who lives in Wiarton, Ontario, to come out of his hole. The belief is that, if it is a bright sunny day and Willie sees his shadow, he will jump back in again, and winter will remain for another six weeks. Willie's predictions, however, have to be taken with a pinch of salt, as his accuracy rate is rather low.

The change in the seasons is usually a time for rain and wind. March and April are cold, wet and windy months. Spring season is mud season. Thawing ice causes mud slides, very bumpy roads and pot holes. Drivers must be careful.

Thaws can make many places very muddy and bog a car down in a back road.

Long, Hot Summer Days

It often comes as a surprise to learn that Canadian summers can be really hot. Somehow, one's picture of this northern country is one of constant cold, ice and snow. However, except for the North, other parts of Canada can experience fairly warm summers because of the intrusion of tropical air from the Gulf of Mexico and the hot deserts of the American south-west. Some days in the months of June, July and August can even be tropically hot and humid.

The days are usually long. The sun rises as early as 4:00 am and does not set until after 10:00 pm. Those who can take advantage of these long warm, sunny days to be outdoors. Gardens blossom. There are activities like camping, hiking, fishing, baseball, tennis, golf ... the list goes on and on; so many reasons to hurry home from work every Friday and take off to that cottage by the lake.

The smell of summer is the smell of steak grilling on a barbecue pan. Increased outdoor activity is echoed by the renewal of nature. Flies emerge as if from nowhere, and the swarms of mosquitoes and blackflies can make life a misery. There are literally clouds of these little insects, especially in wooded campsites, all through May and well into June.

For many Canadians, especially those who live in apartments, summer brings a longing for a way of life that cannot be found in the towns and cities and for which proximity to water is an absolute necessity. This explains the phenomenon of the 'summer cottage', a home away from home that is a prized possession of many families. Some cottages have been in the same family for several generations, and some change hands regularly. However, they all share the same basic purpose: to allow their owners to get away from the hurried pace of their ordinary

Schools close from the end of June to the end of August, and this is the long summer break for most families who go on holiday at this time of the year. Community and all other organised group activities take a break too, because there is seldom anyone around to participate.

Fishing: a favourite pastime for Canadians.

lives and spend time doing water-based leisure pursuits such as fishing, canoeing, water-skiing and sailing. Others simply sit around enjoying the sun and watching the surrounding flora and fauna.

After Labour Day on the first Monday of September, the unofficial end to the summer season, most cottages are left unvisited, though the ritual of closing and securing them for the winter months is a long and elaborate one. However, there has been a trend in recent years to winterise some of the larger cottages, so as to be able to stay there all year round.

Autumn Colours

Summer's heat is tempered at this time, but the days are still sunny and warm, and the nights sharply cool. The trees take on the loveliest colours of flaming reds, deep browns and vivid gold. But the planting season is almost over, and it is time to clear the weeds and leaves.

Some people are depressed by the retreat of nature, and the shorter days. By late October and especially in November, these shorter days really begin to affect one's life. Children leave for school in the morning when it is still dark, and office workers come home after the sun has set. It can be rather depressing if you come from the tropics and are used to a fairly even distribution of 12 hours of light and 12 hours of darkness all year round. It gets dark very early in the afternoon, and when you come home from work it can be pitch black outside. Although it is only 5:00 pm, your instinct tells you that it's already late, and you should have had your dinner and gone to bed.

LIVING IN THE NORTH

When Canadians speak of 'the North', they generally mean the part of Canada north of the 60th Parallel. This area, made up of the North-west Territories, Nunavut and the Yukon, is not as economically developed or heavily populated as the provinces to the south, and living in the North has its own special requirements.

Nunavut was created out of the central and eastern part of the North-west Territories, roughly following the tree line. Iqaluit, the capital, is just three degrees south of the Arctic Circle. It receives a full 24 hours of daylight during the month of June, but only six hours in December.

Yellowknife

In the North-west Territories, 38 per cent of the population (about 17,000 people) live in Yellowknife, the area's capital and centre of government. It is on the extreme southern edge of the region. Transport in and around Yellowknife is good and prices are relatively low.

In the Yukon, about three-quarters of the people live along the Alaska Highway. Whitehorse, the capital, has about 19,000 people, and Dawson City, the second largest town, has about 2,000 residents. The rest of the population live in villages and small settlements of a few hundred people, almost always very isolated. In the Yukon, there are also 'company towns' in which the population depends upon a mining company for jobs and municipal facilities.

Travel into these areas is by air, and often one has to catch as many as four or five planes (each time a smaller one) to get there. Commercial air carriers operate scheduled services to most communities and charter services everywhere else.

The remoteness of these northern communities means that the cost of living is much greater than that in the southern parts of Canada. Since few consumer goods are produced in the North, most of these have to be air-freighted. One can expect to pay anything from 20 per cent to as much as 60 per cent or more above average for food and other essentials, depending upon the remoteness of the area where one lives. The local people consequently eat 'country food'—game like moose, beaver, rabbit, fish, caribou, bear and little else. The Inuit live almost exclusively on meat, fish and fowl. The Dene eat some vegetables and grain, but very little.

Most of these small settlements do not have the rudimentary services that Canadians in the south take for granted. There is seldom any hotel or motel, no café or restaurant. But there is usually a school and some sort of library, a mounted police detachment and several churches. Groceries, clothing and other supplies are often sold by Northern Stores, the successor to the Hudson's Bay Company. Health services are the responsibility of a nurse, supplemented by occasional visits from a doctor. A dentist and an optometrist may visit several times a year. A patient requiring major medical treatment must be flown out to Yellowknife, Inuvik or Edmonton.

Housing is standard, provided by the federal government under the Homeowner's Assistance Programme. Although almost every community has electricity, provided mainly by local diesel generating units and sometimes by hydroelectric power, only a few have running water. Water comes from wells or is trucked in. Sanitary facilities are inadequate and modern conveniences such as a flushing toilet are scarce. Sewage disposal systems are rare because of the difficulty of keeping sewers from freezing. Houses either have a holding tank with a pump-out service, or more often, what is euphemistically termed 'honey buckets', in which sewage is collected in plastic bags which are then picked up and trucked to a dump.

Alcohol abuse is a problem in the North, especially with the native people, and much of the police work has to do with alcohol-related problems. Because of this, some communities prohibit the import of alcohol, and anyone wishing to buy alcohol in such 'dry communities' must apply for a permit.

When driving north, the motorist must prepare himself for conditions that are quite unlike those in any other part of Canada. Northern roads are characterised by long distances and infrequent traffic. Most all-weather roads have gravel surfaces and parts of some major main roads, like the Alaska Highway, Klondike Highway and Hay River Highway, are paved.

The principal main road of the North-west Territories is Mackenzie Highway. It provides a link with Alberta in the south, while the Liard Highway is NWT's road link with British Columbia.

Because of the long distances one has to travel between communities, weather forecasts and information on road conditions are regularly given on the radio. Nevertheless, whether you are driving north in winter or summer, survival equipment is important. Your vehicle must be in good condition. You should carry a tow rope or chain, at least one spare tyre, an axe, a box of matches, tools, first aid kit, fan belts and fuses. Extra gas (as petrol is known in Canada and the United States) and oil are necessities as petrol and service stations are few and far between. Bringing extra food like chocolate bars, canned food and fruit is also a good idea. If you are travelling in winter, add a snow shovel to your emergency equipment, a good winter coat, mitts, a sleeping bag and some blankets. In summer, you should have insect repellent and water.

Major Roads

The main road into the Yukon is the Alaska Highway, built during World War II. Other major roads in the Yukon are the Robert Campbell Highway, the Klondike Highway, the Dempster Highway which links the Yukon with the North-west Territories and the Top-of-the-World Highway running west into Alaska.

How Cold Is the North?

Nowhere else in Canada does climate rule human activities as in the North. The type of housing, work patterns, leisure activities and transport are all largely determined by weather conditions.

Winters are cold and long, with temperatures in February averaging between -15°C and -30°C. Low temperatures (it is not uncommon for temperatures to fall below -40°C) and strong winds produce what the weather forecaster calls a 'wind-chill factor' that creates severe, sometimes dangerous, winter conditions for people.

Most outdoor activity and movement come to a halt when there is a blizzard (snow or blowing snow) and visibility is cut down to less than a kilometre. Fog is another problem, especially in summer in the Arctic islands, when the presence of open water creates high humidity. In winter, ice fog is a common occurrence because of the freezing of warm, moist air from buildings and vehicle exhaust fumes.

But in the summer months, temperatures average 12°C to 13°C south of the tree-line, and 3°C to 8°C in the Arctic islands. Warm air currents from the Pacific Ocean can even make the mercury rise above 25°C in some parts of the Yukon and the Mackenzie Valley.

FINANCIAL MATTERS

There are five major chartered banks within Canada, and most Canadians have at least one bank account with one of these. They are the Royal Bank, Bank of Montreal, Bank of Nova Scotia, Toronto Dominion Bank and the Canadian Imperial Bank of Commerce. These five banks have branches in all major towns and cities, and several of them have an extensive network in smaller centres as well. However, in urban areas, there are also a number of trust companies and credit unions, which also provide banking services, sometimes at a lower rate. Major banks and most trust companies provide a wide range of services, including supplying regular current (chequing) and savings accounts, issuing major credit cards, arranging investments, providing mortgage and loan services and individual financial planning. However, in addition to the services provided by the banks, there are now also a number of private individuals in many towns and cities in Canada who are licensed as Certified Financial Planners (CFP), and who will provide (usually free) advice on individual money management. CFP's will also give advice on investment strategies and tax issues, as will the many Chartered Accountants who can be found all over the country.

Taxation in Canada operates on many levels. The main income for the federal government comes from income tax, which every resident Canadian must pay, and for which an income tax return must be filed at the end of April each year. For people in the work place, income tax is usually deducted from their pay cheque at source, and the rate of deduction will depend on their individual income. Self-employed people must keep their own records and report their own annual gross income directly to the Canadian Customs and Revenue Agency. Other income from the federal government comes from the collection of customs duties on goods brought into the country, and from the Goods and Services Tax (GST), which is levied at seven per cent on a wide range of products and services in all provinces and territories of Canada. There are other federal taxes, too, such as capital gains tax and gasoline (petrol) tax, but these are largely hidden taxes, the details of which are best explained by a competent tax accountant or financial planner.

The provincial government also collects its share of tax directly, the majority of which comes from a provincial sales tax (PST) set at various rates, except in the province of Alberta which has no PST at all! The provincial government also receives a share of the personal income tax collected by the federal government in the form of transfer payments. Income from such other things as the sale of various licences and traffic violation fines also goes to the provincial government.

In addition to the federal and provincial governments, the municipality in which you live also collects its share of tax, mainly in the form of property taxes, which are assessed and collected locally on your home, the amount varying depending on its size. Money from property taxes go to support such community services as schools and hospitals as well as local road maintenance, street lighting, rubbish collection, etc.

In addition to taxes, most people will also have to pay for various kinds of insurance, the cost of which will vary from province to province and region to region. The main two are car insurance and home owner's or tenants' insurance, both of which can be arranged through private insurance companies in all provinces (and some government sponsored organisations in a few areas) and for which you will be billed annually or semi-annually. There are other types of insurance also available, such as life insurance, business insurance, long-term disability insurance, etc., which can usually also be purchased from these same companies.

Mainly as a result of all these different taxes and insurance policies which most Canadians have to pay, a system has been developed to keep track of how well people make their payments. The diverse information fed into this system by the different organisations comes together as what is known as a personal credit rating. This record will be consulted by most organisations and companies before they issue you a credit card, be it a bank card such as VISA or MasterCard, a department store card or even a card enabling you to buy petrol for your car on credit from one of the major oil companies. It is important to maintain a good credit rating by paying the bills you receive promptly, as otherwise, it may well become more difficult to obtain further credit, including mortgages and car purchase loans.

In the 'worst case scenario', any credit account which is in arrears can be referred to a collection agency, which will try increasingly more legally forceful methods to collect the money owing on behalf of the company to which you owe it. If you get into trouble and owe more than you can pay, there are credit counselling agencies which can work with you and your creditors to find a solution or, in extreme cases, you may formally declare personal bankruptcy, but this will have severe consequences on your ability to obtain credit in the future.

HEALTH AND HOSPITALS

Canada has a very comprehensive health care system, which covers everything from coughs and colds to major surgery. In all provinces of Canada, basic health care is provided free of charge to Canadian residents under the coverage of a provincial medicare plan. A health card is required to access this service and can be obtained on application to the provincial Ministry of Health.

The first level of health care in Canada is usually provided by family doctors, most of whom maintain offices in most Canadian cities and towns. However, due to the recent increase in the Canadian population and a growing shortage of Canadian certified family doctors, it has become difficult in some areas to find a physician who will be willing to provide ongoing health

Many non-emergency normal medical procedures such as child birth are also covered by the heath care system at no charge, as is elective surgery though there is often a long waiting list for this.

care for you and your family. For those who are unable to find a family physician where they live, often the only alternative is to visit a public clinic or the emergency department of a local hospital. However, these are often very crowded and it is unlikely that there will be any consistency in the medical personnel who treat you there. In some provinces, there is also a telephone health service provided by nurse practitioners. Nurse practitioners can be reached 24 hours a day at a toll-free telephone number and will give basic advice on minor medical problems. Most local hospitals also have emergency departments, which will see anyone as quickly as possible if there is a genuine medical crisis. Ambulance services staffed by qualified paramedics can also be summoned by telephone if a medical situation develops at home which requires very speedy treatment.

If the family doctor or the doctor in a clinic is unable to treat a particular problem, you will then be referred to a specialist. Most communities in Canada have specialists available in all the major medical disciplines but you have to be referred to them by a local medical practitioner and there can sometimes be a lengthy wait to get an appointment. If your condition requires hospitalisation, most communities have a local hospital which can deal with common ailments and provide a range of medical and surgical procedures. Hospitals in larger centres also have specialised clinics, such as those for the treatment of cancer, renal dialysis, etc, and you will be referred to one of these if your local hospital is unable to provide the service you need. Specialists in all of these hospitals will also usually perform any required medical or surgical procedures, the cost of which will be totally covered by the provincial health care plan.

Within a Canadian hospital, medical services and food are provided at no charge, but accommodation can often be upgraded through private insurance plans from basic ward type accommodation to a semi-private or private room. These same plans can also provide complete or partial coverage for prescription drugs, as well as alternative medical services such as chiropractors, physiotherapists and dentists, none of which are covered by most provincial health care plans.

Outside of major medical procedures provided by the government, there are a number of private nursing homes, which provide basic medical services, especially for senior citizens and the disabled. The facilities and quality of service provided by these homes can vary widely, as can the rates which they charge, depending on the type and location of the home, and to what extent it is subsidised by the provincial health care system. However, homes of various sizes and costs can be found in most urban centres in Canada and are becoming increasingly common as the population ages.

Charitable organisations also provide some limited medical services, such as hospices for the terminally ill, the rates for which will depend on the charity and the ability of those concerned to pay for them.

KEEPING IN TOUCH

Canadians statistically use the telephone more than any other nation on earth and it would be a rare house which did not have a telephone in this day and age. After all, the inventor of the telephone was himself a Canadian, and his legacy certainly endures in his adopted country.

The Birth of the Telephone

Born in 1847, Alexander Graham Bell came to Canada from Scotland with his parents in 1870. Originally trained as a speech therapist like his father, Bell first settled in Brantford, Ontario, and spent much of his time working on a device that would help his speech-impaired clients communicate more clearly with one another. In 1876, during the course of one such experiment, Bell uttered the immortal words 'Come here Watson, I need you' into his end of the speech device and the telephone was born. Bell patented the Bell Telephone, revolutionising long distance communications and leading to the opening of the first commercial telephone exchange in 1878.

Telephone services today are provided through various public and private companies, the biggest of which is appropriately named Bell Canada. These various telephone companies own and maintain the telephone lines throughout the country and have different plans for their use, which they offer to their customers. The basic rule of thumb is that local calls, namely calls within a designated area, are free while those going further afield are charged according to distance. Most communities in North America are now accessible to one another through direct dialling and many countries of the world can also be reached via satellite by simply dialling the telephone number without any need to resort to an operator. Special services are also offered by many telephone companies, including telephones for the deaf and a variety of public information services. In recent years, more and more Canadians have also been subscribing to local and national Internet service providers, either via phone lines or through cable modem services, and often at high speed. As a result, within Canada, the use of email and information from the World Wide Web, both for business and for personal use, has grown significantly.

Getting a home telephone installed is not a complicated process any longer. In most areas, phones will be installed within a day or two of being requested, and all lines are private in the major areas. In addition to renting their lines, the telephone companies also sell and service equipment, but they no longer have a monopoly on doing so. The telephone user now has a number of options as to what equipment can be bought and installed, and there are many retail outlets that sell a range of telephone instruments and other telephone related merchandise. Such alternative telephone services, for example voice over internet protocols (VOIP), are also now becoming much more widely available and have helped to reduce the cost of telephone services significantly. Mobile telephones are also now in widespread use in Canada, and there are a number of companies who provide these services for a comparatively reasonable cost.

By contemporary standards, the telephone service in Canada is not expensive. Most families will have a basic telephone bill that runs to about C$ 20 to C$ 25 per month for service and equipment with the long distance portion of the bill depending on the time, distance and duration of the calls made. Using the telephone is very much a part of the Canadian lifestyle, which may be one of the reasons why the Canadian postal service has fallen on hard times in recent years!

GETTING AROUND IN CANADA

Because of its vast size, moving from place to place in Canada has always been a major undertaking. As a result, ways of moving about inside the country have changed and evolved just as the country itself has done. The transition from canoes, sleds and pack animals to the sophisticated air, rail, road and sea services that now link Canada together has been a long and complicated one, and not without its problems. But modern Canada now boasts a transport and communications system which is another factor that cements the various regions into a unified whole.

The Heyday of Canadian Railways

Many historians have commented that Canada was built by the railway. Canada as a country was created by the joining of the older, well-established provinces in the east with the former colony of British Columbia in the west through the building of steel rails from the Atlantic to the Pacific shore. Between these two populated areas was what was considered to be a vast area of nothingness— a plain inhabited only by the native peoples and the buffalo which they hunted. Early explorers had crossed this vast space on foot, horseback or by canoe where stretches of water allowed, but little settlement of any permanent kind took place until the building of the first transcontinental railway line.

Canada's largest ever engineering project, the Canadian Pacific Railway was finished in 1885, linking Montreal in the east with Port Moody and Vancouver in the

Scenic Train Rides

The ride on the Algoma Central Railway from Sault Ste Marie to Hearst, traversing the Agawa Canyon in the Canadian Shield area of the country, is breathtaking, especially in the autumn when the leaves turn amazing shades of colour along the way. The Polar Bear express, which travels north from the Ontario town of North Bay to Moosonee, the southernmost town on James Bay, which is still inaccessible by road, is another worthwhile ride for the train enthusiast.

west. This was a tremendous achievement considering the kind of territory that those who built the railway had to contend with; the muskeg and swamp of the Canadian Shield, the desolation of the vast prairie and the seemingly impenetrable barriers imposed by three sets of mountain ranges in the west. That it was accomplished at all was a tribute, both to its engineers and designers, but also to the labourers who worked long and arduous hours clearing the land and laying track. Many of these workers were Chinese immigrants brought to Canada especially for this task, who endured immense hardship and worked with the ever present reality of being killed on the job, as indeed many of them were.

The construction of the Canadian Pacific Railway created the opportunity to bring settlers from overseas to farm the empty spaces on the prairie. In the process, it created the towns and cities which are now parts of the provinces of Manitoba, Saskatchewan and Alberta. After its construction, and for more than 50 years, the Canadian Pacific Railway, and later also the Canadian National Railway, provided the only link between many isolated communities and the rest of the country as many settlements grew up which could only be reached by the railway. Many generations of visitors to the country marvelled as the CPR's trains passed through the wilds of the Rogers Pass and looped round the spiral tunnels of the Selkirk Mountains.

The Rise of the 'Canadian'

The CPR's fastest and most luxurious train was the 'Canadian' which ran daily from coast to coast in both directions, and from whose windows many new arrivals had their first glimpse of the vastness of Canada. For more than 50 years, this train and the other transcontinental expresses held the country together, both economically and socially, while the Canadian railway system as a whole provided both the freight and passenger transport that made Canada viable as a country.

However, by the middle of the 20th century, with the advent of internal flight and the gradual development of a complex national highway system, the popularity of the railway system had started on a continuous decline, finally reaching the point at which both the Canadian National Railway and Canadian Pacific Railway began to lose substantial amounts of money. To prevent the complete collapse of passenger service in many parts of the country, the government eventually agreed to let both companies give up their passenger operations and to hand responsibility for passenger trains over to the government. As a result, although the two large railway companies, and a number of smaller ones, still operate their own freight services and maintain the actual track, all passenger service is now operated by a government subsidiary, VIA Rail. The 'Canadian' still runs but only three times a week, using the less spectacular northern route through the Yellowhead Pass and not the original CPR track through the spiral tunnels of the Kicking Horse Pass.

VIA Rail

VIA Rail was created by the federal government specifically to bring under one umbrella all passenger rail services in Canada, and thus to increase their efficiency and profitability. Unfortunately, VIA has never had a real chance to do this effectively, as the number of passengers travelling by rail has continued to decline ever since its creation. This means that passenger service all through the country has now been pruned to the point at which some communities no longer have access to any passenger train service at all and others have much less than they used to.

For the traveller, these cutbacks to VIA Rail mean that many small communities are no longer accessible by train. Services between the major cities remain intact, however, and the service between the two largest cities in Canada, Montreal and Toronto, although reduced from what it was, still remains quite frequent and efficient. Rail travel is still possible in all of the maritime provinces, except for Prince Edward Island, which has no rail lines, and Newfoundland, where the famous 'Newfie Bullet', a narrow gauge train that crossed the length of the island, has also been eliminated by the government. Halifax and Fredericton remain served by VIA rail, but the service is neither as frequent nor as fast as it used to be.

However, in spite of all the cutbacks, if time and convenience are not absolute priorities, a trip by rail through part of Canada is still a very scenic and comfortable way to travel. Canadian trains are not the cheapest available form of transport between two places, but they are spacious, well-maintained and have good service facilities both at stations and on board. In fact, crossing any part of the country by train is still one of the best ways to appreciate the diversity of this vast country. There are still a few train trips which allow the traveller to get into some of the country's most scenically beautiful areas.

Buying Tickets

Tickets for train travel anywhere in Canada (with some minor exceptions on private lines) can be bought through the computerised system available at any VIA Rail station, and also through most travel agents. Tickets can be bought in advance, and for many trains they must be. For travel of any distance or on very popular train services, it is advisable to make a reservation. Via Rail's fare structure means that travel is more expensive on the two peak travel days of the week, Fridays and Sundays, with substantial travel discounts being offered for those who travel on the less popular days. As in any other country, trains also tend to be more crowded at holiday times, so that travel around Christmas and in the summer months on scenic routes may need to be planned and booked well in advance. Many of VIA Rail's services also connect with those of Amtrak (American travel by track) in the United States with the result that it is possible to start out from the major Canadian cities and travel well into the United States without having to change trains.

Trains in the City

Paradoxically, while the main line train service has now been reduced to the point at which it is no longer really attractive to the business traveller, commuter rail services in and out of the major cities have been improved over the last few years and service to the city centres is now quite frequent and efficient from suburban areas. The GO (Government of Ontario) transit service that looks after the needs of commuters into and out of Toronto is run by the provincial government and has an extensive network of lines that reach all the major suburban communities from which people commute into Toronto. Montreal and Vancouver also have similar commuter networks from their outlying bedroom communities.

Inside the major cities themselves there are also extensive subway (underground) networks, and in the case of Toronto, streetcar lines. These urban rail lines are cheap and efficient and operate long hours, making it fairly easy, in conjunction with an extensive network of buses, for people to move from one side of the city to another. One interesting feature of Canadian urban transport systems is that the distance travelled does not relate to the price of the ticket. There is a flat fare regardless of the distance travelled, and if more than one means of transport is used, a transfer ticket can be obtained at no extra cost.

Flying Visits

Travelling by air in Canada has replaced the railway for long distance and business travellers. For those travelling out of the country, Canada has nine international airports. It also has a national air carrier, Air Canada, that provides international as well as scheduled services between all the major cities both in Canada and the United States, and a regular shuttle service between Toronto, Ottawa and Montreal. To promote business travel on these routes, both of these airlines offer special incentives in the form of rebates and/or free travel privileges to those passengers who use them more than a set number of times during the course of a year.

Outside the major cities, many smaller communities have

Flying with the smaller airlines, and on the smaller planes that they use, can be an interesting experience for those not used to it. Travellers can rest assured that the government imposes stringent inspection standards to ensure that the safety regulations controlling these planes and their pilots are complied with.

a municipal airport, served by provincial or local airlines. Some of these are affiliated with the major carriers and others are independent. Where no railway exists, it is usually possible to find some sort of air service linking virtually any community of any size in Canada with a major hub, especially in the southern areas of the country. In the northern areas, some form of bush plane service usually serves isolated communities on a regular basis, bringing in supplies and mail as well as passengers. Like travelling on the smaller rail lines, flying between the smaller communities, especially in the North, can also be a superb introduction to the splendours of the country and to places not readily accessible by any other means. Even if you need to get somewhere in the country which is not served by any regular scheduled service, charter aircraft service is usually available at most small airports, but for quite a hefty price!

The Ubiquitous Bus

Intercity and 'in-city' bus services have been a large part of the Canadian transport scene ever since Canada developed an extensive and efficient road network. This often helped to contribute to the decline of rail travel. Usually cheaper than travel by air or by rail, buses run regularly between most of the major centres in Canada and across the country. Companies such as Coach Canada in Ontario and Quebec operate the intercity services, while the long-distance buses of Canadian Greyhound and its subsidiaries provide an interprovincial service. Most bus companies operate specially-equipped vehicles for very long distances and they run 24 hours a day. Therefore, a trip that involves more than a 12-hour journey will usually continue through the night. The driver of the bus will change periodically, but the passengers will go stoically on to their destination without any delay.

Fortunately, Canadian buses are well adapted to the road conditions and are comfortable and fast. All of them have reclining seats and many now have washroom and refreshment services available. The drivers are meticulously trained, and a bus trip can be quite a relaxing way to travel for those who want to travel between two points in an

9 Broadway to Boundary

2861

9507 FS

A Vancouver city Translink bus.

economical and reasonably speedy fashion. Tickets can usually be purchased in advance at local bus stations for most long trips, and, in fact, this is often a wise thing to do, as buses are occasionally fully booked. This is especially true on Fridays and Sundays and around holiday times.

Bus companies in Canada are either privately or provincially owned and are required to meet stringent safety standards so that their passengers are assured of comfort and efficiency. Many bus companies also provide charter service facilities and/or operate a regular school bus service in their local operating areas, for which they use special buses, in co-operation with the local school board.

The Two-car Family

One of the reasons why public, long distance, ground transport services in Canada have been steadily eroded and are not as comprehensive as in many other countries is that most Canadians, like their American cousins, have a long-standing love affair with their cars. Ever since the automobile became easily available and within the budget of the ordinary person, a private car (or even on some occasions two cars) has been considered a necessity by most Canadians. Cheap petrol has contributed to this overwhelming use of cars since the end of World War II, and it is only quite recently that Canadians have begun to reconsider jumping in their cars at any time—even for a trip down to the shop on the corner—as the price of petrol has begun to creep relentlessly upwards. However, having access to a car remains an important part of the Canadian lifestyle, especially in the country, where there is little or no public transport available.

As with petrol, cars are no longer as cheap as they once were. A new car can cost anywhere from C$ 15,000 and up and up. The competition to sell new cars is fierce and buyers are well advised to shop around carefully for price, options and length of warranty before they settle on which model to buy and what price to pay for it. But even if a new car is not within budget, there are plenty of used cars on sale in every community. Prices for these used cars are lower than for new cars, although there are some problems that can obviously come with the purchase of a used car. However, the sale of used cars is government controlled so that practices, such as turning back the odometer are illegal, and most dealers are honest. But care should still be taken when buying a car that appears to be too much of a bargain. As the old saying goes, 'you get what you pay for'.

Car Rental

Leasing and renting cars are also options for those unwilling or unable to put a large sum of money into the purchase of a car. Leasing plans enable the user to rent a car on a long term agreement from the dealer. Leasing a car can often be tax deductible if done through a business, and so is growing in popularity at the moment. Renting a car is generally too expensive for anyone who is interested in getting a car for long term use, but attractive on a casual basis. This is especially so for many people who live in cities with good public transport systems and who only need a car occasionally to make trips that take them out of the city.

> As selling petrol is a very competitive business in Canada, the various oil companies usually make their own credit cards easily available to anyone who wishes to buy petrol in this way. They often use incentives, such as issuing coupons for cheap accessories or free car washes, to get people into their stations.

Car Maintenance

Maintaining and servicing a car can be done in any number of ways. Either through the dealer from whom the car was purchased; at one of the many specialist repair shops which can be found in most towns and cities; or even by the owner himself using parts purchased at one of the many retail shops, such as Canadian Tire, which specialise in the automobile business. Canadian winters require some special preparation for the car in the autumn. This can include checking the anti-freeze in the radiator and making sure that the tyres are suitable for winter road conditions, for example. Those who are uncertain about what has to be done, or how to do it, will be able to find plenty of garages and automobile care centres where this can be carried out for a very reasonable charge. Petrol can be bought in a similar way as petrol stations will often have two kinds of service at the pumps—full serve (where the attendant will do everything for you, including checking your oil and cleaning your windshield) and self-serve where you do everything yourself and then just pay a cashier for what you have bought. The vast majority of cars (and all new ones by law) now use unleaded petrol, which is universally available and comes in three kinds—regular (the cheapest), superior and premium. The names of the specific kinds of petrol may vary depending on the oil company, but the basic types remain the same.

Driving Regulations

Regulations for driving in Canada are determined by each province with the result that some of them do vary from region to region. Specific provincial laws cover areas like the legal driving age, driving tests, vehicle fitness and rules of the road, such as turning, stopping and parking. In fact, the only really accurate way to determine what specifically applies in any given area is to visit an office of that province's Department of Highways and obtain a copy of the provincial Highway Code. However, there is enough similarity between what is allowed in one province and another to make driving throughout the country quite possible for anyone, providing that common sense always prevails. Throughout Canada, all drivers must be licensed by a provincial authority (licences from outside the country are valid only for a specific period of time after arrival and then a Canadian test must be taken). The driver must also be covered by some form of insurance, which includes protection from at least personal liability and property damage. The cost of car insurance varies from area to area throughout the country and also depends to some extent on your personal driving record.

Roads

Canada boasts a marvellous network of roads, many of which are four-lane or wider. Major main roads or highways are scrupulously maintained by the provincial highway departments, whose responsibility also extends to snow clearance in the winter months. Regional and local governments look after the smaller roads, many of which are still gravel surfaced, and can thus be more difficult to navigate, especially in winter. In fact, most Canadian drivers who do a lot of driving on smaller and more isolated roads usually carry basic emergency supplies in the car, in case of a breakdown some distance from a source of immediate help. However, on the whole, travelling by car from place to place, whether short or long distances, can be easily accomplished at any time of year. In fact, it is not uncommon for people to drive 50 kilometres or more just to go out for dinner or for a medical appointment.

There are several ways of crossing Canada by road, and although to do so takes several days, there are many people who prefer to cross the country this way. Along the major roads, networks of service stations and motel chains have been developed so that long distance travellers can find somewhere to buy petrol or stay the night more or less whenever they wish. During the summer months, many Canadians travel long distances on holiday, and recreational vehicles or RVs (motorised camping vehicles) are a common sight on main roads all over the country.

Transport Alternatives

In addition to the traditional methods of transport, Canada has also developed some which are unique to its particular needs.

With the long coastline and the millions of lakes and rivers, ferry service is a common method of transport. This ranges from the major ferries which link Canada's offshore islands, such as Vancouver Island, Prince Edward Island and Newfoundland to the mainland, to small car and passenger ferries across rivers and bays. These are considered to be an integral part of the road system.

During the summer months, other boats of all shapes and sizes can also be seen on practically every lake and waterway throughout the country. These boats range from large excursion craft to private craft. The large excursion craft run public tours for visitors through scenic areas inaccessible

The boat is still very much in use as a means of transport. Canadians love to spend time on boats and on the water.

in other ways. Private craft are used either as transport to 'summer homes' often located on islands, or simply as pleasurable forms of recreation.

The land equivalent of the boat is probably the All-Terrain Vehicle (ATV), a kind of four-wheeled dune buggy, whose popularity has grown in recent years. It can often be seen travelling through parts of the country where there are no roads or where it is more fun not to use the road even if it does exist!

Canada's winter months make the use of boats impractical and different forms of transport emerge to take their place, although ATVs are often used all year round. The snowmobile— a form of motorcycle adapted for use on snow—has become almost as common a form of winter transport as the boat is in summer, while in the northern regions of the country, the sled and dog team can still be found. However, its use has become much less common during recent years as the snowmobile has grown in popularity.

'Food is our common ground, a universal experience'
—James Beard, chef

IS THERE ANY SUCH THING as Canadian cuisine? Canadian food is hard to define. It varies tremendously across Canada, especially since each ethnic group has brought to its new country the tastes of its people. Canadian food is therefore French in Quebec and British in most parts of Canada. In the cities, you will find Jewish, Chinese, Italian, Indian and other cuisines. Chinese food is especially easy to find. Even in small towns, cafés and restaurants offer 'Canadian and Chinese smorgasbord' which is a western-Chinese assortment of food that is sold buffet style. *Chow mein* (fried noodles), sweet and sour pork and *wonton* (meat dumplings) soup are standard offerings.

CANADIAN SMORGASBORD

Some may argue that there is no typically Canadian cuisine in the same way as there is Chinese, Indian, French or Italian cuisine, but over the years, immigrants have brought many ethnic foods with them that have now become associated with those areas of Canada where they settled.

'The basic Canadian meal is meat and potatoes plus other vegetables. Eggs, cheese and fish are common meat substitutes, while spaghetti, noodles and rice or beans are a few common substitutes for potatoes. Vegetables and fruit are included in most meals. Generally speaking, Canadians do not spice their food heavily.'
—from the admissions handbook 1990/91 of the University of Victoria, British Columbia, giving students an idea of what to expect in Canadian food.

Going Native

There are some foods that are native to Canada, for example, Saskatoon berries, maple syrup (which is also produced in the north-eastern American states), fiddleheads and Arctic char.

It must also be mentioned that, as with many other things, there are some standard foods such as corn on the cob, clam chowder, baked beans, sourdough bread and pancakes that are as much Canadian as American, whether this fact is well known or not.

Certainly, there are many regional delicacies to explore. Here is a sampling of some of them:

- In Newfoundland, hunting seals for their fur and oil has resulted in a culinary by-product called flipper pie. This is made from the flippers of young harp seals. Many organisations hold flipper pie suppers during April and May. Fish, especially cod, is available all year round, and served fresh, dried or salted. It is so plentiful that finding sufficient cod tongues for a recipe is no problem in this province. Cod tongues apparently have a delicate flavour and a texture much like that of scallops or clams. Fried in batter, cod tongues can be served as an appetiser or for breakfast or brunch.

- Nova Scotia has a varied cuisine which was brought by Scottish, English, French and German settlers. Try Solomon Grundy, a traditional Mennonite recipe of salted herring pickled with vinegar, sugar and spices. Alternatively, try Acadian blueberry grunt in which spoonfuls of a soft dough mixture are cooked in a hot blueberry sauce.

- New Brunswick is known for its clam chowder. This is a rich, thick broth that has New Brunswickers ecstatic when it is made with large clams from the Shediac area. When in the province, also look for a distinctive vegetable called fiddlehead. This is the young curled shoot of the ostrich fern. While it grows all along the east coast of North America, from as far south as Virginia to New Brunswick and a little way inland, not many places have embraced it as a culinary delight.

However, in New Brunswick, it is gathered from the woods in the spring almost as soon as it pokes its head above the soil. It is not very well known in western Canada, where supermarkets have to introduce it to their customers. Recipe books recommend that fiddleheads should be lightly boiled and served either buttered and seasoned or with Hollandaise sauce.

Another 'vegetable' that is associated with New Brunswick is an edible seaweed called dulse. It is harvested in the summer time from Grand Manan Island, where it grows on the rocks.

- Prince Edward Island is well known for its potatoes, the main product of its farmlands. It is also famous for seafood. Oysters from Malpeque Bay are used to make oyster bisque, a kind of rich soup. Fresh lobsters, which are plentiful, can be steamed, boiled, added to salads or used to make delicious Lobster Thermidor.

- In Quebec, look for *tourtière*, pea soup, maple syrup and Oka cheese. *Tourtière* is a French-Canadian meat pie. It is traditionally made with pork and served on Christmas Eve after midnight Mass. There are many cheeses made in monasteries in Quebec. Oka is one that is well known. It is a soft and highly flavoured cheese made by the Trappist monks.

Special mention must be made of maple syrup, which is harvested or 'sugared off' in the early spring. Most of Canada's maple syrup is produced in the east—in both Quebec and Ontario. Spring is the only time it can be harvested because that is when the days are warm and the nights still cold. This weather signals the sap to move up from the roots to the tree. Mature maple trees are tapped by driving a spigot into the side of the tree. A bucket or plastic tube attached to the spigot collects the sap. The sap is sweet but thin. To make a gallon of syrup, you would have to collect about 40 times the amount of sap, place it in special containers and boil it down until the syrup is of the right consistency.

'Sugaring off' is a great social event. Everybody in the village and on the farms gathers for this. It is a time the

During the early spring, maple syrup is collected in buckets such as these.

kids love, when they can enjoy 'sugar on snow' (chewy bits of maple syrup toffee which is made by just splashing some of the hot, thick syrup onto the clean snow still on the ground. The snow cools the syrup into toffee which you can then pick up and sink your teeth into).

- Ontario cuisine has a rich heritage to draw from. Mennonite settlers brought *schmier kase* (a buttermilk curd) and smoked sausage, while British Loyalist settlers preserved such English recipes as creamed kippers and minced lamb pie. In fact, in recent years, the presence of ethnic communities from all over the world has added extreme variety to both the cooking ingredients and prepared food available in Ontario, especially in Toronto.

- When in Manitoba, try the Winnipeg Goldeye, a small herring-like fish that is smoked over oak logs and then dyed a deep coral red. Ukrainian settlers have contributed *pirozhki* (a meat pie appetiser).

- Saskatchewan has many native wild berries, of which the Saskatoon berry is perhaps the most well known. It is also famous for many migratory birds that could end up on the dinner table, such as the partridge and prairie chicken. The Saskatoon looks like a blueberry, and is often made into Saskatoon berry pie. Having a corn roast is also a popular pastime. With the husks pulled back and the silks removed, freshly picked corn is soaked in water, cob and all, for about half an hour to ensure that the husks are wet through.

  Note that fresh corn should be eaten almost immediately after being picked as the natural sugar in the corn turns to starch as time goes on. The soaked corn is then drained and brushed with melted butter. The husks are put back on the corn, and the whole thing is covered with aluminium foil and placed over the glowing coals of a bonfire. After 20–30 minutes, the corn is ready to eat.

- Albertans are proud of their cattle which they believe produce the best beef steaks. An unusual beef dish is Chuck Wagon Stew, which acts as a reminder of days when the covered wagon used to bring dinner to cowboys on the range.

A beef barbecue Canadian style.

- British Columbia is noted for its salmon, of which there are five varieties—chum, coho, pink, sockeye and spring. From tiny Saltspring Island off the coast of Vancouver comes tender Saltspring lamb, which is best roasted and eaten with fresh mint sauce.
- Game food must certainly be mentioned when thinking of the Yukon and North-west Territories, for it still forms a large part of the local diet. When in the North, you might have an opportunity to try moose roast but the meat must be marinated for as long as one to two days to counteract its gamey flavour. Buffalo stew is another to try. Pemmican, a mixture of pounded buffalo meat and berries, no longer finds its way onto the dinner table but it used to be a staple of the early explorers.

Eat My Boots!
Any discussion of food in the North is never complete without mention of sealskin boots, which Inuit women actually chew upon to soften them before use. In 1909, the Bishop of Yukon, Isaac O Stringer, and his companion became lost but survived the ordeal by eating their sealskin boots, toasted and boiled!

A TYPICAL CANADIAN MENU

After briefly acquainting yourself with the tremendous variety that makes up Canadian cuisine, you might like to try an all-Canadian dinner menu as described by Pierre and Janet Berton in *The Centennial Food Guide, A Century of Good Eating*:

- Oysters Canadian
- Pea soup
- Brome Lake duckling with wild rice dressing
- Fiddleheads
- Young PEI (Prince Edward Island) potatoes
- Mashed pumpkin
- Blueberry whip with lemon
- Oka cheese
- Coffee

Oysters Canadian

Finely chop lamb's quarters (pigweed), fresh young dandelion greens, romaine lettuce, fresh celery leaves and curly endive. Make sure you have enough of each to fill ¼ of a cup. Also finely chop 4 sprigs of fresh parsley and 2 large fresh green onions, tops included.

Add the following: 2 strips of lean bacon which has been fried until crisp, then cooled and well crumbled; 1 tsp of anchovy paste; 1 tsp of tarragon; 1 tsp of dry English mustard; ½ tsp chervil; 4 well crushed fennel seeds; 1 tbsp of well chopped, fresh chives; 1 tbsp onion juice; 1 tsp lemon juice; ½ cup bread crumbs; ¼ cup grated cheese; a dash of Worcestershire sauce, Tabasco sauce and Angostura bitters; salt and ground fresh pepper to taste. Pound the whole mixture in a mortar until it reaches the consistency of a paste. Add ¼ of a cup of creamed butter and blend slowly in a blender. Open on the half shell one dozen Malpeque oysters and cover each with the mixture. Top with grated cheese. Broil in a pan of wet heated rock salt for 10 minutes.

French Canadian Pea Soup

Soak 1 cup of yellow or green split peas in cold water overnight. Drain. Put in a pot with: a ham bone to which some meat is still clinging; 2 chopped onions; 2 chopped carrots; 4 stalks of chopped celery; 5 peppercorns; 1 bay leaf; a little salt; Worcestershire sauce and monosodium glutamate. Simmer for several hours or overnight until the peas and vegetables have the consistency of smooth purée. Serve with crisp, crumbled bacon.

Brome Lake Duckling with Wild Rice Dressing

Place 1 cup of wild rice and 1½ tsp salt in 5 cups of chicken stock and slowly bring to the boil, stirring to prevent sticking. Cook without stirring for about 45 minutes until tender.

Drain and add: 1 tsp of celery salt; 1 tsp of thyme; 1 tsp of sage; ½ an onion, chopped; 1 celery stalk, chopped; 1 cup of sliced sautéed mushrooms; salt, pepper and butter to taste. Lightly fill each duck with rice, add ½ an orange per duck. Baste while roasting with red wine and orange juice.

Fiddleheads and Young PEI (Prince Edward Island) Potatoes

The Bertons do not give any recipe for fiddleheads and young PEI potatoes, but the fiddleheads may simply be boiled very quickly over a high heat and seasoned to taste. The potatoes can be roasted.

Mashed Pumpkin

Cook the pulp of one pumpkin until tender. Mash together with: ½ tsp of dill; 1 tsp of cracked pepper; ½ an onion, chopped; ½ a cup of sour cream.

Blueberry whip

Soak 1 tbsp of gelatine in ¼ of a cup of cold water. Then dissolve the mixture in ¼ of a cup of boiling water. Mix the grated rind of 1 lemon with ¾ of a cup of sugar. Dissolve the sugar in boiling water and gelatine.

Add: 3 tbsp of lemon juice; 1 cup of lightly crushed blueberries; 1 tbsp of Cointreau. Chill the mixture until it is partially set and then beat until frothy. Whip 4 egg whites with

⅓ of a tsp of salt. Then whip the mixture into the gelatine and blueberry mixture until it holds its shape. Set in a wet mould and serve with Cointreau-flavoured whipped cream.

SHOPPING FOR FOOD

In Canada, most people do their food shopping in supermarkets, which have the standard offerings found in supermarkets worldwide. Meat and vegetable counters are well stocked, but the same cannot be said for fresh seafood. Unless you live along the coast, the selection of fresh fish and other seafood is often poor. Cod, trout, mackerel, halibut, salmon and snapper can usually be found. Prawns and shrimp are often sold in cooked or frozen form. Live crabs are hard to find and therefore expensive. Instead, there is crab meat of the artificial kind. Fresh mussels, clams and oysters are also scarce, and when there is squid, it is often bought by fishermen for bait.

Sometimes there are speciality sections that cater to the needs of a large minority population. So even in a small shop, there might be Chinese, Japanese or Indian spices and condiments if there is a sizeable Chinese, Japanese or Indian population. Moreover, with the current trend in health food, soyabean products are a familiar sight on the shelves. Western taste buds are more educated now when it comes to Asian, especially Chinese, cuisine. Soya sauce can be found next to tomato ketchup, bean sprouts and *bok choy* (Chinese cabbage) next to alfalfa sprouts and broccoli, and *tofu* (soyabean) products range from curd and milk to burgers and cheese.

Pick of the Crop

As in many other countries that have large agricultural areas, journeying through farm country in the summer or autumn often provides the traveller with an opportunity to stop by fruit and vegetable stands along the secondary roads. It is both a delight and a relief after a long and tiring car journey to pause and buy freshly picked fruit and vegetables of the season, such as corn, melons, apples, cherries and strawberries. A variation of this is the numerous farms where you can pick your own fruit. These farms often advertise along the road with 'pick-your-own' signs. The whole family is encouraged to get out there and enjoy picking the fruit. There is great satisfaction in knowing that you have truly 'farm fresh' produce. You can also eat a few berries as you pop your harvest into your containers, but it is good etiquette not to eat more than you collect.

CANADIAN CHEER

Canada produces its own wine and beer. The brewing industry in Canada has long been dominated by the large national beer manufacturers, whose products have become, in some ways, an indispensable part of Canadian culture. Beers such as Molson's Canadian and Labatt's Blue are available coast to coast and enjoyed by millions of Canadians, who love their beer served cold. There are also a number of small local breweries, called 'micro breweries', whose products, although not so widely available as those of their giant competitors, are increasingly catching on with connoisseurs of fine beers. Many of the small breweries base their brewing procedures on European models, manufacturing their beers without additives and following traditional guidelines to preserve the character of their products. Some of these guidelines are as old as the German Bavarian Purity Act of 1516.

Such local beers are usually available through the beer retailing outlets in each province, and are also increasingly being sold in special local 'brew-pubs' whose clientele dedicate themselves to sampling beer which is different from those conventionally served.

Canadian wine is generally the cheapest type one can buy here. C$ 10 will get you a 750 ml bottle of decent-tasting red or white wine. The main wine-making regions are British Columbia's Okanagan Valley and Ontario's Niagara region.

Canadian whisky is made with rye, and so is known as rye whisky. Two leading Canadian brands are Seagram's VO and Hiram Walker's Canadian Club Whiskey.

Alcohol licensing laws vary from province to province, but alcoholic drinks are generally available only from government alcohol shops and licensed wine and beer shops, and not from the local corner shop or supermarket, except in Quebec. The legal drinking age varies according to province too, but is either 18 or 19 years old.

DINING OUT

In Canada, dining out can be an experience ranging from the mundane to the exotic. Small café-restaurants offer inexpensive lunch and dinner buffets or smorgasbord meals as well as à la carte selections. A decent meal can be had for about C$ 6 to C$ 12. Franchise establishments which range, for example, from the all-familiar A&W and McDonald's hamburger restaurants to regional chains, Whitespot and ABC restaurants in the west, offer a comparably-priced menu. Naturally, given Canada's immigrant history, there are many small speciality places that cater to ethnic tastebuds and the adventurous epicurean. Expensive restaurants are also found where one undoubtedly pays not only for the food, but also the quality of ambience and service.

Unlike in some countries, such as Australia, the practice of bringing your own wine or alcoholic drinks to the restaurant (BYO or 'bring your own') is not a common or accepted

There is no automatic service charge, so tipping is necessary. This can be hard to remember if you are used to having a service charge included in the bill. In Canada, a charge for service is added to your bill only if you consent to it. If you are unsure of what to do, most tourist guide books recommend that you leave anything from 10 to 20 per cent of the total bill as a tip.

one in Canada. However, some restaurants are now beginning to allow patrons to bring their own wine, providing a 'corkage fee' is paid to them for each bottle opened.

As for portions one can expect to get, this is really a subjective matter. However, if one had to generalise it would not be wrong to say that Canadians are big eaters and you can therefore expect portions to be very generous.

POT LUCK

Pot luck is an easy and popular way for organisations to hold social gatherings without the headaches that accompany feeding the hungry. Each family that attends brings something to contribute to the common table. If you are invited to a pot luck supper, it is a good rule of thumb to bring enough to feed your own family. You should be responsible for what you bring, including reheating the food, refrigerating and serving it and taking home your pots and utensils when you leave. If it is an unusual cuisine that you are offering, make sure you let your hostess know so that guests can be warned if a dish is particularly hot and spicy, or if it contains unfamiliar ingredients. A pot luck function, therefore, can be a great adventure and it usually works out such that there is a great abundance and variety of food to enjoy.

THE PERFECT GUEST

It is difficult to decide what you should bring when going to a friend's for a meal. It seems to be just as much a Canadian custom as it is an Asian one not to arrive empty-handed, but what should one bring? It is best to play this by ear. If you know your host fairly well, you might offer to bring something for the table, a dessert perhaps. Canadians are often clever at preserving and pickling, and a jar of home-made jam often makes a perfect gift. A bottle of wine, if your host drinks, or a box of chocolates are safe bets. If you have a well-established garden, some blooms that are in season will also do.

Visiting Etiquette

When you arrive at your host's house, do you take off your shoes or keep them on? There is no established custom regarding this. Rather, it depends upon personal preference. Some Canadians do and some don't. A friend said he found the habit more prevalent in the west of Canada than in the east, while another said city folk did not, but country folk did, on account of the fact that their shoes might be dirty from working on the farm! Also bear in mind that most homes have wall-to-wall carpeting. Your host or hostess might not wish to have the carpets muddied. So again, one should play this by ear. A quick glance around the entrance will tell you what is expected.

If a Canadian friend invites you to spend a weekend at home with his family, you will want to make a good impression. A good guest is one who does his best not to disrupt the normal functioning of the household, so you should find out when meal times are, at what time the family gets up in the morning and at what time they go to bed. An offer of help from you when you see your host and hostess working in the kitchen or garden, for example, may be declined but will always be appreciated. After you have returned home, remember to send a thank-you card or letter for the hospitality that you have received.

CANADA AT PLAY

CHAPTER 7

'You just jot down ideas as they occur to you. The jotting
is simplicity itself—it is the occurring which is difficult!'
—Stephen Leacock, Canadian humorist

CELEBRATIONS

Canada's diverse and multicultural people celebrate many different kinds of holidays and festivals during the course of the year. Some of these are official in nature (with some unofficial and locally limited ones too), some primarily religious and others are just traditional with no political or religious overtones at all! The major festivals, holidays and celebrations observed throughout the country are described below:

January
- 1 January—New Year's Day
  On this day, all public buildings and most shops are closed as people celebrate the final holiday of the Christmas season before returning to a normal work routine.

February
While there are three different days to celebrate in this month, none are public holidays!
- 2 February—commonly known as Groundhog Day
  On this day, people keenly watch for the first appearance of the groundhog (a small rodent-like animal) which is supposed to indicate how much longer the winter season is going to continue. Tradition has it that if the groundhog sees his own shadow wintery weather will continue for six more weeks, but if he does not, the cold

weather of winter is close to an end and there will be an early spring!

- 14 February—Valentine's Day
  The traditional time to send an expression of love to your sweetheart. Many people also use this day as an excuse for a good party!

- Third Monday in February—Heritage Day
  It has developed into a semi-public holiday to celebrate Canada's history and traditions. For many years, various people have been trying to get the federal government in Ottawa to make this an official holiday. Though this has not been done, certain institutions will close on this day (many universities, for instance), but the people of Canada as a whole still have to go to work!

March

- 17 March—Saint Patrick's Day
  It is an unofficial holiday and is celebrated mainly by the Irish community, but many Canadians use it as an reason to hold a parade and have a big party, and as an excuse to drink green beer!

- March Break—second week of March
  In certain regions of the country, the second week of the month is called 'March Break'. It is a time when public schools will traditionally close down for a week and all the students get a week off.

April

- Easter (As Easter is a 'moveable' holiday, it sometimes occurs in late March)
  Easter is an extra-long weekend which begins with Good Friday (the Friday before Easter) and finishes with Easter Monday (the Monday following Easter). Although a traditionally Christian celebration, like Christmas, it has been commercialised and shops sell hot cross buns, Easter bunnies and chocolate Easter eggs when this time of the year comes around.

- 22 April—Earth Day
  Although not a public holiday, this is a day on which

everyone is encouraged to help to clean up their local area in some way and to study the effects of pollution on the environment as a whole.

May

- Second Sunday of May—Mother's Day
  All Canadians try and do something special to show their regard for their mothers on this day, e.g. send her a card, take her out for a meal etc.
- Nearest Monday before 24 May
  It is the first of the summer public holidays and, in fact, this day is regarded by many as the start of the summer season. The whole country takes the day off and goes outside to play, and to celebrate the return of warm weather after the long, cold, winter season.
- Victoria Day, celebrating Queen Victoria's birthday, falls on the Monday before 25 May.

June

- Third Sunday of June—Father's Day
  It is not a public holiday, but is a chance for families to do for their father what was done for their mother the month before!

July

- 1 July—Canada Day
  The biggest public holiday for all Canadians. On this day, celebrations, parades and parties are held throughout the country to celebrate Canada's independence from Great Britain in 1867. It was formerly called Dominion Day. The main ceremony takes place on Parliament Hill in Ottawa, the nation's capital, but many other celebrations take place in communities large and small all around the country. Firework displays are traditionally held on this day.

August

- First Monday of August
  Most communities in Canada have a public holiday in August—usually the first weekend of the month—called the August civic holiday. As this has no special national significance, it is commonly left up to the various municipalities to declare that it will take place. It does, however, mark the mid-point of the summer season, and provides yet another opportunity for families to get away to the countryside for a long weekend.

September

- First Monday of September—Labour Day
  Labour Day is the first Monday in September. For school children, it is the last fling before a new school year begins. It marks the end of summer and the beginning of school.

October

- Second Monday in October—Thanksgiving Day
  Thanksgiving is celebrated both in America and Canada, but on different dates. In America, Thanksgiving falls on the fourth Thursday of November but in Canada, it is celebrated on the second Monday in October. It is a day of thanksgiving for a bountiful harvest.
- 31 October—Halloween
  Halloween on 31 October is not a public holiday, but is a big event for children. They look forward to dressing up

"Trick or treat!" Halloween is a festival much loved by children who dress up in scary fancy dress. Notice the jack o' lantern in the bottom right-hand corner.

in costumes and going from house to house getting treats. Shops sell all kinds of Halloween costumes and offer free pumpkins. The pumpkins are hollowed out to make glowing jack o' lanterns at night. Younger children often go out accompanied by their parents or older siblings. Adults stock up on sweets to give out when the children come calling. Older children and teenagers often disdain 'trick or treating'. For them, Halloween is a time to throw firecrackers at passing cars perhaps, and eggs at anything. In the morning, buildings, pavements and parked cars can look a mess.

Tips for the Perfect Ghoul!

If you want to get into the Halloween spirit, here are some make-up tips from a Hollywood special effects master: use corn syrup and red food colouring to make fake blood and apply it liberally on your face. Chalk or some dark eye make-up around the eyes will give you a ghoulish look. Colour your tongue and teeth with a lot of yellow and green food colouring.

Unfortunately for the children, some people apparently think it is 'fun' to give 'treats' of apples and sweets with needles or poison in them. So parents are warned to check the sweets and treats brought home before allowing children to eat them.

November

A rather dismal month in Canada; the weather can often be quite unpleasant and there is no real public holiday to break up the time.

- 11 November—Remembrance Day
  Remembrance Day is a time to parade the old uniforms and medals and remember the dead of the two world wars. It is held on 11 November because the armistice which officially ended World War I happened at the 11th hour of the 11th day of the 11th month—11:00 am on 11 November, 1918. Members of the Royal Canadian Legion, together with other uniformed groups, gather at the court house, city hall or other town centre where the cenotaph is and pay their respects to the fallen. The ceremony often includes a religious service, the playing of the Last Post and Reveille, a traditional two-minute silence and the laying of wreaths. Remembrance Day, however, is no longer an official public holiday.

December

- 25 December—Christmas Day
- 26 December—Boxing Day
  You can tell Christmas and New Year are coming when the postman brings you a Christmas mail-order catalogue so you can get all your gifts. This, plus the advertisements and shops, all try to persuade you that Christmas begins in early November, almost as soon as Halloween ends. Then, even before 25 December arrives, you are plagued with Boxing Day sales.

  In fact, Canada celebrates Christmas with a two-week holiday for schools that begins the weekend before Christmas. For offices and businesses in most of the country, both Christmas Day (25 December) and Boxing

Day (26 December) are public holidays, as is New Year's Day (1 January).

Apart from the commercialisation of the season, there is still a good deal of Christmas tradition alive. Thus, parents and teachers may encourage little boys and girls to write to Santa Claus, who lives in the North Pole, making toys for them with his elves. Even Canada Post plays the game and will reply on Santa's behalf to all letters addressed to Santa Claus, North Pole, Canada, HOH OHO.

Families get together at this time, and a highlight is the Christmas dinner, often featuring a roast turkey, ham and a Christmas pudding.

HOLIDAYS ACCORDING TO PROVINCE

In addition to the above, there are holidays that may be celebrated in some provinces but not in others. Newfoundland seems to be the province with the greatest number of other holidays with Commonwealth Day celebrated on the second Monday in March.

Alberta has Alberta Family Day (the third Monday in February) and Heritage Day (the first Monday in August). Ontario, Manitoba, Saskatchewan and the North-west Territories celebrate Civic Holiday (the first Monday in August). In British Columbia, that same day is called BC Day. Quebec celebrates Saint Jean Baptiste Day (the patron saint of Quebec) on 24 June and the Yukon holds Discovery Day on the third Monday in August.

THE LONG WEEKEND

Many Canadian public holidays occur on Fridays or Mondays to give people the opportunity of enjoying a three-day weekend. This is especially important in a country where many live and work away from their families. Canadians are extremely mobile people, changing provinces, or moving from one city to another or from city centres to small towns and vice versa. The Friday preceding a long weekend is often marked by an exodus of people heading for the country (if they come from the city), the city (if they come from the country) and home, wherever that may be.

CULTURAL PURSUITS

As has been mentioned earlier in this book, Canadians are often accused of having no culture themselves, or at least not one that is distinguishable from the American culture. To some extent, this appears to be a valid theory, certainly from a cursory look at the kind of television programmes that are common fare in Canada, or at the kinds of films that are most popular in the cinemas.

In reality, however, although this might have been true 20 years ago, times have changed and in all aspects of the arts there are signs that a distinctly Canadian culture is becoming identifiable, and this is becoming a lot more assertive than it ever was before.

Canada in Print

Traditionally, Canada's two best-known writers internationally have been the humourist Stephen Leacock, whose *Sunshine Sketches of a Little Town* depicts life as it was in many small communities in Canada in the late 19th century, and the children's writer Lucy Maud Montgomery. Born on Prince Edward Island in 1874, Lucy Maud Montgomery led a lonely childhood. To pass the time, she invented a fictional surrogate, Anne, who lived in a house close to hers with the rather attractive name of Green Gables. Anne was everything that Lucy was not—outgoing, meddlesome and perpetually in trouble, but with a heart of gold when it came to dealing with misfortune, whether hers or other people's. When Lucy Maud Montgomery wrote down the adventures of her fictional friend, they were immediately taken to heart by the Canadian public as a whole, who identified with Anne and were thrilled to be able to read the adventures of a real and likeable Canadian girl, rather than the imported tales of the Americans and the British. Her best-known book, *Anne of Green Gables*, has been made into a very successful play which enjoys annual runs at the Charlottetown Festival, and has also been made into a television drama which draws substantial viewer support wherever it is shown.

Other Canadian writers have also acquired international status in recent years, and many of their works have been

A book about Canada displayed in a shop window.
Canadian writing is gaining more popularity and cities
like Toronto are important centres for publishing.

made into films that have had international distribution. Margaret Laurence's books, *The Stone Angel* and *The Diviners*, centre on Canadian experiences with which Laurence was familiar, but also deal with themes and issues much bigger than national boundaries. One of Margaret Atwood's books, *The Handmaid's Tale*, presents a frightening view of a future which should disturb anyone. In addition to these two literary women, well known Canadian writers also include Morley Callaghan, Mordecai Richler and WO Mitchell. All of these writers write from their own experiences in various parts of Canada, and there is much to be learned from these novels about growing up in Canada, whether on a prairie farm during the Depression or in the Jewish quarter of Montreal in the 1950s.

Over the last 20 or 30 years, a surge of popular interest in Canadian writing has encouraged libraries and bookshops to develop specific Canadian sections where books both about Canada and by Canadian writers can easily be found. The increase in the quantity and quality of this writing has also led to the foundation of several large, exclusively Canadian publishing houses. The oldest and most famous of these is probably McLelland and Stewart, a publisher of many of the best-known Canadian writers. However, there are now also legions of small publishers, producing not only fiction but everything from self-help books on a wide range of topics (Self-Counsel Press of Vancouver) to complete Canadian encyclopedias (Hurtig Publishing of Calgary). Many of these publishing houses have spent a lot of effort trying to make sure that Canadian writers get the kind of exposure outside the country that they deserve, and slowly—very slowly—Canadian writing has been emerging as distinct and different from American writing.

Canada on Stage

Canadian theatre has also enjoyed the same kind of recent revitalisation experienced by Canadian writing. In fact, it is one of Canada's best-kept secrets that a large number of actors who became famous on the American stage or in film were, in fact, Canadians to begin with. Mary Pickford, Lorne

Greene, Christopher Plummer and William Shatner are some big-name actors who have been lured south of the border by the fact that, up to very recently, to make one's name in the theatrical world required exposure either in Great Britain or in the United States. Slowly, that is changing, as theatres become more plentiful in Canadian cities and the Canadian public becomes more attuned to what Canadian playwrights have to say through Canadian actors. Currently, most Canadian cities have small theatres presenting the works of Canadian playwrights on a full-time basis, and have developed a loyal and devoted clientele for them.

Strangely enough, however, Canada's best-known theatrical company is dedicated not to the works of a Canadian playwright, but to the works of one of the world's best-known dramatists. The Canadian Shakespeare Festival at Stratford, Ontario, has acquired a reputation for its presentation of Shakespeare that is matched by few other theatrical companies in the world. Many people claim, in fact, that the Canadian Stratford productions are preferable to those staged by the Royal Shakespeare Company in Shakespeare's own birthplace of Stratford-upon-Avon. Started in a tent by the Irish director Tyrone Guthrie in 1953, the Stratford Festival now has its own custom-built theatre and a season which runs from early April until late November. The Stratford Festival Company has also spawned other festivals celebrating other playwrights in many other parts of Canada, ranging from the Shaw Festival (now an integral part of the scene at Ontario's Niagara-on-the-Lake) to the Robert Service Festival in Dawson City in the Yukon.

Buying Tickets

Tickets for major theatrical performances can be bought through the computerised telephone ticket services, such as Ticketron and TicketMaster, which operate in most major centres. Sources of tickets for local events are usually advertised through local newspapers and radio. Dress for the theatre in Canada is usually casual, although for premieres and special events, rather more formal.

In communities without easy access to theatres and concert halls, popular productions are put on by touring theatre companies through arrangements made by local entrepreneurs. Amateur theatrical groups are also a prominent part of most local cultural scenes, presenting works by both Canadian and foreign dramatists, and the standard of their productions is often impressively high.

Canada on Film

The making and distribution of films in Canada, not unlike Canadian theatre, was, until a comparatively short time ago, totally dominated by the Americans—with one notable exception. In cinema, in fact, the American cultural stranglehold has proved to be, in many ways, a harder grip to break than in other branches of the arts.

So most of the Canadians who wanted to make a name for themselves in the film industry were forced to go south of the border to develop their careers, and the Canadian film industry has remained dominated by the big American studios. Recently, however, partly due to financial encouragement by the Canadian and provincial governments, Canada has become a great place for the shooting of films on location, and not only in the more scenic parts of the country, such as the Rocky Mountains. The city of Toronto, for instance, has been transformed on many occasions into incarnations of various American cities or even into the nameless cites of such films as *Batman* and *Superman*. Without them being aware of it, in fact, many people watching highly publicised feature films all over the world have become familiar with the landscape of the city. The same thing has happened in Montreal and Vancouver, with the result that, although there may still not be many well known Canadian names among the actors in Canadian films, there are large numbers of well-trained and qualified technicians in the country with expertise on everything from sound recording to the directing of an entire film.

The one notable exception, however, is Canada's National Film Board which has been known worldwide since the 1930s, and its expertise has never really been duplicated anywhere else. The National Film Board was founded just before World War II by a Scotsman named John Grierson, who was brought to Canada for the express purpose of creating an institution whose films would 'interpret Canada to Canadians'.

Beginning initially as a kind of celluloid propaganda machine for the country in the years leading up to and during the war, the NFB has since made many films about the country, including some of feature length. However, its directors have become particularly expert in the making of short films, especially those using experimental animation techniques. NFB films have won a large number of Oscars and other film awards for their innovative ideas and their technical excellence, and have given rise to generations of young filmmakers who have gone on to found their own studios and specialise in the making of short, high quality films. Some of these studios have come and gone, but there are still a substantial number of young, vital film companies in Canada which make award-winning short films. One of the most well known of these companies is Atlantis Films, founded by three young Toronto filmmakers and which is now gaining a reputation as one of the best and most creative studios in the world.

Going to the cinema is still a popular pastime in Canada, particularly among young people, and most towns of any size have at least one 'movie house', showing current releases. Unfortunately, entrance prices to Canadian cinemas have risen steeply over the past few years and are now about C$ 7 to C$ 8 per admission. However, many cinema chains—which own the majority of Canada's 'movie houses'—offer specially priced admission on specific nights of the week (usually Tuesday or Thursday), and on those nights, it can be quite difficult to get to see popular films!

In most provinces, a classification system determines the age of those who can be admitted to specific films, with degrees of restricted admission possible. The actual way this system is enforced varies from province to province. Basically, it divides films into those that are 'general' or 'family' in nature to which anyone can be admitted, through various other categories. These can include 'parental guidance' or 'adult accompaniment', where the age at which unaccompanied minors can be admitted is specified, to the restricted film to which no one under 18 can buy a ticket. Advertisements for films also often carry warnings about the nature of the content, for example, 'violence' or 'graphic language'.

Canadian Home News and Entertainment

Like the film industry, all types of Canadian media have been extremely influenced by the styles of the Americans. Much of the programming on Canadian television is still American in origin, and a large number of Canadians who live close to the American border have 24-hour access to American television stations.

To counter this American influence, the Canadian government set up the Canadian Radio and Television Communications Commission which is now the controlling body for the entire communications industry in the country. The CRTC has laid down very stringent regulations for the content of Canadian radio and television, stipulating that a substantial percentage of the programming has to be of Canadian origin, including music of any kind that is played. Each radio or television station licensed by the Commission is required to file a 'promise of performance' with the Commission, outlining the ways in which that station is going to meet the requirements of Canadian content through its proposed kind of programming. The result of these stringently-enforced requirements is that there is now a significantly higher proportion of Canadian content on air than there used to be and much of it is of very good quality.

Canada's national radio and television service is provided by the Canadian Broadcasting Commission which was originally established as a Crown Corporation in 1936. This happened after a couple of earlier attempts to establish a private national broadcasting network along the American model failed. The CBC network then comprised only eight broadcasting stations and 16 affiliates, in contrast to the hundreds it now has. Although originally only concerned with the promotion of a national AM radio broadcasting network, over the intervening years, CBC has added a number of other services. These include FM and FM Stereo, national and regional television services in both official languages, services to listeners in the far North and multi-lingual services overseas. They have also taken responsibility for broadcasting the proceedings of the federal House of Commons to the nation at large.

CBC is 80 per cent government funded, with the remaining 20 per cent coming from commercial sponsorship and the sale of its programmes overseas. This has, unfortunately, led to some recent cutbacks in the variety and availability of its regional services, but CBC remains an important cultural link between the diverse regions of the country. Much of its programming is an insightful and thorough examination of current Canadian events. CBC has produced plays and films dealing with practically all Canadian issues, and has dramatised some of the most well-known Canadian classic books, including a superlative adaptation of the children's classic *Anne of Green Gables*. News specials on major Canadian concerns have also been dealt with exhaustively by CBC with the result that most Canadians are very well served with information about current issues of concern in their country.

Canadian newspapers have managed to remain much more independent of their American counterparts than other segments of the media. Due to its vast size, Canada has not really developed a truly national newspaper, but rather a series of large regional ones. The country's biggest newspaper, *The Globe and Mail*, is Toronto-based but comes the closest to being a national newspaper, while other newspapers, such as the *Vancouver Sun*, the *Toronto Star* and the *Montreal Gazette* deal largely with both international and regional news for subscribers in their own areas. Curiously enough, unlike other forms of media, American

Local News

Local newspapers can also be found in many small towns throughout the country, often coming out weekly and dealing with events of interest to the surrounding community.

publications have never really caught on, and although papers like *USA Today* are readily available on the streets of Canada's large cities, they have never enjoyed the success with Canadians which their electronic counterparts have done.

Conversely, the Canadian magazine market does defer largely to the American one—both *Time* and *Newsweek* enjoy a large circulation in the country and are read by many Canadians. However, Canada does have its own news magazine, named *Macleans*, which enjoys a large and dedicated subscriber list. In other areas of magazine publication, although American magazines are readily available, there has also been a steady growth of Canadian-based magazines dealing with matters of interest from computers to the environment.

Canadian Art

The Canadian art world was, for a long time, dominated by the scenic painter. The works of Paul Kane, who first depicted the Canadian wilderness in the 19th century, still give to modern Canadians a sense of the visual history of the country. Canada's most famous landscape artists, collectively known as the Group of Seven, also dedicated their lives to depicting the Canadian countryside, especially around the area of the Canadian Shield.

The Group of Seven was formed in 1911 by seven Canadian painters, all of whom were thrilled by the potential of the Canadian landscape as artistic material, and wanted to investigate, through their work, the relationship between nature and art. Franklin Carmichael, Lawren Harris, AY Jackson, Franz Johnson, Arthur Lismer, JEH MacDonald, FH Varley and Tom Thompson were the original members of the group. In addition, AJ Casson joined in 1926 and Edwin Holgate of Montreal and LL Fitzgerald of Winnipeg were added at a later date. Their paintings are a celebration of the wilderness of Canada and its colours as the seasons change. Many of these pieces have now become collector's items. Although the Group of Seven was disbanded in 1933, their influence on Canadian painting has remained very strong,

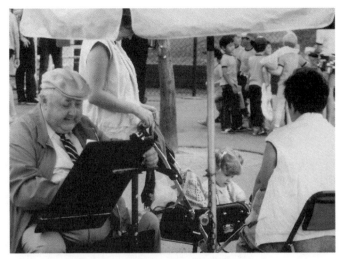

A street artist doing sketches while passers-by pause to look.

and artists in other parts of the country, such as Emily Carr in British Columbia, have followed in their tradition. The result is that the scenic splendour of Canada is well represented in Canadian painting.

The contemporary Canadian art scene is much more varied, and modern Canadian artists work in a number of different media and styles. The influence of the natural beauty of the country is still strong, however, and native art work, particularly that of the Inuit people of the North, has become very popular and influential. The works of the major native artists, such as the west coast's Bill Reid, are in great demand among collectors and have led to a renewed interest in the folk roots of Canadian art. As a result, many modern Canadian artists are now experimenting with traditional folk art styles and incorporating them into contemporary works. This has led to a peculiarly Canadian blend of homegrown tradition and modern international art influences.

To display the works of Canadian artists, both public and private art galleries have proliferated over the last 10 to 15 years. Practically every city in Canada now has some form of art gallery and/or art society which present regular collections of the work of both nationally known and local artists. The federal government's Art Bank, which purchases and distributes Canadian paintings all over the country for exhibition in federal buildings, has done much to bring an awareness of the art scene to every Canadian. During the summer months, much local art is also displayed at outdoor exhibitions, where those interested in art can purchase good contemporary pieces.

CANADIAN MUSIC

Canada has a musical tradition which goes back well before it became a separate country. The influence of musical traditions from both France and England can be seen from the time of its original settlers back in the 1500s right through to the present day. The influence of French musical traditions, dating back to the songs of the Voyageurs and the ballads celebrating popular events, heroes and heroines of early French Canada, is still very clearly reflected in the music of Quebec. This is true in the music festivals of rural Quebec and New Brunswick, where such traditional music is kept alive. It can also be seen in modern folk music, as many of French Canada's contemporary popular singers clearly celebrate their heritage in the songs which they compose and sing.

English Canada has a similar heritage; the sea shanties of the original sea faring folk of the Maritimes, the ballads of the early musicians from Upper Canada as well as the songs of the extremely ethnically diverse settlers of the western prairie can still be heard at Canadian folk festivals all over the country. Many of these songs have also been interpreted, modernised and added to by such well known contemporary folk singers as Stompin Tom Connors, Gordon Lightfoot and Anne Murray.

Some Canadian folk groups have even gained a respectable amount of attention outside the borders of Canada—Ian and Sylvia, Stan Rogers, the Brothers Four from the 1960s and more recently Tanglefoot, Great Big Sea, Buddy Whatisname and the other fellas, and Celtic artistes such as Natalie McMaster and Jimmy Bowskill.

This tradition of folk music also continues to be reflected today in Canadian classical and popular music. However, it has been overlaid over the centuries by other musical influences both from the United States and the many other nations whose people have come to Canada as immigrants over the last two centuries.

Canadian classical composers such as R Murray Schafer, Harry Somers and James Rolph regularly have their works performed by the many symphony orchestras and smaller chamber groups which abound throughout Canada—and many of which have international reputations strong enough to attract conductors of the calibre of Mario Bernardi, Zubin Mehta and Seiji Ozawa. As one would expect, most of these are located in the major Canadian cities, which have venues dedicated to the performance of classical music. These include the Place des Arts in Montreal, Roy Thompson Hall in Toronto and the Orpheum Theatre in Vancouver, but there are also many fine classical ensembles which exist in the smaller communities throughout the country. Several Canadian universities have very fine music departments also, many of which put a strong emphasis on composition, and there are many well international known artistes, such as Ofra Harnoy, Liona Boyd and Glenn Gould, who got started in Canada.

Opera and ballet are also well represented in Canada, with the Canadian Opera Company in Toronto and the Vancouver Opera Company introducing world calibre performers in that field. Examples are Ben Heppner, Jon Vickers and Maureen Forester, while the National Ballet of Canada and the Royal Winnipeg Ballet have also produced major international stars such as Karen Kain.

Canadian jazz and popular music is also very strongly represented not only on the national scene but the world stage too. Canadian jazz has produced such world class performers as Oscar Peterson, Guido Basso and Jeff Healey, while, in the pop field, singers such as Neil Young, Bryan Adams, Celine Dion and Avril Lavigne have established international reputations.

Country music's Shania Twain is also a Canadian—from Timmins, Ontario—as are singers Sarah MacLachlan and Lorena McKennit. There are also several internationally known Canadian rock bands, such as Rush, Blue Rodeo, The

Tragically Hip and The Bare Naked Ladies (all of whom are fully clothed and none of whom are female!)

OUR SPORTING SELVES
The Great Canadian Sport

There can be no doubt that, if there is a national sporting obsession in Canada, it is with the game of hockey. A careful distinction has to be made here, however, for what a Canadian would call hockey does not refer to the game played on a conventional outdoor field (this is somewhat derisively known as field or ground hockey) but rather to the great Canadian-invented game of ice hockey. Most Canadian males grow up playing hockey on frozen ponds and streams during winter and many of these boys become starry-eyed at the thought of becoming a member of one of the NHL (National Hockey League) teams whose members are now among the highest paid sportsmen in the world.

As ice hockey is undoubtedly the great Canadian sport, the hockey player is naturally one of Canada's most enduring heroes. Current National Hockey League players are paid extremely large salaries to play a game that is second nature to all Canadian small boys, while famous hockey players of the past are celebrated in their own Hall of Fame. Among the members of the Hockey Hall of Fame are such people as Bobby Orr (inducted 1979), Bobby Hull (inducted 1983), 'Rocket' Maurice Richard (inducted 1961) and Canadian born and bred Wayne Gretzky (inducted 1999), who is widely regarded as one of the all-time greats. The current hockey player on whom all Canadian eyes are focused on is newcomer Sidney Crosby who plays for the Pittsburgh Penguins and who is strongly felt to be the next outstanding player with the potential to measure up to the recently retired superstar, Wayne Gretsky. The NHL includes both Canadian and American players, but most of the well known players for all the major teams—which include the Toronto Maple Leafs, the Los Angeles Kings, the Edmonton Oilers and the New York Rangers—are Canadian in origin. Many players past and present are household names and their pictures appear on a vast variety of memorabilia ranging from T-shirts and caps to hockey cards, which are regularly traded among fans of the game. In fact, some of the rarer hockey cards can reach collector prices as high as several thousand dollars if they represent an all-time great player.

Watching a hockey game is almost a ritual experience for many Canadians, whose Saturday nights are dedicated to the hockey game on television or in the local arena. There are various levels of hockey available, both to players and spectators, and there is a vigorous selection procedure for those youngsters who wish to make it up the ladder of playing expertise. Many Canadian parents in all parts of the country rise every day, early in the morning, to take their offspring to hockey practice. This is because the sport is so popular that it is hard to find a time when the local ice surface is not being used for practice.

Other Less Popular Sports
While there is no doubt that hockey is the sport of choice in Canada, other international sports are commonly played in

Canada. Among these are baseball, tennis, basketball, squash and lacrosse (which is itself Canadian in origin). Initiation into these sports begins early for young Canadians as the fundamentals of these games are widely taught in all school systems during Physical Education classes. All of them are also played in a strong league structure across the country, and for some sports, also in competitions with American leagues. Canada is also represented at the Olympic Games and the Commonwealth Games, where it has, in recent years, become particularly noted for its track and field athletes.

Outdoor Sports

Canadians love the outdoors. With such a large country and so much of it still wilderness, it is scarcely surprising that all kinds of sports which encourage people to take to the countryside are extremely popular.

Canoeing is universally popular throughout the country, with many of the large national and provincial parks offering facilities for both the experienced and the novice paddler. Canoes and lessons for the inexperienced can be purchased in most major centres, and certainly travelling in this way is one of the most attractive ways to see the Canadian wilderness.

Another way of getting involved with the Canadian wilderness is to take part in winter sports which are well represented throughout Canada. For the less energetic, snowmobiling is one way of travelling through the Canadian countryside, although it is inevitably accompanied by the din of the motor and the smell of petrol. For the environmentally conscious, there is always cross-country skiing, a sport that has been growing in popularity over the last few years with the development of the environmental movement. There are a large number of trails all over the country set up for those who wish to use skis. Many of these trails are closed to snowmobilers who have their own trails in other places.

For the ski purists, facilities for downhill skiing abound. In the western Rockies, one finds downhill skiing to challenge even the most intrepid skier, such as the runs at Whistler and Blackcomb, north of Vancouver. However, there are also fine downhill ski runs in the east, especially in the Laurentian mountains above Montreal and the Muskoka region, north of Toronto. In fact, wherever one lives in the country—except on the vast flatness of the prairies—skiing facilities (both cross-country and downhill) are usually not far away, often within an hour's drive of home.

Hunting and fishing are also popular summer and autumn sports. With its many lakes and great expanses of wilderness, Canada is a hunter's and fisherman's paradise. There are strictly enforced seasons for most species, however, and catches are limited by law. Those wishing to hunt deer and/or moose with a firearm must take a special hunter safety course before setting out, and penalties are quite severe for those who do not.

Like most avid outdoors people, Canadians are great campers and many camping sites can be found in all areas

Canadians learn to ski at a young age. As snow covers the whole country in winter, skiing is a favourite Canadian winter sport.

of the country. The tent has now been supplemented with the convenience of the tent trailer or the mobile home . The only difference between the two is the cost of the equipment and the comparative luxury which they offer. But whatever the camper chooses to drive around in, a vast variety of camp sites are available for his use—and very inexpensively in most cases! The majority of sites now have shower and toilet facilities, and quite a few of them have special hook-ups for power and water for those who wish to travel in more comfort.

Many of the most scenic areas in all parts of the vast Canadian outdoors have been set aside as protected parkland for the permanent enjoyment of their visitors. In fact, as soon as the transcontinental railway was completed in 1885, bringing with it the beginning of tourism to the most scenic spots in Canada, it was realised that many of these areas would need protection if they were to be kept in their natural scenic condition. As a result, in November 1885, Banff Hot Springs was the first to be designated a National Park. From this beginning came today's extensive National Park system. In 1964, a National Park policy was formulated and national parks were divided into several regions and types, from those in the High Arctic to the Pacific Rim National Park, from Point Pelee Bird Sanctuary to the Fundy National Park on Canada's east coast. These parks are now managed by Parks Canada which is a department of the federal government. Any type of development within these areas is strictly controlled.

Provincial governments have also developed a similar network of parks, ranging from those protecting and conserving resources to those developed to allow the citizens of a particular province to see its scenic variety for themselves. Information on these parks, including which ones contain camping facilities, can be obtained through the various provincial Ministries of Tourism. They also maintain information centres during the summer months at strategic locations throughout the province. These include in shopping centres, motorway service centres and at major scenic and historical attractions.

Canadian Wildlife

One of the joys of being in the Canadian outdoors is the contact with Canada's abundant wildlife. Animals from the large moose, bear and caribou to the smaller fox, beaver, groundhog and tiny chipmunk can be found in most parts of Canada. However, most of them are best admired from a distance, as direct contact with some will frighten them badly and can even be quite dangerous on occasion! Canada is also home to a large number of species of bird, ranging from the large eagle and hawk to the tiny hummingbird.

Moose and bear are the largest species of Canadian wildlife and are often found in abundance in the north. Moose—which look like a larger version of the deer—are usually quite bashful and non-aggressive (unless they are in heat or with young), although they can be a menace if they wander onto the roads at night. There are three species of bear in Canada; polar, grizzly and black/brown bear. The polar bear is found only on the arctic coasts and islands, and although usually quite easy to spot, must be approached with extreme caution. The grizzly bear, large and often dangerous, is restricted to the north and west of the country, especially in mountainous areas. Black or brown bears can be found almost anywhere, and often make a nuisance of themselves

The grizzly bear is an endangered species. This young bear was photographed at the Metro Toronto Zoo.

in small communities and camping grounds by trying to get into unattended food or rubbish.

The beaver is the symbol of Canada and lives almost everywhere in Canadian swamps and wetlands. Beavers are nocturnal animals, however, and so are not always easy to spot, as they tend to remain in their specially constructed houses during the day. Beavers can often cause great damage to wooded areas and crops, due to their annoying habit of using their strong front teeth to cut trees down for their own use. Other small mammals, such as the groundhog and chipmunk, are equally abundant, and easier to find. The latter will even sometimes come and take food from your hand.

Two Canadian birds also deserve special mention—the Canada goose and the loon. Both of these birds are migratory and can usually only be seen during the summer months on ponds and lakes all over the country but especially in the Canadian Shield. In the spring and autumn, the migration of the Canada goose is considered to be one of the signs of seasonal change.

Indoor Pursuits

Not all Canadians are outdoorsmen, at least not all the time. There are many indoor pursuits which are equally popular in the country. These can range from collecting—a passion among many of those people who haunt flea markets and auctions at weekends—to model railroading to card playing. Hobby shops, found in all urban centres, cater to all kinds of interests and there are a number of clubs and associations in all regions of the country. Here. devotees of a particular pursuit can join to practise and/or learn whatever skill or pastime it is that takes their fancy.

Canadians also have a great and enduring interest in all kinds of crafts, from appliqué to quilting to weaving, with a tremendous variety in between. For the newcomer interested in a particular skill, finding a teacher is usually not difficult. Many of them are, in fact, taught through night school classes, sponsored by local educational organisations. The products of local craftsmen are regularly displayed at craft shows and exhibitions, especially during the summer months. Here, many examples of extremely fine workmanship can be purchased quite inexpensively. Many areas also have small, privately operated craft shops which are often run by local art collectives and are open all year round.

If indulging in a private passion or acquiring a specific skill is not one's idea of an indoor sport, there are even some common pursuits which combine the sporting instincts of Canadians with the desire to participate in some kind of social experience. One of the most popular indoor pastimes in Canada is probably the game of bingo, and bingo halls are common sights in every community of any size (*see* Chapter 3, *The Canadian Vision*). Bridge and curling are also popular indoor pursuits and facilities for both of these are equally common. Perhaps the most common indoor pursuit of all in recent years, however, has become the viewing of home videos, and the growth of businesses renting these to customers for one or two nights has been phenomenal.

CANADIAN LANGUAGE

CHAPTER 8

'I didn't know at first that there were two languages in
Canada. I just thought that there was one way to speak
to my father and another to speak to my mother!'
—Louis Saint Laurent, former Canadian Prime Minister

BECAUSE OF ITS UNIQUE HERITAGE and composition, Canada is, in reality, a country of many different languages. Travel through the breadth of the country and you will hear a variety of native languages (Cree, Ojibwa, Iroquois etc.) as well as the widest possible range of languages imported into the country with early immigrants and still widely spoken in ethnic pockets through Canada. German, Dutch, Spanish, Ukrainian, Polish, Tamil, Hindi and Chinese in all its dialects can still be heard somewhere in the country, and all contribute to the rich linguistic mix of Canada as a whole. Officially, however, Canada is a country of two languages. Services in either of these two languages are accessible to all its citizens no matter where they live. However, neither the French nor the English spoken in the country is exactly the same as the language spoken today in their countries of origin. The reason is that each Canadian language has changed and evolved on its own. Both have acquired a distinct character over time, and to the practised ear, they identify the nationality of their speakers just as clearly as the maple leaf flag pins which Canadians abroad often wear in their lapels.

THE ENGLISH CANADIAN LANGUAGE

So how can you tell just by speech tell if the stranger you are talking to is a Canadian? Here are the secrets.

Most people will tell you that the most tell-tale giveaway in Canadian speech is the addition of 'eh' at the end of a remark, as in 'Is that right, eh?' or 'How y're doing, eh?' This is true for a lot of people, but if you think this method will enable you to instantly identify the speaker as a Canadian the first time he opens his mouth, you're in for a disappointment. Not all Canadians speak like that, and even those who do, don't do it all the time. So take this advice with a pinch of salt, eh?!

In fact, many features of Canadian English can also be found in either British or American English, and it is probably this very combination of both which really distinguishes the English spoken in Canada. For example, a Canadian will use the American words 'fall, French fries or garbage can' rather than the British terms 'autumn, chips or dustbin'. But interestingly enough, he will also often say 'tap' rather than 'faucet'. The spelling of Canadian English usually follows the British rather than the American model too, e.g. 'colour' not 'color', and 'centre' not 'center'.

But these are only generalisations and there are many other factors to take into account when analysing Canadian English, such as regional and ethnic differences. Newfoundlanders, for instance, speak English with an accent quite different from their Ontario counterparts, while a family with a strong European background may pronounce the same word differently from one with a Chinese background. There have been many learned attempts to define Canadian English and standardise it, but as it is still constantly changing, its nature remains a subject of disagreement. There are, however, dictionaries which deal with Canadian English, such as *The Gage Canadian Dictionary* and *A Concise Dictionary of Canadianisms* which can be consulted if you are in doubt about the proper word to use.

Apart from the British and American influences, there are also some words and expressions which have arisen from circumstances peculiar to being in this country, and yet others which have been borrowed from people of native and other origin. In fact, the name Canada itself was probably derived from *kanata*, a Huron-Iroquois word for 'village' or 'small community'. It was first recorded by French explorer Jacques

Cartier in his journal and referred to the Saint Lawrence area, but was later adopted as the official name for the new country.

ENGLISH CANADIANISMS

There are some words which are not exclusively Canadian, either in origin or in usage, but which you'll certainly hear often enough in Canada:

- 'Huge', 'enormous' and 'gigantic' are all big words for a very big country. However, none of them seem to be big enough for Canadian purposes, so try 'humongous'—that appears to be a particularly Canadian way of describing the vastness of the country.
- At the other end of the scale, try using 'tad' to describe something that's just a little bit of whatever, such as being 'a tad out of line'.
- If you go to the Canadian north, you'll certainly come across 'muskeg', meaning swampy or marshy land that goes on for miles and miles. It is an Algonkian Indian word which has been adopted into the English Canadian language.
- While up north, you might find yourself eating 'pemmican' or 'bannock'; the first being dried meat, often rather tough and stringy, and the second relating to the traditional flour and water pancakes guaranteed to keep hunger at bay anywhere you go.
- Coming further south, visit southern Alberta or British Columbia and experience the 'Chinook', a dry warm wind that blows from the south-west. During winter, it often causes a sudden warming of temperatures that melts the snow into unwelcome slush.
- And speaking of wintertime activities, what about 'curling'? Not something you do in bed with a good book, but a winter sport which enjoys tremendous popularity among Canadians. Played on ice, it is a little like lawn bowling, as two teams compete against each other to slide special smooth stones (called 'rocks') down the ice, trying to get their rock closest to the tee in the centre of the target area.

- Another winter word is 'black ice', which forms on the roads when rain or a slight thaw is followed by freezing temperatures. This turns the water into a transparent sheet of ice which cannot be seen by drivers. Many a winter accident has been caused by 'black ice'.
- Canadian winters also introduced the 'toque', a knitted woollen cap, indispensable for keeping your head warm in the freezing temperatures of January and February.
- And finally, Canadian winter creates the 'snowbirds', not always of the feathered variety, but as a term often used to describe the human cousins of the snow geese. During the winter months, they migrate to warmer temperatures in Florida or California. Many use recreational vehicles or the planes of Air Canada to escape!
- There are lots of other Canadianisms which you will hear used commonly, ranging from the word 'hydro' used to describe both the electricity supply and the company which provides it; 'medicare', the government health insurance plan; a 'chesterfield' on which you sit (you might want to call it a sofa); and finally 'zip' or 'zilch', which means absolutely nothing at all!

LANGUAGE AND 'THE TWO SOLITUDES'

Depending on where you live in Canada, it is easy to forget that there is not one official language, but two. English is the most frequently used, but there are large sections of the country in which French is the mother tongue and English very much a second language. In 1945, one of Canada's most well respected authors, Hugh MacLennan, wrote a now famous novel called *The Two Solitudes*. It is about this aspect of the Canadian experience and its effect on the relationship between the two linguistic groups. MacLennan, at that time a professor of English Literature at McGill University in Montreal, attempted to analyse the nature of Canadian society and reflect upon its divisions through a fictionalised account of the English/French tensions in Quebec at the time of World War I. *The Two Solitudes* caused much controversy at the time of its publication, and although events in Canada have changed many of the opinions in MacLennan's book,

MacLennan, who died in 1989, is still remembered as one of the first prominent Canadian literary figures to draw attention to the need for all Canadians to regard themselves as part of one complete entity rather than submerge themselves in regional differences.

the issues of division between the French and English cultures are still debated in the Canada of today. In fact, MacLennan's phrase, 'two solitudes', is still used to describe the nature of the relationship between the French and the English.

FRENCH AND ENGLISH

According to the census of 2001, nearly seven million people in Canada, or approximately 25 per cent of the population, list French as their mother tongue, with the main concentration of these being in Quebec and New Brunswick. In addition, over five million Canadians (approximately 18 per cent) indicate a language other than French or English as their first language. Of these, the most widely spoken is Chinese.

The federal government, which has often been headed by a French Canadian prime minister, has been increasingly aware during this century of the divisions which can be caused by ignoring or mishandling the importance of the French language to its native speakers. This is particularly so for those in Quebec. As a result, after many decades of ill feeling over language issues, an Official Languages Act was passed in 1969. This declared that English and French had equal status in Canada, and that all services throughout the country were to be provided for all citizens in both of these languages.

Thus today, from the box of cereal on your breakfast table to any other product you buy in Canada, the information and advertising are in both official languages, no matter where in the country you buy it. All federal government forms have a French and an English side, and all federal offices are equipped to provide public services in either language.

However, you don't have to speak both languages yourself to get by in Canada. Currently only about four million of the nearly 32 million Canadian population are

Signposts to everywhere at Signal Hill in Saint John's, Newfoundland. The names of the world's cities are in English and French, the two official languages of Canada.

bilingual and most of them are in Quebec. However, this number is increasing all the time through various special language programmes. The most widespread of these is French immersion, a type of schooling in which students are taught all, or some, subjects entirely in the other language than that which they speak. Pioneered in 1965 among kindergarten students in the English-speaking community of Saint Lambert, Quebec, the concept of French immersion has spread widely throughout the country. It is now a common part of school systems in nearly all provinces. The idea of teaching a second language by total immersion in it when young has been internationally recognised as a successful concept, and graduates of French immersion courses have found that their language skills are much in demand in an increasingly bilingual Canada.

CANADIAN FRENCH

> ### Contributions to the Language
> French universities in Quebec do considerable research in linguistics and terminology. Jean Claude Corbeil, a linguist and terminologist at the University of Montreal, and Claude Poirier, a linguist and lexicographer at Laval University, are well known for their contributions to the French language.

The French spoken in Canada, mostly in Quebec, is, for the greater part, very similar to the French spoken in France. It is not a dialect nor a patois, as it shares France's linguistic heritage and is an integral part of international French.

However, there are also differences between France's French and that of Quebec. Both the geographical situation and the historical and socio-cultural North American context have given birth to linguistic forms which are called 'quebecisms'. The term 'quebecism' refers to words peculiar to Quebec such as *motoneige* (snowmobile), *âge d'or* (the age at which one becomes a senior citizen), *epluchette* (corn roast), *dépanneur* (newsagents or variety/convenience store) and *tabagie* (tobacconist).

In order to contribute to the collective growth of French language in Canada, and to facilitate communication between French-speaking people, the Office de la Langue Française du Quebec has the responsibility for officially accepting such 'quebecisms'.

HERITAGE LANGUAGES

Slightly over 13 per cent of the population speak neither English nor French as their native tongue. Two-thirds of these 3 million people speak a language of European origin, such as Dutch, German or Polish. Since the 1960s, the use of Asian and Middle Eastern languages, especially Chinese, Vietnamese, Punjabi, Hindi and Urdu, has grown considerably. This fact, too, has been acknowledged by the government and the provincial education systems. Many now have heritage language programmes in the schools to ensure that these native languages survive in a multicultural Canada and are not swamped by the all-pervasive use of English or French.

Unlike the United States, Canada is actively trying to preserve its multilingual, multiethnic and multicultural society and, at the same time, mould the population into one people with a common outlook on their country and the world. It is a very difficult task, but preserving language is a very important component of its success.

BODY LANGUAGE

Read All About It

There are several excellent books available for those people who want to bone up on this area, and the best thing to do to thoroughly understand body language in Canada would be to read one of them. The very best of these is probably one simply called *Gestures*. This is the result of a long and thorough study of the subject taken all over the world by renowned anthropologist Desmond Morris and his two co-authors. It was published by Stein and Day publishers of New York in 1980.

Non-verbal communication in Canada is not really different from that used in most other societies whose background is culturally English. Those who have some familiarity with both the polite (and not so polite) gestures made by both Englishmen and Americans will find most of them fairly commonly used in Canada. They will have no trouble interpreting their meanings.

For those not so familiar with Western culture, it is probably best to beware of non-verbal gestures at first, as there are some significant differences between those used in non-Western cultures and those in use in Canada. An over eager use of a particular gesture (unless you are absolutely sure of its meaning) could lead to embarrassment.

DOING BUSINESS
IN CANADA

CHAPTER 9

'Four things an executive ought to know:
what ought to be done, how it should be done,
who should do it, and has it been done!'
—Joseph Atkinson, Canadian newspaper publisher

THE IMPACT OF THE UNITED STATES pervades all business dealings and dictates many of the practices which are followed in organisations, both large and small.

Canadian manufacturing industries are acutely aware that the largest customer for all of Canada's products has always been the United States, and the impact of their large neighbour is felt nowhere more profoundly than in their pervasive control of the marketplace. For instance, in 1988, three of Canada's 10 largest companies were wholly US owned, while a number of other major companies had extensive American stock holdings. Although the Canadian government has tried to minimise the effect of this fact on Canadian industry over the years, it does have extensive ramifications, both for those who run businesses and for those who seek jobs.

Businessmen have to be aware that the David and Goliath syndrome is very much at work in Canada. So much of Canadian business is American dominated, either physically by being a subsidiary of an American parent company or simply through the need to compete viably in a more and more North-American-oriented market. Such domination means that managing any kind of business which may come into direct competition with a much bigger and better funded American one is always risky, especially in today's era of free trade legislation. In struggling economic times, it is usually the Canadian companies which fold first.

The impact of the United States on the Canadian employee has become frighteningly more apparent since the implementation of a free trade agreement between Canada, the United States and Mexico. In times of plenty, free trade can mean more and greater job opportunities for the Canadian worker, but when times are not so good, jobs have a tendency to move south of the border and away from Canadian workers. This is particularly important for those who seek jobs for the first time, because the seniority system is generally the yardstick which is applied in any case of redundancy. The shorter the time that a worker has had his job, the more the chance of losing it when hard times loom.

Goliath apart, however, there is still plenty of room in Canadian business, both for the potential employer and employee. This is especially true in areas related to the service sector which is much less susceptible to domination by the Americans. Those who choose to invest either their capital or their labour in Canada can be amply rewarded, both in material terms and in their quality of life but only if they understand the peculiarities of the Canadian way of doing business.

ENTREPRENEURSHIP IN CANADA

In fact, the spirit of entrepreneurship has certainly been flourishing in Canada over recent years. In his book, *The New Entrepreneurs*, author Allan Gould lists 75 Canadian success stories in starting new and enterprising new businesses. Among those he lists are: Cultures Restaurants, specialising in fresh produce served in a fast food environment; Japan Cameras, a chain of retail photography shops; College Pro, a painting and decorating service started by a college student; Noma, an electrical company which specialises in making Christmas lights; Tilley Endurables, specialising in rugged products that are guaranteed never to wear out; Annick Press, an adventurous publisher of children's books; and Homestead Computing services, which brings computerised technology to the family farm. All of these businesses were started in different areas of Canada by people with limited

The Canadian National Exhibition, held in Toronto, gives a good overview of what the Canadian industry is capable of. As it attracts many visitors, trade is brisk for the small entrepreneurs who set up stalls in the exhibition grounds.

capital who used, instead, their knowledge and good sense to take an idea whose time had come and turn it into a viable and successful business.

STARTING A BUSINESS IN CANADA

As in any country, starting a business in Canada is always a risky proposition, especially in hard times. Out of any 100 businesses that start to operate, more will fail than make it through the first year. Of course, this obviously indicates that some are going to succeed as well—again, probably those who have carefully studied the current trends of successful business in Canada.

Understanding Canadians and what they want is obviously the first step to a successful business. Service industries are always much in demand by Canadians, who are constantly looking for any ways in which a task can be done faster and more efficiently. Similarly, environmental issues are a preoccupation with the Canadian public with the result that products and services which do not pollute and in fact reduce the likelihood of this happening will be popular for some years to come. Leisure products and activities will also enjoy similar popularity as work practices change and Canadians have more time to spend on their own choice of activities.

Starting a business, however, is not just a matter of picking a product or service and hanging up a sign. Because of Canada's vast size, the ideal location is also important, depending on the nature of the product or service offered. Something which might have overwhelming success in Vancouver or the west might be completely inappropriate for eastern Canada, where both the people and their needs are different. Similarly, the manner in which a business can be started in Canada may depend on national, provincial and local regulations, depending on the province and the type of business. This may also depend even on local restrictions which could be in force. All of these considerations should be closely investigated prior to attempting to start any business. Contacting local business associations such as the Chamber of Commerce or Board of Trade—both of which promote business growth—can often be very helpful in these investigations. However, generally speaking, businesses in Canada can be owned in one of four ways: either as a sole proprietorship, a partnership, a limited company or as a franchise.

All four of these methods of starting a business in Canada have their advantages and disadvantages and all are commonly used methods. The choice of which method to use usually depends on the proposed size of the business to be started and the capital available to start it with. Financial assistance to start a new business is usually available from either the federal or provincial government, through such agencies as the Federal Business Development Bank, Provincial Development Corporations or through special legislation such as the Small Business Loans Act. The latter allows specially underwritten low cost loans to be obtained through Canadian chartered banks.

Sole Proprietorship

A sole proprietorship is a business owned by one person only who is legally responsible for all its debts and other obligations. To start and operate a business in this way usually requires only a permit from the local municipality. The individual also needs to be willing to observe all the necessary regulations concerning operating hours, employment practices, fire and sanitary requirements. The great advantage is the ease of operation. There is no one else to consult and the owner is completely free to make any decisions he thinks fit whenever he feels they are appropriate. Financially, too, the sole proprietorship has some advantages. Namely, the sole owner need not publish a financial statement as companies are obliged to do. This is because the annual net income from his business is included in his own personal income tax return, which is a private document.

Partnership

A partnership can be one of two kinds—a general partnership and a limited partnership. A general partnership is one in which all the partners share equally in the management of the business and the profits, and have unlimited liability for any losses incurred. With a limited partnership, the liability for loss for some of the partners is limited to the amount which they have invested in the partnership. General partners—of which there must be at least one in any partnership—can be either active (a partner whose name appears in the firm's name), dormant (someone who has an interest in the business but whose name does not appear in the firm's name) or ostensible (someone who lends his name to a partnership, but has no financial interest in it). In most provinces, the setting up of a partnership must be registered within a specified period of time, and the partners are encouraged—and in some cases required—to file, at the same time, a written agreement of partnership in case of any later disputes among the partners. Partners often find it easier to raise funds through the chartered banks or other loan agencies as there are at least two or more talents involved in running the business. However, there are obviously some individual disadvantages when it comes to spending this money as its disbursement must be agreed upon by all the partners. As with the sole proprietorship, no special tax returns have to be filed with the government.

Limited Company

The limited company, or business corporation, is a more complicated way of starting a business, but in some ways, also a safer one. A limited company can be registered either with the federal government (if business is to be done in more than one province) or with a specific province (if the operations are limited to that province alone). Incorporation is possible as either a private stock company (up to 49 stock-holders) or as a public stock company, whose charter determines the maximum number of stockholders and permits trading on any of the three public stock exchanges.

Limited companies can be established in one of four ways: by special act of the federal parliament (such corporations as banks, etc.); through adherence to the terms of some special act of a provincial parliament (loans and trust companies, for instance); by incorporation under the federal Canada Business Corporations Act; or through a provincial Corporations Act.

Federal incorporation requires the registration with the federal government of information on the location of the head office, the names of the directors and the ways in which shares in the company are to be issued and divided.

Provincial incorporation is achieved either through a registration system or a letters patent system, depending on the province. Note, however, that both federal and provinical incorporation procedures require the filing of information concerning location, directors and shareholders. The financial affairs of a limited company have to be declared and made available to all the shareholders and regular annual reports must be issued. The main advantage of a limited company is the fact that all the shareholders are limited in their liability only to the amount which they have paid for their shares. Thus, in case of financial trouble in the company, their personal assets are not at risk.

Franchise

A very popular way of entering business in Canada is through the purchase of a franchise operation. A franchise is a licence to operate a business which has already established its name and proved that it has a good and expanding market. The food industry, especially fast foods, has traditionally been an area in which franchising is a common practice. This is now extending to all facets of the service industry structure too.

How a Franchise Works

When a franchise is purchased, it is often on a turnkey basis, which means that training and facilities are provided by the franchisor to the purchaser, who follows a strict set of guidelines laid down by the owner of the franchise in operating the business. If these guidelines are followed and the right location has been chosen, chances are the business will have much greater success than an unknown company whose products have not yet been available on the market in other locations.

To protect themselves, local franchise holders usually also incorporate themselves as an independent private stock company, thus limiting their liability.

FINDING A JOB

There are many different ways of finding a job in Canada, and businesses and companies will use one or a combination of these to find employees, depending on who they are looking for and where the company is located.

For management level employees, the most common place to find out about possible openings is through the advertisement columns of national, provincial or local newspapers and on the Internet. *The Toronto Globe and Mail* carries nationally advertised positions according to clearly defined categories. These are placed either directly by the company or by employment agencies (sometimes called 'headhunters'), and invite applicants to apply in writing for a specific position, which may often involve a substantial relocation. Candidates for these positions will usually have to be well qualified in their field and have a university degree or similar academic qualifications. A personal résumé or CV (curriculum vitae) will usually also be

Certain questions and practices are not allowed by law during the hiring process in Canada. For example, no applicant has to state his religious or sexual preference nor is any discrimination allowed in hiring on the basis of sex, race, creed or age.

required to be submitted with any application, prior to the short-listed candidates being called for an interview. In fact, having an impressive personal résumé can be extremely important, especially in hard economic times. Many advertised jobs attract literally hundreds of applicants, and many employers will short-list candidates for interview based on the impression created by these résumés. There are even professional résumé preparation companies which, for a fee, will make sure your personal presentation is eye-catching!

For those wishing to restrict their job search to a specific region of the country or to a more local area, provincial and local newspapers provide similar information on job opportunities, as does the local office of the federal government's Human Resource Development Centre. Jobs at all levels are placed with these federally-run employment centres and the screening of applicants is usually done by them. These centres are also heavily involved in retraining and upgrading programmes for workers who find it hard to get jobs in their fields. Finally, perhaps, there is no substitute for old-fashioned leg work in the job search, as a high percentage of vacant jobs never get advertised at all. It is the diligent seeker who often unearths such vacancies and benefits from the employment that they can provide.

The actual application process for a job varies, again according to the location, the company and the type of position. It could require some or all of the following: filling out a specific application form, having a preliminary interview, completing various aptitude tests required by the company, having an investigation conducted by the organisation into previous employment, a medical examination and/or a follow-up interview by a panel of people.

WORKING FOR A LIVING

Those who succeed in obtaining a job find that they are usually paid either weekly or fortnightly. However, regardless of whether you are paid an hourly rate, a salary or on a commission basis, certain deductions will inevitably be made from the pay cheque of all employees by the employer. These include income tax, pension plans and specific forms of medical insurance, for example. All these deductions will be itemised in the pay statement, and the remaining money paid to the employee, either in the form of a cheque or directly by pre-organised deposits into a specific account. This account has been opened by the employee with some kind of financial institution, such as a bank or credit union.

Some employees may be required to join some form of staff association as part of their employment, but this is usually conditional on an agreement that the employer has with his staff. The terms of such memberships will be made clear to the new employee as soon as he begins work. The purpose of any union or federation (similar to such organisations in other parts of the world) is to protect the employee and make sure that he or she is not the victim of any discrimination or unfair practices. Trade unions exist in many fields in Canada, and among the largest are the teachers' federations, public employees' unions, automotive workers' unions and steel workers' unions. All of these organisations undertake collective bargaining on behalf of their members or oversee such bargaining and represent individual members in the event of disputes with management.

There are also a number of laws which regulate the manner in which a business can operate in Canada and what can be reasonably expected of an employee. The Canada Labour Code requires that there be no discrimination in either hiring or employment; that female workers must be paid the same as a man for the same work; that specific maximum hours of work and minimum rates of pay must be observed depending on the province; that safe working conditions must be provided for all employees; and that bargaining for wages and working conditions must be conducted in good faith and be subject to an arbitration process if negotiations become deadlocked.

For the worker who might be injured on the job, a Workmen's Compensation system is also operative. This body provides a guaranteed income for any worker who has to take time away from work due to a work related injury, and also arranges for retraining for any worker who is permanently unable to return to his former occupation. Similarly, benefit packages provided by employers to their employees often tend to be generous, including such items as long term disability insurance, life insurance and dental or optical services.

JOB SECURITY

All employees, whether seasonal or not, who are hired by their employers on an hourly or weekly basis, are vulnerable to downturns in the economy which may make their jobs less secure. In the event of a company making some of its workers redundant, seniority is usually the determining criteria for redundancy, with those most recently hired being the first to go. Unions will try and prevent as many workers being made redundant as possible, and will support those of their members who are, but redundancies do still occur in hard times. Government programmes, such as unemployment insurance, exist to cushion the impact of being made

Farming work can be found in the rural communities of the prairie provinces. Here, herring gulls are searching for worms in a newly cultivated field.

redundant and, in many cases, those made redundant will be called back to work as soon as the economic climate improves.

If a worker is made redundant or dismissed after having worked for a business for a specified period of time, he may also be entitled to severance pay (this depends on the circumstances of the termination and the level of the job). He is certainly entitled to unemployment insurance benefits, for which payments will have been deducted during the period of employment. This benefit will continue either until he has found another job or until a specific period of time has elapsed, after which local welfare systems can help the worker who has fallen on exceptionally hard times and is unable to find another job.

For those whose employment is permanently terminated, most employers will provide assistance with finding a new job, and will often sponsor some form of retraining programme to help him find another job successfully, even in a new field of work. In any case, many of these programmes are available through government sources.

TYPES OF WORK IN CANADA

Canada's economy has traditionally been resource based, and certain occupations have long been practised. Farming, fishing, mining and logging still account for a large number of jobs in Canada, but there are a number of other areas in which there are now a large number of Canadian jobs to be had, especially in the service industries.

Farming employment can be found in most provinces, although it tends to be centred around the prairie provinces of Manitoba, Alberta and Saskatchewan. Fishing is centred on the east and west coasts, mining in the Maritime Provinces and logging in the interior of British Columbia. Employment can also be found in the oil and gas industries of Alberta, although jobs are not as plentiful now as they once were, and many Canadian oil experts have gone overseas to work for much higher salaries.

The manufacturing base of the country is located in the southern section of the province of Ontario, stretching from

Windsor in the south-west to the Quebec boundary on the eastern side of the province. Heavy manufacturing is located in the Toronto-Hamilton area where the majority of the automobile factories and their suppliers, including the steel industry, are situated. Most of the more recent high-tech industries are also located in the Toronto area. The smaller centres, which are connected to Toronto by the MacDonald Cartier Freeway (the main road artery of the region) have a number of light industrial plants providing an infrastructure of jobs for their communities. Manufacturing jobs can also be found in other major Canadian centres, especially around Montreal and Vancouver, but outside these areas, they are scarcer and usually less well paid.

The service industry sector is the fastest growing in the country, and Canada is well on the way to having a mainly service-based economy. Tourism (including the hotel and restaurant industry) and management consultancy are two of the biggest service areas in the country and employment in these industries can be found all over the country. This is especially true for those who have prior experience. Most of the new businesses which are starting in Canada are also

The construction industry is one in which part-time jobs are usually available, if you do not mind working out of doors.

service based and many of them address environmental concerns as well.

Home-based businesses have also become more and more common recently, and this is often the result of the entrepreneurial skills of a employee who has been made redundant. These small one- or two-person operations offer a wide variety of skills and services, ranging from income tax preparation and home cleaning to management and computer consulting. They are operated from houses, apartments and condominiums, in which part of the space has been specially designated for office use (and tax breaks given accordingly). What they all have in common is the desire of their proprietors to make a living to the best of their abilities in a difficult economy.

Jobs with predetermined Canadian standards—which may differ from standards prevailing overseas—are more difficult to enter for newcomers. The Canadian Medical Association has strict standards for doctors who wish to practise in this country, as do the associations of other health professionals. Teachers and lawyers also require special certification by the province, which has to be obtained before seeking employment and which may require some degree of retraining or a competitive examination before it can be achieved.

COMMON MANAGEMENT STRATEGIES

Management and direction in Canadian business has become much more decentralised in recent years. The strict hierarchy in which the boss makes the decisions, then passes his wishes down the chain of command for implementation, has almost passed. The employee is now encouraged to make appropriate decisions, in consultation with his peers if necessary. Strategies, such as those of 'quality circles', are commonly employed and divergent thinking encouraged as long as it complements the ultimate aims of the company.

This means that most Canadian managers of large and small industries have a vested interest in keeping their employees efficient and contented. Many companies encourage substantial employee input into decision making. They also provide opportunities for workers to upgrade or refine their skills at regular intervals so that they have the knowledge and the tools to be productive and useful. Safety concerns are also strictly regulated and attended to, with any job which requires any kind of exposure to hazards being strictly monitored.

Companies also sometimes assume responsibility for problems in the behaviour of employees. Problems with absenteeism, alcohol or drugs, or with fellow workers, which might in the past have resulted in dismissal, are now often dealt with through employee assistance plans that give workers a chance to come to grips with and change disruptive behaviour before facing any long-term disciplinary action. Even problems within a worker's family which could be affecting his performance on the job are sometimes dealt with by this method, as companies realise that their best resource is a productive and contented worker, as free from stress as the demands of the job will allow.

CANADIAN BUSINESS ETIQUETTE

Whether you are a manager or a worker, the way in which you will be expected to conduct yourself in the workplace is not far different from business practices prevailing in most westernised societies.

For example, the way in which you dress should be appropriate to the job that you are doing. Managers and executives are expected to come to work conservatively dressed—a suit or jacket and tie for men, an appropriate dress or trouser suit for women. Those who are required to wear some form of uniform to denote their position will usually be supplied with one by their employer. Production workers may or may not be provided with working clothes, and if not, are usually free to wear more or less what they like, provided no part of their attire (including their hair) presents any kind of safety hazard.

Working hours in Canada again conform to the acceptable Western standards, usually 8:30 am or 9:00 am in the morning, to 4:30 pm or 5:00 pm in the evening, five days a week. Those in service industries, especially the retail and banking business, may be required to work on Saturdays from time to time, but often, part-time workers are used to replace or supplement workers in businesses which open late or at weekends. In fact, there is a great deal of part-time work available in most Canadian centres, although much of it is low-paying and often taken by students who wish to work in their non-school hours.

The working day usually includes scheduled meal and rest breaks, 15–20 minutes morning and afternoon and one hour for lunch. Most working locations provide some form of rest area for their staff, and larger companies often have a caféteria which serves reasonably priced food at appropriate times.

Managers and executives may often be required to host and/or attend business lunches and dinners for visiting delegations or clients, which are usually held away from the office. These are usually low-key get-togethers at a local restaurant, at which routine items of business are dealt with or sales are concluded. However, the formal business dinner does exist and managers will be expected to attend them whenever or wherever they may be held. Travel is often a part of an executive's job description as well, and, because

Smokers Beware!

One word of caution for smokers. Many public areas are now designated as non-smoking locations, and some companies, in fact, have outlawed smoking on the premises completely. There is still a certain amount of controversy about this in the workplace, but, at the very least, smokers had better be prepared to find restrictions on when and where they can smoke!

of the size of the country and its close business relationship with the United States, travel on business can often involve going a considerable distance and therefore frequent overnight stays.

Most companies are also most concerned about staff development and require employees to attend upgrading courses and workshops on a regular basis. This, too, can involve travel to attend conferences and meetings in locations away from the home office. However, as the time used for this purpose is generally considered to be part of the overall working requirement, fees and expenses for staff development purposes are often absorbed by the company.

Meetings and consultations, for whatever purposes, are very much part of the working environment in Canada and nearly all employees will find occasions when they become involved. Most businesses encourage their employees to participate as much as they can in ensuring that the work of the company goes smoothly, and often have in-house committees which meet regularly for that purpose. Most Canadian meetings are not unduly lengthy and there are no special rules for their conduct other than to be prepared and to follow the directions of the chairman on whose shoulders the smooth running of any meeting rests. Participants are encouraged to speak their minds and to say what they feel— within the obvious limits of politeness and decorum—and to achieve a consensus acceptable to everybody on the points being discussed. At most meetings, there is no expectation for newcomers to be particularly reticent, but, of course, it is important that you familiarise yourself with all aspects of the issue at hand before voicing an opinion! Those who don't or who try to monopolise meetings will usually be put in their place by the chairman, who will endeavour to ensure that all points of view are heard and that the whole meeting is conducted in a fair and constructive manner.

Equality in the workplace is considered to be an important right and is respected by most Canadian employers and workers. No one should be made to feel in any way 'inferior' or 'subservient' to anyone else, including the boss, and obvious discrimination or harassment of any kind, be it racial, sexual or religious, is usually severely dealt with, especially if, as is often the case, it contravenes laws and/or practices specifically put in place to prevent that happening.

MADE IN CANADA

CHAPTER 10

'... Following many increasingly acrimonious decades
of constitutional haggling, an exasperated English Canada
has asked, 'What does Quebec want?' And Quebecers ...
have countered with a question of their own. 'What does
English Canada want?' I can answer both questions.
Quebec, as usual wants more. English Canada, fearful
of being snookered, wants a little peace and quiet.'
—Mordecai Richler, *Oh, Canada! Oh, Quebec*

Official Name
Canada

Capital
Ottawa

Flag
A base red flag with a white square in its centre, featuring a red stylised 11-pointed maple leaf

National Anthem
O Canada

Time
Canada uses six primary time zones. From east to west, they are Newfoundland Time Zone, Atlantic Time Zone, Eastern Time, Central Time Zone, Mountain Time Zone and the Pacific Time Zone. In the winter months (from the last Sunday in October to the first Sunday in April), Canada operates on Standard Time. In the summer months (first Sunday in April to last Sunday in October), most parts of Canada, with the major exception of the Province of Saskatchewan, use Daylight Saving Time. During the summer, clocks are advanced by one hour, and the names of the time zones change from Eastern Standard Time (EST) to Eastern Daylight Time (EDT) and so on.

2006 may be the last year that Canada springs forward in April and falls back in October. In the next year (2007), time changes may take effect in March and November, following the practice of the United States.

Telephone Country Code
1

Land
Northern North America, bordering the North Atlantic Ocean on the east, North Pacific Ocean on the west and the Arctic Ocean on the north

Area
Total: 9,984,670 sq km (3,855,102.7 sq miles)
Land: 9,093,507 sq km (3,511,022.7 sq miles)
Water: 891,163 sq km (344,080 sq miles)

Highest Point
Mount Logan (5,959 m / 19,550 ft)

Climate

The Official Canadian Temperature Conversion Chart
4.4°C (40°F)
- Californians shiver uncontrollably
- Canadians sunbathe

1.6°C (35°F)
- Italian cars won't start
- Canadians drive with the windows down

0°C (32°F)
- Distilled water freezes
- Canadian water gets thicker

-17.9°C (0°F)
- New York City landlords finally turn on the heat
- Canadians have the last cookout of the season

—from the website on Canadiana Connection
http://www.canadianaconnection.com/quips.htm

The general climatic conditions range from the extreme cold characteristic of the Arctic regions to more moderate temperatures. The Canadian climate is marked by wide regional variations.

Natural Resources
Iron ore, nickel, zinc, copper, gold, lead, molybdenum, potash, diamonds, silver, fish, wildlife, timber, coal, petroleum, natural gas, hydropower

Population
32,805,041 (July 2005 est.)

Ethnic Groups
British Isles origin (28 per cent), mixed background (26 per cent), French origin (23 per cent), other European (15 per cent), Amerindian (2 per cent), other, mostly Asian, African, Arab (6 per cent).

Religion
Roman Catholic (42.6 per cent), Protestant (23.3 per cent—including United Church 9.5 per cent, Anglican 6.8 per cent, Baptist 2.4 per cent, Lutheran 2 per cent), other Christian (4.4 per cent), Muslim (1.9 per cent), other and unspecified (11.8 per cent), none (16 per cent) (2001 census)

Official Languages
English and French

Government Structure
A constitutional monarchy that is also a parliamentary democracy and a federation

Adminstrative Divisions
10 provinces: Alberta, British Columbia, Manitoba, New Brunswick, Newfoundland, Nova Scotia, Ontario, Prince Edward Island, Quebec, Saskatchewan
3 Northern Territories: North-west Territories, Nunavut, Yukon

Agricultural Products
Wheat, barley, oilseed, tobacco, fruits, vegetables, dairy products, forest products, fish

Currency
Canadian dollar (CAD or C$)

Gross Domestic Product (GDP)
US$ 1.023 trillion (2004 est.)

Industries
Transportation equipment, chemicals, processed and unprocessed minerals, food products, wood and paper products, fish products, petroleum and natural gas

Exports
Motor vehicles and parts, industrial machinery, aircraft, telecommunications equipment, chemicals, plastics, fertilisers, wood pulp, timber, crude petroleum, natural gas, electricity, aluminium

Imports
Machinery and equipment, motor vehicles and parts, crude oil, chemicals, electricity, durable consumer goods

Airports
1,326 (2004 est.), 503 with paved runways

FAMOUS NAMES
Think of America, and you think of Hollywood, apple pie and football. Think of Canada, and what comes to mind? Probably the maple leaf, ice hockey, sub-zero temperatures and the Mounties.

But there is more to Canada than that. Here are some other interesting examples of Canadian ingenuity:

- Trivial Pursuit is a made-in-Canada board game, invented by Chris Haney, photo editor of the *Montreal Gazette*, and Scott Abbott, sportswriter for *Canadian Press*, in just 45 profitable minutes.

- The electron microscope was developed by members of the Physics Department of the University of Toronto. The team was headed by Professor EF Burton and included C E Howe, Ely Berton and James Hillier. Although the basic concept of the microscope came from Germany, it was Burton's team that eventually made it into a practical, commercial device.

- Instant mashed potatoes: Dr W H Cook, director of the division of bio-sciences at the National Research Council, was responsible for developing a new way of making frozen dried food. This turns potatoes, fish or meat into a powder which can be reconstituted with water to make croquettes.

- The first pre-cooked, vitamin enriched baby cereal was developed by doctors Frederick Tisdall, Theodore Drake and Alan Brown at the Hospital for Sick Children, Toronto, in the 1930s. It was first marketed internationally by Mead Johnson in 1930 as Pablum.

- The gas mask which saved the lives of so many Allied soldiers during World War I is an example of necessity being the mother of invention. It was developed by a Canadian doctor, Dr Cluny McPherson, when the German army released poison gas at Ypres in France in 1915. This first gas mask was improvised with metal and cloth. It was gradually improved to become the standard mask for Allied soldiers.

- It is to Dr Gideon Sundbeck, chief engineer of the Lightning Fastener Company at Saint Catherine's, Ontario, that we owe thanks for keeping much of our clothing together. In the 1940s, Dr Sundbeck redesigned the old slide fastener to make the modern zipper. He also invented a series of machines for zipper manufacture. However, Dr Sundbeck was not the first man to think of the idea. This honour goes to an American, W L Judson, but he never succeeded in selling the idea.

- The paint roller is a simple invention, but it revolutionised the painting and decorating industry and did much to usher in the do-it-yourself era in home decorating. It was invented by Norman Breakey of Toronto in 1940.

- The snowmobile, or 'skidoo' as it is called, was invented by Quebec manufacturer Joseph-Armand Bombardier in 1922. The motorcycle-like machine has tracks like a tank that enable it to run on snow and ice, and is used for both recreation and work.

- The discovery of insulin for the treatment of diabetes was the work of four medical researchers at the University of Toronto—Frederick G Banting, Charles H Best, JB Collip and JJR Macleod. Banting and Macleod were awarded the 1923 Nobel Prize for Chemistry, which they shared with their two colleagues.

- Ice hockey was invented by a group of soldiers in Kingston, Ontario, who tied blades to their boots and used field hockey sticks and an old lacrosse ball to keep boredom away one Christmas Day in 1855.

- Canola oil was developed from the rapeseed plant that produced an edible oil in Canada in the 1960s. When research identified certain potential health problems with the oil, Canadian breeders, using traditional plant breeding methods, developed a healthier product with lower levels of saturated fat which they named canola to differentiate it from the original rapeseed plant.

- Basketball was the invention of a Canadian, Dr James Naismith, who was an instructor at Massachusetts School. The need for a competitive indoor team sport led him to devise this game played under 13 basic rules with a ball and round hoops.

CANADIANS OF NOTE

Ask a non-Canadian to think of some famous Canadians and don't be surprised if he cannot recall the name of even one well known son or daughter of this country. But in truth, there are many well known Canadians, although it is doubtful if many people realise the true nationalities of these people. One reason for this is that many Canadians have had to go south of the border where the opportunities to seek fame and fortune are greater by far.

Consider, therefore, this list of famous Canadians whom most people think are Americans:

- Former presidential adviser John Kenneth Galbraith
- Novelists Saul Bellow, Arthur Hailey, Jack Kerouac, Margaret Atwood, Stephen Leacock
- Actors Raymond Burr, Genevieve Bujold, Raymond Massey, Lorne Greene, Christopher Plummer, Donald Sutherland, William Shatner, Margot Kidder, Mary Pickford, Michael J Fox, Shania Twain, Avril Lavigne and Neil Young.
- Singer Paul Anka
- Cosmetics queen Elizabeth Arden

Of course, Canada has its heroes and heroines too and others who have left their mark on their various fields. References to many of them and thumbnail sketches are sprinkled throughout this book. In addition, here is a purely arbitrary list of more famous Canadians:

Susanna Moodie and Catherine Parr Traill

Among the early Canadian books that give one a glimpse of the pioneer life are those written by two immigrant English women, Susanna Moodie and Catherine Parr Traill.

Susanna was already a published author when she and her husband left England in 1832 to settle in the backwoods of Upper Canada. In her two most well known books, *Roughing it in the Bush* and *Life in the Clearings,* she describes the difficulties of pioneer existence, as experienced by an English lady used to the comforts of life.

While the pioneer life did not agree with Susanna, who returned with relief to a more civilised life after a few years in the bush, her sister Catherine had a more positive outlook. She undertook to give those who would follow her a 'survival manual' entitled *The Canadian Settler's Guide*, in which she describes how to grow corn, make your own soap and gather wild rice, among other things.

Louis Riel

A controversial figure, once considered a traitor to his country but now acknowledged as hero and martyr, is Louis Riel, a Métis born in 1844 in Manitoba. He was a deeply religious man, educated in Montreal, who felt he was chosen to save his people and protect their rights. He led them in the Red

River Rebellion and set up a provisional government, but was forced to flee into exile in the United States when his revolution failed. He returned home when summoned to help lead his people in another revolt, the North-west Rebellion, which also failed. Riel surrendered, was tried for treason and hanged in 1885.

Emily Carr

One of Canada's great landscape artists, Emily Carr was born in 1871 in Victoria, British Columbia. She studied art in San Francisco but had to turn her home into a boarding house and find other ways of making a living. She held her first major exhibition of paintings when she was 56 years old, when she was 'discovered' by the director of the National Gallery in Ottawa. Her paintings of the Coast Indians of British Columbia won her much recognition.

Norman Bethune

Canada has a Chinese connection in Norman Bethune, a medical doctor from Ontario. He practised medicine in Montreal and served in the Spanish Civil War, where he organised the world's first mobile blood-transfusion service. Early in 1938, he joined the Eighth Route Army of the Chinese Communists in the hills of Yenan, where he formed the world's first mobile medical unit. He died in 1939 of an infection. Chairman Mao Tse-tung wrote an essay in which he extolled Bethune's 'boundless sense of responsibility'. The Chinese government donated a statue of Bethune which stands in downtown Montreal.

Bata

The Bata shoe company, which is the world's largest manufacturer of footwear, was established by Thomas J Bata, a Canadian. The company was actually founded by his shoemaker father in the Czech Republic. Bata, an 11th-generation cobbler, moved it to Canada when he emigrated in 1939. Bata company now produces about 300 million pairs of shoes a year in 61 countries, supplies shoes in 115 countries and has 6,000 retail outlets, many of them in the East.

Terry Fox

A recent Canadian hero is handicapped athlete Terry Fox. Fox was a 21-year-old track star who was stricken with cancer at the height of his career. In his courageous fight against the disease, he set out to run from one coast of Canada to the other in order to raise money for cancer research. It turned out to be his last event and he collapsed outside of Thunder Bay, Ontario, on 1 September 1983, and died nine months later. Every year since then, on the anniversary of his death, Canadians from coast to coast take part in Terry Fox runs to raise money for cancer research.

David Suzuki

Through radio and television, scientist David Suzuki has brought, and continues to bring, science into the homes of Canadians in a way that can be easily understood. He is especially noted for his TV series, *The Nature of Things*. He gained an international reputation when, as a professor of zoology at the University of British Columbia, he embarked upon a research programme on the common fruit fly and bred a strain that died in hot weather. His work caused him to be concerned about the effect that scientists have on the world. Science, he felt, was too important to be left to experts, so he set out to explain it to the public.

ACRONYMS

2-4	A slang term for a case of 24 bottles (or cans) or beer
26er	A slang term for a 26-ounce bottle of alcohol
401	The main highway between Ontario and Quebec
aka	also known as
AB	Alberta
AUCC	Association of Universities and Colleges of Canada
BEd	Bachelor of Education degree
BC	British Columbia
BCIT	British Columbia Institute of Technology

BLT	Bacon Lettuce and Tomato Sandwich
.ca	All Canadian websites
CA	Chartered Accountant
CBC	Canadian Broadcasting Corporation
CFL	Canadian Football League
CFP	Certified Financial Planner
CFS	Canadian Federation of Students
CIBC	Canadian Imperial Bank of Commerce
CIC	Citizenship and Immigration Canada
CIDA	Canadian International Development Agency
CMA	Canadian Medical Association
CMHC	Canada Mortgage and Housing Corporation
CPP	Canada Pension Plan
CCRA	Canada Customs and Revenue Agency
CRTC	Canadian Radio and Telecommunications Commission
CUSO	Canadian University Service Overseas
CSIS	Canadian Security and Intelligence Service
CUPE	Canadian Union of Public Employees
DND	Department of National Defence
DIY	Do-it-yourself
ESL	English as a Second Language
FAQ	Frequently asked Questions
GG	Governor General
GIC	Guaranteed Investment Certificate
GPS	Global Positioning System
GVRD	Greater Vancouver Regional District
GST	Goods and Services Tax
GTA	Greater Toronto area
HRDC	Human Resources and Development Canada
HST	Harmonised Sales Tax
IMF	International Monetary Fund
LCBO	Liquor Control Board of Ontario
MB	Manitoba
MLA	Member of Legislative Assembly
MP	Member of Parliament

MPP	Member of Provincial Parliament
MOT	Ministry of Transport
MSP	Medical Services Plan
NDP	New Democratic Party
NGO	Non-Governmental Organisation
NHL	National Hockey League
NRC	National Research Council
NSF	Not sufficient funds (on returned cheque)
OAS	Old Age Security
OPP	Ontario Provincial Police
OHIP	Ontario Health Insurance Plan
OISE	Ontario Institute for Studies in Education
ON	Ontario
PEI	Prince Edward Island
PST	Provincial Sales Tax
QC	Quebec
RRSP	Regsistered Retirement Savings Plan
RESP	Registered Education Savings Plan
RCMP	Royal Canadian Mounted Police
RMT	Registered Massage Therapist
SFU	Simon Fraser University
SIN	Social Insurance Number
SK	Saskatchewan
TESOL	Teachers of English to Speakers of Other Languages
TOEFL	Test of English as a Foreign Language
UBC	University of British Columbia
UCC	Universities and Colleges of Canada
UVic	University of Victoria

A–Z FAST FACTS
911

In most Canadian cities, this is the number to dial in case of an emergency when you need either the police, fire department or ambulance.

Some small communities may not have 911. In these places, check the front pages of the local telephone directory for the local emergency number.

Alphabet

The letters of the alphabet are identified by first names. Those who have been used to saying 'A as in Australia' and 'B as in Bangkok' will now have to change to 'A as in Andrew' and 'B as in Betty' and so on.

Box Number

Many Canadians have two addresses—their street address and their postal address. The street address is where they actually live (you would need it if you were visiting a friend). The postal address is what you need to post a letter to a friend. It might be a 'box number' or an 'RR number', followed by the town, province and postal code. For example:

PO Box 123,
Townsville, Alberta,
A1B 2C3

or

RR#1, Site 2, Compartment 3,
Townsville, Alberta,
A1B 2C3

The system of rural postal routes and box numbers is gradually being replaced in favour of the use of 911 emergency house and street numbers, which are in the process of being assigned to every dwelling in Canada.

Canuck

This is an affectionate term that Canadians use to call themselves. Johnny Canuck was a very early personification of Canada in political cartoons in 1869, later reborn during the World War I as a comic book hero—a captain in the Allied air forces fighting Nazi oppression.

Eh?

This is supposedly a Canadian habit of tagging 'eh' to the end of sentences, as in 'Nice day today, eh?' While this is true of some Canadians, not all of them speak like this!

Environment
Canadians are increasingly aware that they have to be responsible for the health of their environment. Recycling is an important aspect of Canadian life today.

Flag
Although Canadians say they do not openly display their patriotism, there are many who proudly fly their national, as well as their provincial, flag from a flagpole in their yard.

From Sea to Sea
This is Canada's motto. It is an extract from the Latin version of verse 8 of the 72nd Psalm: 'He shall have dominion also from sea to sea, and from the river unto the ends of the earth'.

GST
This is the federal Goods and Services Tax (known as TPS in French) which you must pay in addition to the price of any goods and services you purchase. It adds an extra seven per cent to your bill.

Health Insurance
There is a national health insurance programme that provides insured health care services to all Canadian residents. Although national in scope, it is run individually by provinces and territories and therefore varies. To be eligible for health insurance benefits, you must register in the province or territory where you live. In addition, some private insurance companies provide special coverage for newcomers and visitors who are not eligible to register with the provincial schemes.

HST
In Newfoundland and Labrador, Nova Scotia and New Brunswick, the federal GST and provincial sales taxes have been replaced by a harmonised tax of 15 per cent known as HST in English and TVH in French.

Hydro

This is electricity, one of the major forms of heating and power in Canada. Electricity for lights and household appliances is supplied at 110 volts. However, some big electrical appliances such as clothes dryers and electric stoves use 240 volts.

ID

Your driver's licence is an important and useful document that often serves as a form of identification. Teenagers too young to have a driver's licence often use their student cards for purposes of identification.

Loonie

This is the Canadian dollar coin. Canadian currency is counted in dollars and cents. In addition to the loonie, there are coins in the one-cent, five-cent, 10-cent, 25 cent and two-dollar denominations. They are also called the penny, nickel, dime, quarter and toonie. Commonly used notes come in C$ 5, C$ 10 and C$ 20 denominations.

Last Name

This is the Canadian's family name or surname. His own or given name is called his 'first name'.

Late-night Shopping

Most shops and businesses are open from 9:00 am to 5:00 pm while pharmacies and supermarkets often stay open until 9:00 pm or later. Most shops open on Saturdays and offer 'late-night shopping' one day a week. Offices generally function Mondays to Fridays.

Modern Conveniences and Luxuries

The Canadian home is seldom without a clothes washer and dryer (so important when winter makes line drying difficult) in the laundry area, a microwave oven and dishwasher in the kitchen, at least one television set, computer, radio and amplifier in the living room, a telephone and an extension or two in the bedroom.

O Canada

This is Canada's national anthem, and you might want to learn it even though many Canadians are themselves unsure of the lyrics!:

'O Canada, our home and native land,
True patriot love in all thy sons command.
With glowing hearts we see thee rise,
The True North strong and free.
From far and wide, O Canada, we stand on guard for thee.
God keep our land glorious and free,
O Canada, we stand on guard for thee,
O Canada, we stand on guard for thee.'

PST

This is a retail sales tax levied on most goods and services purchased. It varies from province to province and generally ranges between seven per cent and 10 per cent. There is no sales tax in Alberta. Some items are not charged PST. For example, in British Columbia, clothing for children under 16 years and grocery items sold in bulk are exempt from this tax.

Queue

When going shopping or waiting to be served at a counter, Canadians habitually form a queue that is sometimes obvious but at other times invisible. You are expected to take note of those who have come ahead of you and to wait your turn to be served.

RCMP

The Royal Canadian Mounted Police are often called RCMP in Canada even though they are more well known internationally as the Mounties. Established in 1873 for service in the North-west, the RCMP has now become a federal civilian police force. It is the provincial police force in eight of the ten provinces—Ontario and Quebec have their own provincial police—and the police force in about 160 municipalities. It is also the territorial police force in the

North. The official motto of the RCMP is the French phrase *'Maintiens le droit'* or 'Uphold the right'. But the rest of the world has always associated the Mounties with the words: 'They always get their man'.

SIN

The social insurance number is given to every taxpayer using a nine-digit numbering system. A SIN number looks something like this: 737 911 595. It is one of the first things you have to apply for when you live in Canada.

It is required information in many official and government situations, such as applying for a job, joining a medical plan or pension fund or paying income tax. The first digit identifies one of five regional registration offices (e.g. 1 is Atlantic, 2 Quebec, 4 Ontario, 6 Prairies and 7 Pacific). The final digit is a check number and the seven middle digits identify the individual holder. The system permits 99 million combinations.

Stamps

Postal services are available at post offices or at postal agencies in some shops or shopping centres. It currently costs 51 cents for the first ounce to mail a letter anywhere in Canada, 95 cents to the USA and C$ 1.50 to anywhere else in the world. And don't forget, you will be charged another seven per cent GST!

The Weather Network

When living in Canada, you quickly learn to tune in to the Weather Network on television to keep abreast of weather conditions. With its help, you learn to decode the language of warm and cold fronts, high and low pressure systems, arctic fronts and the wind-chill factor. You won't leave home or plan a trip without first checking with the 24-hour Weather Network, as it will tell you what the road conditions are like. If you are a sailor, it will give you wind and wave conditions, too. A skier? Snow conditions at big ski resorts.

Wind-chill Factor

The weatherman has a formula for working it out, but most of us just feel it in the bones. When there is a wind blowing, it can make the effective temperature of the air fall much lower than the reading on the thermometer. Practically speaking, although the thermometer might read -20° C, the temperature you actually experience might be in the region of -30°C!

CULTURE QUIZ

Are you ready for the experience that Canada will offer either the short-term visitor or long-staying friend? Here are some questions and situations for you to test yourself with:

SITUATION 1
You go to the bank to open an account. The bank assistant asks for your personal details—name, age, address, etc.—and then, she wants to know what your SIN is! Do you:

Ⓐ Tell her you've already confessed to your priest and been absolved?

Ⓑ Say it's none of her business and walk out of the bank in a huff?

Ⓒ Lean across the counter to her and get it all off your chest?

Comments
None of the above! SIN is short for a Social Insurance Number which you have to apply for when you live in Canada because you need it for almost anything official, like applying for a

job, joining a medical plan, pension fund or opening a bank account. It is an identification number and looks like this: 737 911 595. That's what the bank assistant wants from you!

SITUATION 2

You have accepted an invitation to a pot-luck supper for members of the ABC club and their families. On the night of the supper, do you:

Ⓐ Bring a big empty pot so that, with luck, you can go back home with it loaded full of goodies?

Ⓑ Ask the organiser how many people are expected to attend and bring a big pot of stew that will be enough to feed the whole company and more?

Ⓒ Bring a dish that you have cooked, but is just enough to feed you and your family?

Comments

It might appear selfish to bring just enough for you and your family only, but **Ⓒ** is the correct answer. You put your offering on the main table where all the food is spread, and then go about sampling all the interesting items that have been contributed by the other guests. Pot-luck suppers are based on the theory that if everyone brings enough food for himself, there will be sufficient to feed the company, and there usually is a lot left over too.

SITUATION 3

You are driving in a small Canadian town and someone suddenly crosses the road in front of you without even looking at you. Do you:

Ⓐ Stop and allow him to cross?

Ⓑ Let him cross but sound your horn in justified anger, stick your head out the window and tell him to look where he's going?

Ⓒ Decide you'll teach him a lesson in road safety by stepping on the accelerator and narrowly missing him as he jumps back in alarm?

Comments

The pedestrian always has the right of way, and he can cross the road at any point, not only at junctions, and expect that the motorist will let him pass. This is especially so in a small town. He also has the right of way in the city, but will have a hard time convincing the motorists of this fact. It would be best and most courteous to do **Ⓐ**. You will find that many small-town Canadian drivers are extremely patient. Some might do **Ⓑ** but you should never choose **Ⓒ**.

SITUATION 4

Still driving in that small Canadian town, you approach a junction and notice that there are two vehicles blocking the way, their drivers having an animated conversation. Do you:

Ⓐ Assume that one of the drivers is lost and is getting directions from the other, and toot your horn to remind them there's somebody waiting to pass?

Ⓑ Assume that this is a chance encounter between two old friends who haven't seen each other for 10 years or more, toot your horn and tell them to go to the nearest café where they can continue their conversation while you hurry on to your urgent appointment?

Ⓒ Assume neither **Ⓐ** nor **Ⓑ** but wait patiently behind until they are ready to move on?

Comments

You will know by now that **Ⓒ** is the correct answer. Curb the urge to press the horn, because it is not polite and restrained, as Canadians like to be. Be assured that when the drivers realise there is someone waiting for them to go, they will limit their conversation (hopefully to not more than five minutes) and move on!

SITUATION 5

You have now left the town and are driving along a country road when suddenly a deer jumps in front of your car. No matter how quickly you react, you cannot avoid the animal and hit it. Do you:

Ⓐ Recover from your fright and drive on, since it was only a deer and nobody else got hurt?
Ⓑ Recover from your fright and drive to the nearest police station to make a report?
Ⓒ Recover from your fright, toss the dead animal into the trunk of your car and bring it home for a venison supper?

Comments

It's against the law to do **Ⓒ**. And no doubt, lots of people decide to do **Ⓐ**, even though **Ⓑ** is the correct course of action, and the most public-spirited thing to do, because **Ⓑ** entails taking a lot of time and trouble. But it is really best to drive carefully, especially in the very rural parts of the country and at around dusk when your chances of encountering wildlife on the main roads and highways are greatest. The consequences can be serious if you should hit a large animal such as a moose!

SITUATION 6

You are visiting Saint John's in Newfoundland and enter a department store to look for some souvenirs. A sweatshirt catches your eye, and the price tag says C$ 24, just what you can afford. You stand in line at the cashier's and when it's your turn to pay, the cash register rings and the cashier tells you your bill comes to C$ 28.56! You are shocked and embarrassed, because you only have C$ 26 in your wallet. Do you:

Ⓐ Get all huffy with the cashier, point to the price tag and demand an explanation?
Ⓑ Retreat in confusion as quickly as you can, without finding out why there was such a discrepancy in the sale price?
Ⓒ Realise that, once again, you have forgotten that there are hidden costs to add to the price of the sweatshirt.

Comments

If you don't know why you had to pay an extra C$ 4.56, you should ask for an explanation, though not in a demanding or self-righteous manner. Obviously, **ⓒ** is what has happened, and the hidden costs that you failed to take into account were the 12 per cent provincial retail sales tax and seven per cent federal goods and services tax. Do keep in mind however, that these hidden costs vary according to each province.

SITUATION 7

You have bought a facsimile machine. You bring it home and excitedly plug it in and try to get it working, but to no avail. Reading the instruction manual is of no help as it is somewhat technical and you can't understand it. Do you:

ⓐ Bring it back to the shop and ask the salesperson to show you how to get it working?

ⓑ Ask the salesperson to send someone to your home to show you how to get it working?

ⓒ Try to find a friend who knows what he is doing and who will help you to get it working?

Comments

All three answers are possible ways of tackling the problem. If you are fortunate enough to have such a friend, **ⓒ** is probably the simplest solution. But you are entitled to get support from the place where you got the machine. Before doing **ⓐ**, however, it is best to call the shop and speak to the person who sold it to you. If it is a reputable shop, the salesperson will be helpful. If you choose **ⓑ** or if the salesperson suggests sending someone from the manufacturer's to see you, it is important that you ask whether this service is free. This is to avoid a nasty shock when you receive the bill.

SITUATION 8

There is something wrong with the lights in your house. You call the electrician and ask him to get to the source of the problem. When he arrives, do you:

A Behave business-like, show him the problem and leave him to it?

B Get him a cup of tea and keep up a running commentary about the weather and current events of the week while he works?

C Something between **A** and **B**?

Comments

It's all right to adopt a friendly attitude, so something between **A** and **B** would be acceptable. If you choose to do **B**, be aware that the service people often charge you is for work done by the hour. The cost of labour and consequently of making a house call to perform a service is expensive. You therefore do not want to waste the repairman's time and your money with inconsequential chatter.

SITUATION 9

You have been invited to dinner. When you arrive, you notice that the hostess greets her guests with a hug and a kiss on the cheek. You are uncomfortable, not knowing how to react. Do you:

A Pucker up and prepare to hug and kiss too?

B Resolve to maintain your reserve and decide a handshake is all you will give?

C Prepare yourself to follow your hostess' lead, and do **A** or **B**?

Comments

Canadians come from different backgrounds themselves, and you will find that some are more openly demonstrative than others. If you come from a more reserved tradition, you will feel uncomfortable when everybody around you is effusively demonstrative. The key to how to behave is how well you know your hostess. If you are good friends, **A** will be acceptable, otherwise a handshake, as suggested in **B**, will do. If you are uncertain, **C** is certainly the best thing to do.

SITUATION 10

You have gone to another country for a holiday and are talking with some people you have met about the Ontario community in which you now live. One of the people listening to you comments "I have a Canadian friend who lives in Vancouver now—have you met him by any chance?" Do you:

A Express surprise that you haven't done so?

B Point out discreetly that it would be unlikely as Vancouver is on the other side of the country from the province of Ontario?

C Realise that the listener has little knowledge of Canadian geography and laugh at him loudly for his ignorance?

Comments

Of course, **B** is the correct answer, as to do **C** would be uncharacteristic of a Canadian, and **A** would certainly reveal your own ignorance of Canadian geography. It is surprising how many people outside Canada don't have any idea of how big Canada actually is, and that most Canadians know comparatively little about what other parts of the country are like or about the people who live there.

SITUATION 11

Another person listening to you knows that French is an important language in Canada and comments that you must speak it well as you have lived in Canada for some years now. Do you:

A Say "*Oui*", and quickly change the subject before she discovers it is just about all the French you know?

B Explain that even though French is an official language in Canada, almost everyone in your community speaks English and that you have never had to speak French in order to get along?

C Explain that it is only in Quebec that French-speakers predominate, and thus, had you been living in that province, you might have learned a little more French?

Comments

You might get away with **Ⓐ** but it would not increase your friend's understanding of the French-English language situation in Canada. It would be far better to do **Ⓑ** and **Ⓒ**.

DO'S AND DON'TS

DO'S

- Take off your shoes when entering a friend's home unless it is obvious that everyone there has his or her shoes on.
- Bring a small gift for the host who has invited you to dinner and do compliment the cook.
- Respect a queue even if it isn't obvious.
- Leave a tip—10 per cent of your bill is the minimum, though 15 per cent to 20 per cent is acceptable if you feel the service was good.
- Say 'yes' when you mean 'yes' and 'no' when you mean 'no'. Canadians expect people to speak their mind honestly, albeit politely.
- Be aware of people around you. Canadians expect you to be aware of their presence and that they should not have to say 'excuse me' in order to have you move out of their way.
- Let the woman make the first move. When introductions are being made, it is the woman who first indicates her willingness to shake hands. You respond accordingly. Hugs are acceptable only between friends.
- Ask 'How are you?' when you meet a friend or acquaintance. This is a common Canadian greeting and usually invokes a standard reply of 'I'm fine. How are you?'
- Make eye contact when you are talking with somebody.
- Say 'senior' and not 'old' or 'elderly'.
- Give cyclists right of way. Lesser road users are given right of way.
- Stop for pedestrians at zebra crossings.

DON'TS

- Don't bring uninvited guests with you or put your host in an uncomfortable situation—ask your host first.
- Don't be a noisy eater. Slurping, burping and other 'eating noises' are anathema at the dinner table.
- Don't bring outside food and drink into another restaurant or café.
- Don't bargain. Prices in a shop are firm and reduced price items would have a sale sticker somewhere visible.
- Don't talk loudly in public. Canadians are generally quiet and will find loud behaviour obtrusive and bad mannered.
- Don't ask 'how much did you pay for it?'
- Don't call a First Nations person an 'Indian'. The most respectful and correct term of address is 'First Nations'.
- Don't ask people their age, unless you know they are quite comfortable with talking about their age.
- Don't have your children call all adults they meet 'uncle' or 'aunty'. Your children should call your friends and acquaintances by their last names, or even by their first names if your friendship is a close one and your friend has asked to be so addressed.
- Don't allow your children to harass the birds.
- Don't honk your horn unless you really have to.

GLOSSARY

anglophone	a native English speaker
Anne of Green Gables	young Canadian heroine of a famous Canadian Book written by Lucy Maud Montgomery and set in the Canadian province of Prince Edward Island in the late 19th century
away	anywhere in Canada outside of Newfoundland
bannock	unleavened bread first baked by native Canadians over a camp fire
Bare-Naked Ladies	a popular Canadian musical group (none of whom are women, and all of whom are fully dressed)
beaver tails	a sweet, light deep-fried pastry shaped like the tail of a beaver, sprinkled with sugar and often sold at winter festivals
black ice	invisible (and highly dangerous) thin layer of ice that forms on main roads during the Canadian winter
blueberries	small round wild blue/purple berry found in rocky areas of rural Canada
boonies (or boondocks)	an isolated place well away from any urban area
break-up	the thawing of the ice in early spring on the many rivers and lakes throughout Canada
Canadian Tire	a chain of automotive and hardware shops found all over Canada

canoe	a cigar-shaped one or two-person boat propelled by paddles, commonly used on Canadian lakes and rivers
Canuck	slang term for a Canadian
caribou	a reindeer found in large herds in the Canadian northlands
chesterfield	a sofa or couch
chinook	a warm wind coming from the west in winter, usually creating a thaw in the snow and ice
clicks	slang term used for kilometres per hour
crown land	land owned by the federal government
curling	a very popular winter sport played on a special ice surface with specially designed large granite rocks
dogsled	a sled pulled by specially trained Husky dogs, still commonly used in the far Canadian north
drunk as a skunk	someone who is completely inebriated
eavestrough	rain gutter on the edge of a roof
eh	a multi-purpose Canadian word that can be used with other words or simply by itself. The tone or slight differences in emphasis can also change the meaning so that it becomes a question marker at the end of a sentence or an exclamation
elastic	a rubber band

First Nations	a description for anyone of direct descent from the original inhabitants of Canada
francophone	a native French speaker
frazzil ice	chunks of ice that form at break-up time in the north and which are very unsafe to walk on
grain elevator	a tall rectangular building used for the storage and loading of wheat into railway cars or ships
Great Lakes	the five major lakes located mainly on the southern border of the province of Ontario (Lakes Superior, Michigan, Huron, Erie and Ontario)
highway	a major paved numbered road, which can be two or more lanes (motorway in British English)
hockey	the great Canadian game played on a specially prepared ice surface. Players wear skates.
hoser	a rude term for a very unsophisticated person
housecoat	bathrobe
Hudson's Bay Company (HBC)	the name of the original Canadian department store, first located in small settlements in the north of Canada but now found in most urban centres also
hydro	an alternative term for electricity and its supply
ice fishing	a popular winter sport where fishermen drill holes in the surface of a frozen lake and drop their lines through the holes

Ididarod	a cross-country race between dogsled teams held annually in the far north of Canada
igloo	a house built with blocks of snow, traditionally made by the Inuit
Indian summer	an unusually warm period of weather, occurring after the first frost in autumn (usually occurring in November)
Inuit	the correct term for the native peoples from the far north of Canada
jacknife	(a) a small folding knife often used by hunters or fishermen, or (b) an accident in which a tractor-trailer ends up 'folded' in two
jamboree	a gathering of people, usually in rural areas and featuring music and games
kayak	a small one-person canoe propelled by a two-ended paddle
kerfuffle	a commotion, or general upset involving several people (not usually serious)
lacrosse	officially the Canadian national sport, introduced by native Canadians, but now rarely played
line-up	Canadian term for a queue of people
loon	a goose-sized black and white speckled Canadian water bird with a very distinctive cry (summer residents)
loonie	a one-dollar coin with a picture of a loon

Lower Canada	name for one of the two parts of the original Canadian settlements (now basically Quebec)
maple syrup	a sweet thick liquid made from boiling the sap of the maple tree in the spring and most commonly used on pancakes
Maritimes	a collective term for the 4 eastern-most Canadian provinces bordering the Atlantic Ocean (New Brunswick, Nova Scotia, Prince Edward Island and Newfoundland)
mickey	12 ounce (375 ml) bottle of alcohol
Mountie	the familiar term for a member of the Royal Canadian Mounted Police (Canada's national police force)
mukluk	a boot with a fur lining, originally introduced by the Inuit
muskeg	a swampy area
Northern Lights	Canadian term for the *aurora borealis* (colourful natural display of light in the night sky)
Northern Territories	one of the 3 territories (not provinces) in northern Canada
Nunavut	one of the 3 territories (not provinces) in northern Canada
Ottawa	the capital city of Canada
outport	a small isolated fishing village, mainly found in the province of Newfoundland
pemmican	dried smoked meat

Prairies	large central Canadian plains found in the provinces of Alberta, Saskatchewan and Manitoba
postal code	a combination of 6 alternating letters and numbers used to indicate the postal area of your house (e.g. K8N 4Z5)
poutine	French fries covered in melted cheese curds and gravy
Quebecois	a native of Quebec province
rest stop	a specially designed area on a main roads for refuelling, food and toilet breaks
runners (or running shoes)	athletic shoes used for everyday wear
rye	Canadian whisky
serviette	a paper napkin
skidoo	a one or two person motorised sled (sometimes referred to as a snowmobile)
snowmobile	a one or two person motorised sled (sometimes referred to as a skidoo)
snowshed	a large, specially designed construction forming a roof over parts of main roads in avalanche areas
snowshoe	a specially designed, flat oval-shaped platform which straps onto your winter boots, and makes walking in soft snow easier
tepee	a cone-shaped native Canadian house, usually made from skins or canvas

Tim Horton's	an extremely popular chain of coffee shops found all over Canada
toonie	a two-dollar Canadian coin
toque (or *tuque*)	a knitted (usually woollen) pointed cap worn by both men and women in the winter
tourtière	a French Canadian meat pie
track pants	sweat pants or tracksuit bottoms
Tragically Hip	a popular Canadian rock band
two-four	a case of beer containing 24 bottles or cans
United Empire Loyalists (also known as UELs or Loyalists)	name for the settlers who came to Upper Canada as refugees from the American Revolution
Upper Canada	name for one of the two parts of the original Canadian settlements (now basically Ontario)
voyageurs	French Canadian explorers and fur traders who opened up much of the interior of Canada during the 18th century
washroom	Canadian term for a public toilet or lavatory
whiteout	severe snow storm which reduces visibility to almost nothing
Yukon	one of the 3 territories (not provinces) in northern Canada
zamboni	a specialised machine used for cleaning the ice surfaces in ice rinks

RESOURCE GUIDE

Canada is such a large country made up of so many disparate parts that it is difficult to give information regarding all parts of the country. Rather, this guide has concentrated upon giving the reader as much general resource information of the country as possible.

GENERAL COUNTRY INFORMATION

- The Citizenship and Immigration Canada
  The Citizenship and Immigration Canada produces several booklets for newcomers to the country. Some of them can be downloaded, including: *A Look at Canada* is specifically prepared for people planning to apply for Canadian citizenship; *A Newcomer's Introduction to Canada* helps ease newcomers into society.
  Website: http://www.cic.gc.ca

- *Canada: A People's History*
  A series of videotapes, compact discs and books based on the Canadian Broadcasting Corporation's television series of the same name. Available from the CBC or in most public libraries in Canada.

- *Government of Canada Services For You*
  Both the printed and the electronic version of this booklet lists numerous services and how to gain access to them, such as finding a job, lifelong learning, retirement planning and tax filing, personal safety and crime prevention. The e-guide on the Government of Canada's website has direct links to the services.
  Website: http://www.canada.gc.ca

- The Government of Canada
  The toll-free telephone number is 1-800-O-Canada (1-800-622-6232).

General Information Websites

- Canadian Government
  Website: http://canada.gc.ca

- Canadian Government News Source
  Website: http://www.news.gc.ca

- Canada Customs and Revenue Agency
  Information for travellers regarding tobacco and alcohol
  restrictions
  Customs, Excise and Taxation Information Services
  2265 Saint Laurent Boulevard
  Ottawa, Ontario K1G 4K3
  Tel: (1)-506-636-5064 (outside of Canada)
  (1)-800-461-9999 (toll free within Canada)
  Website: http://www.ccra-adrc.gc.ca

- About Canada
  Information for newcomers produced by the Canadian
  government.
  Website: http:// www.canada.gc.ca

- Maps of Canada
  Website: http://atlas.gc.ca

- Government Publications about Canada
  Website: http://canada.gc.ca

- Citizenship and Immigration Canada
  Website: http://www.cic.gc.ca
  All you need to know about being a citizen of Canada.

- Government of Canada: Canada International
  Website: http://www.canadainternational.gc.ca

- Statistics Canada
  Website: http://www.statcan.ca
  It provides facts and figures on Canada and its people.

- Canadian Tourism Commission
  Website: http://www.travelcanada.ca

- Canadian embassies and consulates
  Website: http://www.dfait-maeci.gc.ca

- Department of Canadian Heritage
  Website: http://www.pch.gc.ca

- Culture Canada
  Website: http://www.culturecanada.gc.ca
  Issues and articles relating to Canadian culture can be found here.

- Canadian Heritage Information Network
  Website: http://www.chin.gc.ca

- National Capital Commission (Ottawa)
  Website: http://www.capcan.ca

- The Canadian Encyclopaedia
  Website: http://www.thecanadianencyclopedia.com

- National Library of Canada
  Website: http://www.nlc-bnc.ca

- Canada Online
  Website: http://canadaonline.about.com
  Helpful links and information about the country.

EMERGENCIES AND HEALTH

As health services are provincially provided in Canada, these toll-free telephone contacts are for individual provinces, rather than Canada as a whole:

- Alberta   310-0000
- British Columbia   1-800-465-4911
- Manitoba   1-800-392-1207

- New Brunswick   1-888-762-8600
- Newfoundland   1-800-563-1557
- Nova Scotia   1-800-563-8880
- Ontario   1-800-268-1154
- Prince Edward Island   1-800-321-5492
- Saskatchewan   1-800-667-7551

- The College of Family Physicians Canada
  Website: http://www.cfpc.ca

- Health Canada
  General information about health care in Canada.
  Tel: 1-613-957-2991 (not toll- free)
  Website: http://www/hc-sc.gc.ca

- Dial '911' or your local emergency number for the quickest
  response from emergency teams.

HOME AND FAMILY
- Canada Mortgage and Housing Corporation
  Website: http://www.cmhc-schl.gc.ca

- Insurance Bureau of Canada
  Website: http://www.ibc.ca

- Human Resources Development Canada (Job Bank)
  It helps you source for employment in the country.
  Website: http://www.jb-ge.hrdc-drhc.gc.ca

- Canada Customs and Revenue Agency
  It has information concerning benefits and other tax
  related issues.
  Website: http:// www.ccra-adrc.gc.ca

- *Canadian Living* e-magazine
  Website: http://canadianliving.com

- The Vanier Institute of the Family
  Website: http://vifamily.ca

- Seniors Directorate Canada: Seniors Online Canada
  It provides information on government policies as well as publications pertinent to senior citizens' welfare.
  Website: http://www.seniors.gc.ca

- Study Canada
  This is a resource guide giving advice about schools in Canada.
  Website: http://www.studycanada.ca

- Hotel Association of Canada
  It has helpful links to Canadian travel information and various hotel associations in different provinces.
  Website: http://hotelassociation.ca

- Canada Real Estate Directory
  Website: http://www.real-estate-2000.com

- Canadian Association of Home and Property Inspectors
  These real estate building inspectors offer a written evaluation of the structural condition of homes.
  Website: http://www.cahi.ca

- Canadian Real Estate Association
  It provides real estate news, statistics and realtors across the country.
  Website: http://crea.ca

MANAGING YOUR MONEY

- Canadian Bankers Association
  Website: http://www.cba.ca

- Canada Customs and Revenue
  All you need to know about your income tax.
  Website: http://www.ccra-adrc.gc.ca

- Solutions Credit Counselling
  The company will help you with your financial situation.
  Website: http://www.creditsolutions.ca

- Insurance Brokers Association of Canada
  Its members include property and casualty insurance
  brokers across Canada.
  Website: http://www.ibac.ca

Major Canadian Banks

- Canadian Imperial Bank of Commerce (CIBC)
  Website: http://www.cibc.com

- Royal Bank (RBC)
  Website: http://www.royalbank.com

- Scotiabank
  Website: http://www.scotiabank.com

- Toronto Dominion Bank (TD Bank)
  Website: http://www.td.com

- Bank of Montreal (BMO Financial Group)
  Website: http://www.bmo.com

- Credit Union Central of Canada
  Website: http://www.cucentral.ca

ENTERTAINMENT AND LEISURE

- Parks Canada
  Natural resources and parks
  Website: http://www.parkscanada.gc.ca

- Canadian Wildlife Service
  Website: http://cws-scf.ec.gc.ca

- Chapters Bookstore
  A major Canadian bookshop chain
  Website: http://www.chapters.indigo.ca

- National Library of Canada
  You can browse lists of library websites and catalogues.
  Website: http://www.nlc-bnc.ca

- Canada.com
  Entertainment and restaurant listings around Canada.
  Website: http://www.canada.com

- Sympatico
  A popular Canadian website that provides links and information on a variety of items and activities.
  Website: http://www.sympatico.ca

- Virtual Museum Canada
  Look up museums across Canada or find out what's being exhibited.
  Website: http://www.virtualmuseum.ca

- Listings Canada
  It has listings for various vacation, entertainment and leisure ideas.
  Website: http://www.listingsca.com

- North America Tourism Inc.
  Website: http://canadatourism.ca

TRANSPORT AND COMMUNICATIONS

- Air Canada
  Information and flight schedules for Canada's international airline.
  Website: http://www.aircanada.ca

- VIA Rail Canada
  For rail services across Canada.
  Website: http://www.viarail.ca

- Greyhound Canada
  For coach services throughout Canada.
  Website: http://www.greyhound.ca

- Transport Canada, Vehicle Importation
  330 Sparks Street, Tower C
  Ottawa, Ontario, K1A 0N5

Tel: (1)-800-333-0371 (toll-free in Canada and the US)
(1)-613-998-8616 (from all other countries)
Website: http://www.tc.gc.ca
The government department for transport.

- Transport 2000
  A non-profit organisation whose primary purpose is research, public education and consumer advocacy.
  Website: http://www.transport2000.ca

- Canada411
  Online phone directory—it's the Yellow Pages on the Internet.
  Website: http://www.canada411.ca

Some Provincial Telephone Companies
- Bell Canada
  It serves Ontario and Quebec.
  Website: http://www.bell.ca

- Telus
  Phone company operating in British Columbia and Alberta.
  Website: http://www.telus.com

- SaskTel
  It's the Saskatchewan telephone company.
  Website: http://www.sasktel.com

- QuebecTel
  It serves over 300 municipalities in Quebec.
  Website: http://www.telusquebec.com

- NorthwesTel
  It covers the North-west Territories and parts of northern British Columbia.
  Website: http://www.nwtel.ca

- Aliant (Island Tel)
  It serves Prince Edward Island.
  Website: http://www.islandtel.pe.ca

- Manitoba Telecom Service (MTS)
  Website: http://www.mts.mb.ca

- Aliant (Nova Scotia)
  Website: http://www.atlanticzone.ca

- Aliant (New Brunswick)
  Website: http://productsandservice.aliant.net

- Aliant (Newfoundland & Labrador)
  Website: http://www.nl.aliant.net

- Canada Post
  For postal services and information
  Website: http://www.canadapost.ca

BUSINESS INFORMATION

- Business Development Bank of Canada
  It helps clients start their businesses.
  Website: http://www.bdc.ca

- Industry Canada: Business and Consumer
  Website: http://strategis.ic.gc.ca

- Canada Business Service Centres
  For information on government services, programmes
  and regulations.
  Website: http://www.cbsc.org

- Doing Business in Canada
  Read up or download its manual, *Doing Business in Canada: Canadian Business Guide*.
  Website: http://dbic.com

- Canada Customs and Revenue Agency
  (Small Businesses)
  It has information on responsibilities regarding customs,
  income tax and GST/PST.
  Website: http://www.ccra-adrc.gc.ca

- Legal Aid
  Legal Aid Society of Alberta
  Website: http://www.legalaid.ab.ca

- Legal Services Society of British Columbia
  Website: http://www.lss.bc.ca

- Legal Aid Manitoba
  Website: http://www.legalaid.mb.ca

- Law Society of New Brunswick
  Website: http://www.lawsociety-barreau.nb.ca

- Newfoundland Legal Aid Commission
  Website: http://www.gov.nf.ca

- Law Society of the North-west Territories
  Website: http://www.lawsociety.nt.ca

- Nova Scotia Legal Aid Commission
  Website: http://www.gov.ns.ca

- Legal Aid Ontario
  Website: http://www.legalaid.on.ca

- PEI Legal Aid
  Website: http://www.gov.pe.ca

- Legal Aid Quebec
  Website: http://www.gouv.qc.ca

- Saskatchewan Legal Aid Commission
  Website: http://www.saskjustice.gov.sk.ca

MEDIA

- The Globe and Mail
  Canada's national newspaper on-line.
  Website: http://www.globeandmail.ca

- CBC Radio and Television
  Website: http://www.cbc.ca

- The Canadian Press
  It's a multimedia news agency.
  Website: http://www.cp.org

- Al Czarnecki Communications
  It has links to various news agencies.
  Website: http://topstory.ca

LANGUAGE (AND LITERATURE)

- Cornerstone
  It highlights some rules and vocabulary of the Canadian language.
  Website: http://www.cornerstoneword.com

- Canadian Literary Homepage (University of Toronto Libraries)
  Website: http://www.library.utoronto.ca

- Colombo and Company
  It has a list of books written by John Robert Colombo (Canadian Anthologist) and other Canadian authors.
  Website: http://www.colombo.ca

RELIGION AND SOCIAL WORK

- The Anglican Church of Canada
  Website: http://www.anglican.ca

- The United Church of Canada
  Website: http://united-church.ca

- Congregational Christian Churches of Canada
  Website: http://www.cccc.ca

- Canadian Association of Social Workers
  Website: http://www.casw-acts.ca

CLUBS AND ORGANISATIONS
- Kiwanis Club
  Website: http://www.kiwanis.org

- Lions Club
  Website: http://www.lionnet.com

- Rotary Club International
  Website: http://www.rotary.org

VOLUNTEER CANADA
Each city will have a website for volunteer opportunities, e.g:
- http://www.volunteervancouver.ca
- http://www.volunteertoronto.on.ca

FURTHER READING

ABOUT CANADA

Countries Of The World: Canada. Robert Barlas and Norman Tompsett. Milwaukee WI: Gareth Stevens Publishing, 1998; Singapore: Times Editions, 1998.
- A good introduction to Canada, its land, people and events. Written especially for younger people.

Pierre Berton's Canada: The Land And The People. Pierre Berton. North York, Ont: Stoddart Publishing, 1999.
- A very large body of work by Canada's premier historian, featuring items on all aspects of Canadian history and geography and accompanied by stunning photos by some of Canada's best photographers.

Why We Act Like Canadians. Pierre Berton. Toronto: McClelland and Stewart, 1982.
- An interesting attempt to explain what being Canadian means, and how the Canadian lifestyle differs from that of the Americans.

Would You Lend Your Toothbrush? and *What Canadians Do on an Average Day*. Heather Brazier. Toronto: Harper Collins, 1995.

Quick Canadian Facts (annual). Canex Enterprises.

All About Us. John R Colombo. Colombo and Company, 2002.
- A collection of Canadian humour, much of which is unique to this book!

Mysterious Canada. John R Colombo. Toronto: Doubleday Canada Ltd, 1988.

1000 Questions About Canada. John R Colombo. Toronto: Hounslow Press, 2001.
- Written by one of Canada's foremost popular statisticians, this book answers common—and some uncommon—questions about Canada.

How To Be A Canadian (Even If You Already Are One!). Will Ferguson and Ian Ferguson. Vancouver: Douglas and McIntyre, 2001.

Fodor's Guide To Canada. Fodor Guides series. David Mackay Company, 2001 (26th edition).

A Concise Dictionary Of Canadianisms. Toronto: Gage Educational Publishing, 1973.

Canadian World Almanac And Book Of Facts (annual). Global Press.
- The facts and figures about almost everything in Canada.

Canadian Encyclopaedia. Edmonton: Hurtig Publishers. Toronto: McClelland and Stewart, 2001.
- An expensive book, but packed full of up-to-date and useful information. Also available in CD-ROM and at http://www.thecanadian encyclopedia.com.

The Unfinished Country. Bruce Hutchinson. Vancouver: Douglas and McIntyre, 1985.
- The book probes the development of Canada's political institutions and reveals much of what makes the country operate in the way it does.

To Canada With Love And Some Misgivings. Bruce Hutchinson. Vancouver: Douglas & McIntyre, 1991.

Canada: a Travel Survival Kit. Mark Lightbody. Lonely Planet, 2002 (8th edition).

The Story Of Canada. Janet Lunn and Christopher Moore. Toronto: Key Porter, 2000.
- A very good history of the country especially written for young people.

The Canadians. Andrew Malcolm. New York, NY: Times Books, 1985.

Mondo Canuck: A Canadian Pop Culture. Geoff Pevere. Scarborough, Ont: Prentice Hall Canada, 1996.
- An irreverant look at Canada and some of its idiosyncrasies by one of Canada's well known broadcasters.

Reader's Digest Canadian Book Of The Road (2000). Reader's Digest.
- Indispensable for anyone planning a road tour of Canada.

The Canada Year Book (biennial). Statistics Canada.
- All the facts and figures about Canada from the Canadian government's own record-keeping agency. Also available at http://www.statcan.ca.

Hooray for Canada: Special Canadians Talk About What Canada Means to Them. Telemedia Publishing (1989).

The Canadians. George Woodcock. Don Mills, Ont: Fitzhenry and Whiteside, 1979.
- Some very insightful observations from a man who has made the study of Canada and Canadians his life's work.

CANADIAN LITERATURE
Margaret Atwood
Lady Oracle (1966), *The Handmaid's Tale* (1985), *Cat's Eye* (1988), *Wilderness Tips* (1991) and *Robber Bride* (1993).

Morley Callaghan
Our Lady Of The Snows (1985), *A Wild Old Man On The Road* (1988).

Jack: A Life With Writers (The Story Of Jack McClelland). James King. Vintage Canada, 2000.

Margaret Laurence
The Stone Angel (1964), *A Jest of God* (1966), *The Diviners* (1974).

Stephen Leacock
Sunshine Sketches Of A Little Town. (1912).

Hugh MacLennan
Two Solitudes (1945) and *Voices In Time* (1980).

WO Mitchell
Who Has Seen The Wind? (1947).

Lucy M Montgomery
Anne of Green Gables (1908).

Farley Mowat
Never Cry Wolf (1963) and *A Whale For The Killing* (1972).

Mordecai Richler
The Apprenticeship Of Duddy Kravitz (1959), *Joshua Then And Now* (1980), *Solomon Gursky Was Here* (1989) and *Barney's Version* (1997).

Robert Service
Songs Of A Sourdough. (1907).

CULTURE SHOCK
Do's and Taboos Around The World. Roger E Axtell. Hoboken, NJ: John Wiley and Company, 1985.

Survival Kit For Overseas Living Robert Kohls. Yarmouth, ME: Nicholas Brealey Intercultural Press, 2001 (4th edition).

The Art of Coming Home. Craig Storti. Yarmouth, ME: Nicholas Brealey Intercultural Press, 2001.

GEOGRAPHY
Cultural Patterns In Geography. Gary Birchall. Austin,TX: Holt, Rinehart and Winston, 1989.

Investigating Canada. Graham Draper et al. Scarborough, Ont: Irwin Publishing, 1990.

Canada: A New Geography. Ralph R Krueger. Austin, TX: Holt, Rinehart & Winston, 1974.

Hinterland And Heartland, A Geography Of Canada. LD McCann. Scarborough, Ont: Prentice-Hall, 1987.

The Historical Geography Of Canada. Thomas Rumney. Monticello, IL: Vance Bibliographies, 1985.

HISTORY
My Country, The Remarkable Past. Pierre Berton. Toronto: McClelland and Stewart, 1976.

The National Dream. Pierre Berton. Toronto: McClelland and Stewart, 1971.

The Illustrated History Of Canada. Ed. Craig Brown. Toronto: Lester and Orphen Dennys, 1987.

Pioneer Days In Upper Canada. Edwin C Guillet. Toronto: University of Toronto Press, 1973.

A Short History Of Canada. Donald Campbell Masters. Melbourne, FL: Krieger Publishing, 1980.

Reflections of a Siamese Twin: Canada at the end of the 20th century. John Ralston Saul. Toronto: Penguin Books of Canada Ltd, 1998.

True Blue: The Loyalist Legend. Walter Stewart. Toronto: Collins, 1985.

Against the Current: Selected Writings 1939–1996. Pierre Eliot Trudeau. Toronto: McClelland and Stewart, 1996.

GOVERNMENT, LAW AND POLITICS
Civil Rights, The Law And You. Michael P Bolton. Vancouver: Self Counsel Press, 1989.

Lost in the Suburbs: A Political Travelogue. Stephen F Dale. Toronto: Stoddart Publishing, 1999.

Strong and Free: In Defiance of Canadian Cultural Sovereignty. Franklyn Griffiths. Toronto: Stoddart Publishing, 1996.

Ethnicity And Human Rights In Canada. Evelyn Kallen. Toronto: Gage Publishing, 1982. (3rd ed. 2003)

Immigrating To Canada, How To Do It. Gary Segal. Vancouver: Self-counsel Press, 1990.

FAMILY AND SOCIETY
Sex in the Snow: Canadian Social Values at the End of the Millennium. Michael Adams. Toronto: Penguin Books of Canada, 1998.

Canuck Chicks and Pale Leaf Mamas: Women of the Great White North. Ann Douglas. Toronto: McArthur and Company, 2002.

Multiculturalism in Canada. Augie Fleras. Scarborough, Ont: Nelson Canada, 1992.

I Am An Indian. Kent Gooderham. Toronto: J M Dent, 1969.

Towns And Villages In Canada: The Importance Of Being Unimportant. Gerald Hodge and Mohammed A Qaheen. Toronto: Butterworths, 1983.

Canada; Immigrants And Settlers. Ian Hundly. Toronto: Gage Publishing, 1980.

The Canadian Family; A Book Of Readings. Ed. Karigouder Ishwaran. Toronto: Gage Publishing, 1983.

Indians Of Canada. Diamond Jenness. Toronto: University of Toronto Press, 1977.

Just Looking, Thank You: An Amused Observer's View Of Canadian Lifestyles. Philip Marchand. Toronto: MacMillan Canada, 1976.

Urban Sociology In Canada. Peter McGahan. Toronto: Butterworths, 1986.

Sexual Politics. Kate Millet. New York, NY: Simon and Schuster, 1990.

The Vertical Mosaic. John Porter. Toronto: University of Toronto Press, 1968.

Canadian Women, A History. Alison Prentice et al. Toronto: Harcourt, Brace and Jovanovich, 1988.

Profiles of Canada. Kenneth Pryke (ed.). Toronto: Copp Clark Pitman, 1992.

What Teens Really Think. Readers' Digest Canada. Electronic article; http://www.readersdigest.ca/family/home.html.

Canada's Seniors: A Dynamic Force. Statistics Canada. 1988.

Drug Alert, A Provocative Look At Street Drugs. Marilu Weissman. Hoboken, NJ: John Wiley and Sons, 1979.

Women and Social Change. Ed. Jeri Dawn Wine and Janice L Ristock. Toronto: J Lorimer, 1991.

CANADIAN CULTURE

Harness In The Parlor: A Book Of Early Canadian Facts And Folklore. Audrey Armstrong. Toronto: Musson, 1977.

Countries Of The World: Canada. Robert Barlas and Norman Tompsett. Milwaukee WI: Gareth Stevens Publishing, 1998; Singapore: Times Editions, 1998.

Divisions On A Ground: Essays On Canadian Culture. Northrop Frye. Awasi Press, 1982.

Our Own Voice, Canadian English And How It Came To Be. Ruth E McConnel. Toronto: Gage Publishing, 1978.

A Reader's Guide To The Canadian Novel. John Moss. Toronto: McClelland and Stewart, 1987.

Modern Canadian English Usage. M H Scargill. Toronto: McClelland and Stewart, 1974.

Dictionary of Newfoundland English. G M Story *et al*. Toronto: University of Toronto Press, 1982.

DOING BUSINESS IN CANADA

Canadian Business: A Contemporary Perspective. Steven H Appelbaum. Toronto: Dryden, 1994.

Starting A Business. Gordon Brockhouse. Toronto: Key Porter Books, 1989.

Management Challenges for the 21st Century. Peter F Drucker. Toronto: Harper Collins Canada, 1999.

Douglas A Gray. *The Complete Canadian Small Business Guide*. Toronto: McGraw Hill and Ryerson, 1988.

The Financial Post 100 Best Companies To Work For In Canada. Eva Innes. Toronto: Harper Collins Canada, (1990).

Titans: How the New Canadian Establishment Seized Power. Peter C Newman. Toronto: Penguin Books of Canada Ltd, 1999.

Help Wanted: The Complete Guide to Human Resources for Canadian Entrepreneurs. Margaret Butteriss. Toronto: John Wiley and Sons, 1999.

Growing Up Digital: The Rise of the Net Generation. Don Tapscott. Toronto: McGraw Hill and Ryerson Ltd, 1999.

FOOD AND ENTERTAINMENT
The Canadian Living 20th Anniversary Cookbook. Elizabeth Baird. New York, NY: Ballantine, 1995.

Ethnic Eating: The Canadian Scene Cookbook. Canadian Scene editors. Toronto: Hounslow Press, 1991.

Provincial Cooking Of Canada. Culinary Arts Institute. New York, NY: Delair Publishing, 1983.

The Canadian Living Entertaining Cookbook. Carol Ferguson. Toronto: Canadian Living/Madison Press, 1990.

Canada: The Country and Its Cuisine. Victoria Hutton. Godalming, UK: Colour Library Books, 1990.

Canadian Family Cooking. Norman Kolpas. London, UK: Footnote Productions, 1986.

Impossible Pie—A Cookbook of Canadian Family Favourites. Lucy Waverman. Toronto: The Printing House, 1990.

SPORTS AND RECREATION
Bright Waters, Bright Fish: An Examination Of Angling In Canada. Roderick L Haig-Brown. Vancouver: Douglas and McIntyre, 1985.

A Guide to Hunting In North America. Jerome J Knap. Toronton: Pagurian Press, 1975.

One Hundred Years of Hockey. Brian McFarlane. Toronto: Deneau, 1989.

Canoeing Ontario's Rivers. Ron Reid. Toronto: Douglas and McIntyre, 1985.

ABOUT THE AUTHORS

Guek-Cheng Pang was born in Singapore into a large Peranakan (Straits-born Chinese) family. She received her education in Singapore and was a journalist and sub-editor with *The Straits Times* for 13 years. After having written articles for magazines and newspapers, she has naturally progressed to writing books now.

Guek-Cheng has travelled widely. The places she has not been to are South America, China, Africa and Greenland. She believes in travelling as a mind-broadening experience. She lived in England for a year, and is now a permanent resident of British Columbia, Canada, together with her husband and two children.

Guek-Cheng loves reading, music, travelling, hiking, biking, skiing and playing tennis.

Born in England, Robert Barlas has always had wanderlust in his veins. At the age of 19, he migrated to Canada, which has been his home—on and off— for the last 25 years.

A retired teacher, Bob has worked in international education all over the world. Among the countries he has worked in are England, New Zealand, Singapore, the People's Republic of China and Sri Lanka. Bob and his family made many friends in Sri Lanka and he co-authored *Culture Shock! Sri Lanka*. The Barlases have been back in Canada since 1989.

Bob enjoys reading, writing, skiing and sailing, and, of course, travelling, which has taken him and most of his family to over 80 countries so far—the rest of the world he is still working on!

INDEX